KNOWLEDGE
FROM THE WORLD BEYOND

A wealth of information
channeled from the spirit world

Sondra Perlin Zecher
Charles E. Zecher

BALBOA.PRESS
A DIVISION OF HAY HOUSE

Balboa Press books may be ordered through booksellers or by contacting:

Balboa Press
A Division of Hay House
1663 Liberty Drive
Bloomington, IN 47403
www.balboapress.com
1 (877) 407-4847

Print information available on the last page.

ISBN: 978-1-9822-5000-3 (sc)
ISBN: 978-1-9822-5001-0 (e)

Balboa Press rev. date: 06/30/2020

Contents

PREFACE

KNOWLEDGE FROM THE WORLD BEYOND has been written as a sequel to our previous publication *GLIMPSES FROM BEYOND*. It is a reorganized and significantly enlarged and revised edition with much additional information.

The content of this book is the result of many deep-trance channeling sessions that Sondra Perlin Zecher and Charles Zecher held during monthly meetings of the Coral Springs (FL) Metaphysical Group over a period of several years. As a medium, Sondra put herself into an altered state and allowed her spirit guide to speak directly through her. Members of the group were then able to ask questions directly to her spirit guide; questions about their personal lives, world events, ancient history, extraterrestrial influence, the future, etc. Her husband, Charles Zecher, the group leader, prepared approximately thirty questions in advance each month, which he intermingled, with the questions asked by the participants. Unlike the mostly on-the-spot questions asked by the others, his questions were prepared in advance in writing but not shared with his wife before the channeling sessions. The channeling sessions were digitally recorded and then transcribed by Charles. The questions he asked and the answers given by the guide provided the basic material for this publication. After a great number of questions had been asked and the answers written down, he then sifted through them and grouped them into different categories. Those groupings are the A to Z sections in this book. In order to provide some understanding of the process of channeling, the book provides a few introductory explanations to provide a perspective to understanding the information.

The information provided in this book is taken directly from the transcriptions of the questions asked by Charles and group participants and the answers provided by Sondra's spirit guide. On a few occasions information came through that appeared to be contradictory to previous information. There were some answers which were difficult to understand. Nevertheless they are included.

In order to provide an introduction to the information given by the guide, chapters eight through ten are updated passages taken from our earlier book *Glimpses from Beyond*. The grouping of information provided by the guide follows the structure of the organization of that book.

This book is for readers who are willing to receive information that might cause them to think outside of the box. Its objective will be achieved even if it gets you to think about things you never thought about before.

IN REMBRANCE OF SONDRA PERLIN ZECHER

Sondra Perlin Zecher made her transition from the physical world to the spirit realm on April 26, 2020 before this book was intended to be completed for publication. Sondra and Charles had previously decided to continue the channeling sessions of the Coral Springs Metaphysical Group until the June 2020 session, thus providing ample information from the guide to be included in this book. The plan was to continue the channeling sessions of the CSMG after that date to gather information for a subsequent book. However, with Sondra's passing, the March 2020 session was the final meeting of the group.

The following passages are part of a series of papers presented to the Coral Springs Metaphysical Group and other organizations by Charles and Sondra on various occasions to help provide a perspective for understanding the messages from the guide. For that reason, similar information may be included in more than one selection.

Chapter 1

CREATING YOUR PERSONAL BELIEF SYSTEM

Each person creates his own personal belief system regarding metaphysical or paranormal issues. For a great many people, religion does this for them by offering them a codified belief system. This plan can totally satisfy their needs by providing them with explanations of all they feel a need to know. Having faith in accepting what they are told is a significant element in providing them with comfort and security. If certain other concepts are not part of the plan, they can readily discard them.

Religion is vital to billions of people. Religion is important because it encourages positive behavior and consideration for those with whom we come into contact. Each religion is a planned belief system, some with little variation from others. Some are widely diverse but all with the same core value that we refer to as the Golden Rule "Do unto others as you would have them do unto you."

Other people create their own belief system. In creating your personal belief system, imagine that you are making a large painting. The picture that you are painting is your belief system. This picture is in the form of a very large jigsaw puzzle. As you work on assembling the puzzle, initially you have no idea of what the final picture would look like. It is an ongoing life-long paint-as-you-go project. There are a countless number of pieces. Each idea, fact, or concept is an individual piece of the puzzle. Not all pieces will end up being a part of the picture you are creating. Many of the pieces in front of you are beliefs that religions espouse. Some of those pieces will be used in your completed picture. Some are not necessarily part of the codified plans. Others run contrary to religious beliefs and may or may not be included.

As you examine each piece, you decide whether or not it is part of the picture you are creating. If you do not know if a particular piece is relevant to your picture or if you feel that it is not part of your picture, you do not reject it. You simply put it aside and keep it in abeyance. As your picture takes shape, eventually you will know if the pieces put aside are part of the picture you are creating. The important thing is not to reject any piece until after your picture has been created. Only after the picture has been completed will you send pieces to the rubbish bin. Conversely as you are developing the picture, you may realize that some of the pieces you thought were part of the picture were not really part of your picture after all.

The picture you have created is your own personal belief system. As you proceed in life you may meet other people who have created a picture that resembles yours in many ways to varying degrees. You may meet other people whose picture looks totally different from yours. The picture that each person creates is right for only that person. Always remember that belief systems are personal. It is not up to you to judge whether another person's system is right or wrong. Judge only your own belief system. Eventually you may realize that there is no universal belief system that is appropriate for everyone.

Chapter 2

THE EARTH IS NO LONGER FLAT

Many years ago I believed that the earth was flat and that the sun and all the planets and stars revolved around the earth.

Then as time went on, a few scientists made new inventions and were able to think outside of the box. They were able to show that the earth was round and no longer the center of the universe.

There were even a few people who thought the scientists might be correct about this. I was one of the oddball believers in the round earth theory but the Church absolutely forbade such beliefs. Unfortunately the Church wanted control and excommunicated me or maybe even executed me. Of course that was not in this lifetime.

Between that lifetime and this lifetime, the undisputable findings of science convinced the Church that the earth actually was round and was no longer flat. So it was not heresy anymore to openly say that the earth was not the center of the universe.

Yet some people continued to hold the traditional beliefs of the past and were unable to think that the earth was not flat and not the center of the universe.

It is even likely that perhaps some people in the world of today are not ready to think out of the box regarding the position of the earth in the universe.

Now science is in the process of taking another step forward with speculation that intelligent life might exist on other planets throughout the universe, perhaps even more advanced life forms than the people of Earth.

Yet many people, if not most, adhere to the belief that extraterrestrial life is pure science fiction. Nevertheless, little by little, increasing numbers of people accept the speculation that perhaps intelligent life does exist elsewhere in the universe.

Yet, just like in the past, when people adamantly held to the belief that the earth was flat, most people today either hold to the belief that it is ridiculous to believe in alien life or at most hold to the belief that speculation of such thinking is reserved for off-the-wall kooks.

Taking a quantum leap into the abyss of insanity, there is even a small but slowly increasing percentage of people today who say they believe that extraterrestrials were and are instrumental in the creation and evolution of the human beings on Earth.

The great majority of us readily accept that God, or whatever name is given to the creative force, created all the vegetables and now Earth humans are grafting vegetables together or genetically modifying the vegetables in order to make them of more service to humankind.

From that point of departure, it may not be an inconceivable leap of consciousness to envision God creating man and then extraterrestrials genetically modifying humankind to be of more service to them, just as we have done with vegetables. Extraterrestrials genetically modified Earth beings to the point that they created humans in their image. Perhaps that explains why the beginning of the book of Genesis in the Bible says, "Then God said, "Let us make mankind in our image, in our likeness."

Chapter 3

EXTRATERRESTRIALS AND THE PRESENT-DAY WORLD

The following passage consists of information provided by Sondra's spirit guide during the channeling sessions of the Coral Springs Metaphysical Group.

Even though many of you may think that extraterrestrials are the work of science fiction, I assure you that they are indeed real. Since the beginning of time on your planet they have played a very significant role in both the development of your planet and the development and evolution of mankind. They are much more highly evolved than humans and are assisting humans to elevate their level of achievement. They have far greater mental capacities and abilities than you Earth people. Earth humans use only a small portion of their brains. Those on other planets use a much greater percentage of their brains. They can communicate using telepathy. They can create objects and conditions simply with their minds. Although Earth humans are among the least evolved of all humanoid life on the various planets, they are evolving to be more like extraterrestrials. With the forthcoming ascension or, as some say, the movement from the third density to the fourth density, humanity will be much different than it is now. There are thousands of different species of extraterrestrials. Most of them have a humanoid form; a torso, a head, two arms and two legs. Although not all are of a benevolent nature to humans, most of them are here to assist us. Since the very beginning of life on Earth, extraterrestrials have been, and still are, on your Earth.

The current social and political situation in your country and worldwide has its roots eons ago, even before Biblical times and that of Atlantis. It is addressed in your Bible and in the scriptures of many religions. It is a necessary part of the ascension of mankind. It is the struggle between good forces and evil forces. It began as the struggle between opposing extraterrestrial groups, the Luciferians and the Elohim, what you now refer to as the Cabal and the Alliance. Conditions are not always what they appear to be. Until you have attained the power of discernment, make no judgments about what you see or hear. Remember but do not judge. At the current time, evil forces have become energized but they will be defeated by the forces for the good of humanity. Even after defeat, evil will once again eventually raise its head and confront the good. The good will always eventually defeat the evil.

Chapter 4

A SIMPLIFIED OVERVIEW OF HUMAN EVOLUTION BASED ON INFORMATION GIVEN BY THE GUIDE

We tend to think of ourselves as our physical bodies, but we are far more than that. In fact our bodies are only temporary. They are an instrument created for our soul to use to enable our soul to grow and evolve. Everything we sense, think, say, do, or experience is inputted into our soul which is forever expanding and evolving. There comes a time when we discard the physical body (i.e. die) and move on to the realm of the spirit world. In the spirit world, our spirit becomes the instrument for inputting information into our soul.

Some souls do not fully go directly into the spirit world but become earthbound; some a short time before they move on to the spirit world; others become trapped there. We refer to those that are trapped as ghosts. Eventually, even after eons, ghosts can move on to the spirit world.

After many years, sometimes centuries, a new physical body is created for the soul and once again a physical body becomes the instrument for inputting information to the soul. This process of reincarnation can occur repeatedly, even hundreds of times, until the soul reaches a level of evolution where a physical body is no longer needed for its development. The soul then manifests itself in the spirit world until such time as the spirit is no longer needed for inputting information to the soul. The soul then manifests itself at an even higher level. The evolution of the soul is an endless process.

The soul begins as a spark of the divine within a capacity for the development of what we might consider consciousness or awareness. Through each stage of development consciousness reaches a higher level.

To a very limited extent, the emergence of the soul can be compared to the construction of a house. When does it become a house? Is it a house when the construction is completed? Is it a house when it is constructed to the point that it can be recognized as a house? Is it a house when the life force inside an acorn causes the acorn to burst open and start to begin growing into a tree which will provide the lumber that will be used to build the house?

Initially, the development of the soul begins at the lowest level, the mineral kingdom. At that level a minimal form of consciousness is achieved. From there, the development of awareness proceeds to the vegetable kingdom where a greater degree of consciousness is achieved. After the vegetable kingdom, the next stage is the animal kingdom. At the most developed stage at the animal level, individual consciousness occurs. The individual soul comes into existence. Finally animals, most often domesticated animals which have had experience with humans, incarnate as humans.

After the animal state, not all entities develop as humans. Especially those in the flying form, including insects can evolve as angels. At this point, the angel kingdom is totally separate from the human kingdom. Humans never evolve into angels. Angels, however can manifest or show themselves to humans as a human being. The role of angels is to assist humans in their evolution.

Both those in the spirit world and angels help protect humans and guide them to enable them to advance. They are able to project ideas or thoughts into our minds. We rarely recognize the fact that many of our thoughts do not emanate from our own minds. They appear as thoughts from "out of the blue". Whether we respond to those thoughts is totally up to us. Through the exercise of our will, we determine our reactions to those thoughts. Angels project positive, helpful thoughts to us. When we meditate and clear our minds, we become more receptive to thoughts from the outside. Like humans, not all spirits are benevolent. Some can projects malevolent ideas. Our will can always override those thoughts.

The evolution of the soul can evolve far above that of the human level. Very highly evolved souls can manifest themselves as planets, stars or other cosmic bodies, with a level of consciousness far above that of humans. The billions of stars that we see are all energy manifestations of souls. Everything that exists is energy. Energy is vibrations. The lowest level of density is that of the physical world. The world of the spirits is at a higher vibtrational or energy level. The very highest level of energy is the God level.

The thinking of mankind has expanded greatly in the last millennium. You might say that it was once believed the world was flat. You might say that it was once believed that the sun and planets revolved around the earth. Within the last half millennium, scientists have come to the realization that the earth is not the center of the universe but rather only a small speck of matter within the universe. Now scientists say that there may be human or humanlike life on other planets throughout the universe. They are seriously searching for humanlike life elsewhere. Taking a leap forward, you might say that life on other planets might be far more advanced than life on Earth. You might believe that extraterrestrials have created UFO's to explore our world and other places in the universe. Earth people are making explorations of our solar system but have nothing anywhere near comparable to the UFO's of extraterrestrials from other star systems. You might even believe in the heresy of thinking that Earth humans are less evolved than extraterrestrials, even to the point that we are among the least developed humanoids in the universe.

We humans use only a small percentage of our brains. What if those on other planets used a much larger portion of their brains? Taking a further leap forward, you might believe that, with their far greater of intelligence, extraterrestrials may have had an inestimable influence on the development of both the planet earth and its inhabitants. What if extraterrestrials have been manipulating the DNA of the intelligence and physical characteristics of Earth animals and humans for thousands of years? What if the earth and its inhabitants are some kind of experimental laboratory for those of far greater intelligence than that of humans?

What created the life force that animates all beings, whether they are mineral, vegetable, animal, or human? We must admit that, whether we like it or not, there must be only one answer. It is something we refer to as God. It is something that the human mind will never be able to comprehend.

9

Chapter 5

GOD AND PRAYER

There is much truth to the sayings, "As above, so below" and "As below, so above".

Our world and the worlds above us can be compared to a large corporation in which there are numerous levels of guidance, supervision and authority. Corporations can have many levels of bosses: advisors, managers, department heads, supervisors, vice-presidents, presidents, CEO's, all the way up to the Board of Directors.

As workers or employees, some of our wants, needs and problems can be satisfied at the lowest level of our bosses; such as our advisors, others at higher levels such as the department head. It is not at all uncommon for our wants and needs not to even reach the level of the CEO or the Board of Directors. The success of the corporation depends on the success of the bosses. The success of the bosses depends on the success of the lower level bosses. The success of the lower level bosses depends on the success of each individual worker.

Just as in this world, we can have different levels of bosses; there are different levels of "gods" above our world. What we consider these "gods" to be could actually be spirits, angels or even extraterrestrials and many others that we are unaware of. Even though there are many "gods", there is only one God. This God cannot be understood or explained at the human level, the spirit level or even levels above that. The concept of God is too far above that of what we might compare to the Board of Directors for the human mind to even begin to conceive or explain.

When we pray, we are expressing our requests, needs and desires. When we pray to God (whatever we may consider that may be), we are actually broadcasting our requests to all those levels (or heavens) above the physical realm. Our prayers are broadcast throughout creation. They can be responded to by beings in any of the levels above us. Thus, a variety of sources respond to our prayers; including those in the spirit world, the spirits of those in the physical world, the angels, and those in other realms as yet unknown to us.

Sometimes an entity in the spirit would be able to satisfy our needs. Other times a higher-level entity such as an angel might be needed to respond to us. The level of potential assistance is inconceivable. An angel may assist a spirit in responding to our needs. A spirit may assist another human in helping us. All that is above our level is God. All that is at our level is God.

If we choose, we can select specific higher-level entities to address our prayers to. We can call upon entities by name, whether they are an angel or an entity in the world of spirits, including those whom we revere and those to whom we have given the title of saints.

We often receive assistance from spirits and angels. They both have the ability to project thoughts into our minds. We don't usually realize that often our thoughts don't emanate from our own minds. Telepathic thoughts often appear as ideas that just seemed to pop into our heads. These thoughts can help us solve our problems or guide us in our actions.

The degree of telepathic assistance you receive is often related to the level of the entity to which you pray. You can call on your Aunt Becky who died many years ago. Depending on her level of evolution (what we often refer to as "spirituality") she may be able to help you. Spirits have different levels of energy (spirituality) as do humans.

The role of angels is to help humans evolve to the God level for which they are destined. Angels can send helpful thoughts to your mind. They can also manipulate the laws of nature to help you. For example, they can prevent you from drowning when it appears that by all ordinary explanations you should have drowned. Evolved spirits and even some humans have the ability to manipulate the laws of nature. We refer to the manipulation of natural laws as "miracles."

Jesus the man (not Jesus the Christ) dwells in the spirit world. He is an extremely powerful spirit, powerful enough to respond to all those who call upon him regardless of their religion. It does not matter what religion you practice. Jesus will help and guide you.

Our creator has set up the system of prayer to bring assistance to us, to guide us, and to bring comfort to us. Prayer is there for us to use. When, how, or whether to pray or not pray is totally up to us. Prayer is not a requirement for humans. Many people are able to pass through life without tapping into the benefits of prayer. If they choose not to pray, God does not "punish" them.

Choosing not to take advantage of prayer can be compared to people traveling by automobile to a specific destination with no GPS, road signs or maps available to them and not having membership in the American Automobile Association for roadside assistance. If they choose to be on their own, that is there decision. They may eventually get to their destination but not without difficulties, trials and tribulations along the way. The solution is, "Make life easier and better for yourself. Take the easy way out. Pray."

Chapter 6

THE CARE OF
THE EARTH

The earth is not being harmed by the actions of humans. The planet is far too advanced to allow itself to be harmed by humankind. However, the future of the human race is being altered by the actions of man. The altering of the future of Earth humanity is a definite future but can be delayed by the actions of man. Greater concern for the environment is a major factor in prolonging human life on Earth as it now exists. Nevertheless it is inevitable that major Earth changes will occur.

The earth is a very strong conscious entity, fully able to take care of itself as it has repeatedly done in the past when conditions were necessary for action to be taken. The earth must cleanse and renew itself, such as the event referred to as the Great Flood or in the destruction of Atlantis or Lemuria. It will continue to do this countless times in the future.

Perhaps, a parallel can be drawn between the earth renewing itself and a dog standing up and shaking itself to rid itself of fleas. Many fleas will be cast out but it is very likely that some will remain, and thus start the process of infestation over again. The dog will feel better for a while, at least until another shaking is necessary.

When the earth renews itself, a considerable portion of physical human life, if not all, will be destroyed just as it was in the time of Noah. The essence of human life, the soul, will not be destroyed, nor can it ever be destroyed. The physical body is simply a manifestation of the soul. Although some of these manifestations may remain after the earth restores itself, many souls will remain in their spirit manifestation in the earth's sphere of influence but will not be able to reincarnate on Earth until conditions are appropriate for physical life on Earth again. Great numbers of souls will move on to the sphere of influence of different planets where their spirit form will abide. There they will again be able to reincarnate and continue to progress as if they had remained incarnate on Earth.

At the time of the earth's renewal, higher level extraterrestrial entities often come to the rescue of some Earth humans for preserving the continuance of the species for the future repopulation of the new young earth. This has occurred numerous times the earth's ancient past and will occur numerous times in the earth's future. The ascension of the earth from the third to the fourth density which is now occurring is instrumental to the process.

Chapter 7

UNDERSTANDING SPIRIT COMMUNICATIONS

The material presented in this book is based on two underlying assumptions. The first is that our souls are immortal and continue to exist after we leave the physical world. Our existence continues in the astral world; that is, in the spirit realm where non-physical conscious entities dwell.

The second basic assumption is that there are open lines of communication available between the conscious entities of those in the physical world and the conscious entities of those in the astral world.

The information in this chapter is presented as a recounting of my personal thoughts, beliefs, observations and experiences regarding communication from those in the spirit world.

I, Sondra Zecher, want to make it clear at the outset that I understand that others may have had different experiences from mine or have beliefs or truths that are in opposition to mine. Please be assured that I am not trying to convince anybody of anything. All I want to do is to share my personal experiences with you. You can believe or not believe what I say.

You may or may not choose to incorporate anything I present into your own personal belief system. Nevertheless, I avow that everything I am saying here is my own personal truth. I do not proclaim myself to be an expert in anything. All I can do is to talk about what I do.

When we "die" our personal individualities continue to exist in the spirit world. Only the physical part of us dies. The rest continues to exist. Spirits are conscious energy beings that are not encased in physical bodies. Some of the spirits who inhabit the astral world were previously part of our physical world. Others never incarnated in this physical world.

Very few of the spirits who dwell in the astral realm have reached the state of perfection, or completion as my guide corrects me, and are able to move on to another dimension beyond the astral realm.

We must understand that these non-physical entities in the astral realm are not God (or whatever term you may want to use for the highest of all powers) and therefore they are not infallible. Just as in our physical world with some humans more knowledgeable, adept or skilled than others in what they do, so it is with the spirits.

If, for example, you are experiencing severe abdominal pains and you have tried everything you know to relieve the pain, the next logical step is to go to a more knowledgeable person; that is, a medical doctor. Some doctors are more knowledgeable than others but, for the most part, doctors can usually find the source of the pain, sometimes after conferring with other doctors or even researching available information. But doctors are not God. Sometimes the diagnosis is wrong. It is the same in the world of spirits.

Some spirits that channel information to mediums are from a lower energy level in the astral world, others from a higher energy astral level or any level between. The higher the level of the source of information, the greater the probability of the accuracy of the information that is transmitted.

If, for example, your Aunt Millie was someone whose advice you would not take seriously while she was in the physical, treat her advice the same way after she has crossed over to the astral world. In this world, if you had a question about the laws of physics, you could ask your cousin who took a physics course in high school. He just might be able to answer your question correctly. The likelihood of getting the correct answer might increase if, instead of asking your cousin, you asked your neighbor who majored in physics in college. The likelihood of the correct answer might even be greater yet if you asked a university professor of physics. Just as there are different levels of intelligence or abilities in our world, so it is in the spirit world. You might get some kind of answer to your question from Aunt Millie or you might even get an answer from the level of Albert Einstein.

Just because information is channeled from the astral world, this does not mean that you can take it as gospel truth. In fact the Bible says "Try the spirits." meaning "Test the spirits." (I John 4:1 "Beloved, believe not every spirit, but try the spirits whether they are of God: because many false prophets are gone out into the world.") Spirits can be good or evil. They can be right or they can be wrong. Some try to deceive. Some try to help. The important thing is to be very cautious when dealing with the spirits and the information they provide.

Some spirits like to send messages to their loved ones and friends; information mostly about their experiences, relationships and feelings while on this plateau. Other spirits provide guidance in their communications. Their intent is to be helpful and guide the individual. We all have at least one spirit guide who stays with us throughout our lifetime. Even though we may not "hear" them, they do have an effect on our intuition so that we will be more likely to make the right choices in the exercise of our free will.

The exercise of our free will takes precedence over spirit influence. Ideas that come from spirits often appear as thoughts that seem to come into our minds from nowhere or what we might call "inspired" thoughts or even "epiphanies". Sometimes a guide will appear for a specific occasion, such as to give help to a doctor during an operation, or even to give advice to a gambler.

In my book, *Scattered Glimpses: A Mosaic*, I wrote about an interesting case that occurred when one of my physician friends, Dr. Richard Neubauer, spoke to me about the quadruple bypass heart surgery that he needed. He was in considerable pain and was fearful that he might not pull through. He knew me well enough that he had faith in my predictions. My telling him that everything would be okay calmed his nerves. He had the operation and it was very successful. My guide had told me this.

Two or three days after the operation, a doctor whom I did not know came to me in spirit, telling me about what had taken place on the operating table. He told me that when he was alive in the physical world, he had done a great deal of work with heart surgery. From the other side he was guiding the doctor who was performing the surgery, helping him with what he called some kind of loop that he had invented when he was on this plateau. I never spoke to the doctor who performed the physical operation but was curious about how the doctor in spirit had exerted influence on him. Did he actually come to him in spirit as he came to me or did he influence the doctor's thinking (or intuition as my guide calls it) without the doctor even knowing so?

17

When I related this episode to my recuperating friend, I told him the name of the assisting doctor from the spirit world, Christian Bernard. Dr. Neubauer told me that Dr. Christian Bernard was probably one of the most famous heart surgeons ever. It was he who performed the first heart transplant many years ago.

I get the impression it takes spirits a lot of energy to make their presence known to those in the physical world, whether visually or auditorially. On several occasions, after communicating with them for a while, they began to fade or their voice became weaker. They have told me they do not have the strength (I suppose that means energy.) to remain with me any longer. I feel the spirits can sense when they are in the presence of someone like me who can see or hear them.

In addition to the transmission of information from the spirit entities, the receiver (that is, the medium) must also be considered. Very often information from the spirits is not given in words but rather in symbols, or pictures, or moving scenes, or in languages other than English, or by other means less familiar to those in our dimension, such as telepathy. The mind of the medium must handle this information and translate it accurately into understandable verbal language.

The translation of information into verbal language involves the exercise of the medium's psychic ability. A great psychic must be able to shut his mind down, have no conscious thoughts and be devoid of all emotions when in the psychic mode. The same is not true of mediums. Mediums can be simultaneously fully aware of what is occurring in the astral world and the physical world at the same time. Not all mediums are psychics. Not all psychics are mediums. Here also is an area open to wide diversity. Some mediums are more adept in translating the messages with greater accuracy than other mediums because of their varying psychic abilities. A great medium may not be a great psychic. Likewise, of course, a great psychic may not be a great medium. Thus, herein lies another possible reason that a medium might provide information that was different from that which was transmitted by the spirit; in other words, information that was wrong, distorted or incomplete. For truly reliable information, the channeler must be adept as both a medium and as a psychic. Of course, this is all predicated on the energy level of the spirit that is channeling the information.

With all due modesty, I feel that I can say that there are three major reasons for the exceptional level of accuracy of my relating communications from the world of spirits: 1. The high level of the guide that is the source of the information 2. My ability as a medium to clearly receive information from the spirits 3. My psychic ability to interpret the information from the spirits accurately.

Chapter 8

CHANNELING

For me, channeling information from unseen sources is a very natural process. It has always been part of my life on this earth. I receive both psychic and channeled information. By this, I mean that thoughts, ideas, pictures, symbols, feelings, hunches etc. just come into my mind, often when I am thinking about a particular topic but also often when my conscious thoughts are unrelated to the information received. Perhaps this information does come from an unseen outside source (that is, channeled) but I sense a difference between psychic and channeled information. I feel that psychic information comes from my higher self at the soul level or from a source that is not related to specific entities that channel information to me. This I feel but I do not know, nor can I explain the difference.

I do, however, sense four different ways of receiving information from outside sources that I channel. The first is that ideas just flow into my mind. These are not words, but rather concepts that I can easily convert into conscious speech. As I relax, the words flow very easily from my mouth. I sense a difference that I am unable to explain between receiving information through this modality and receiving information psychically.

The second way I receive information is that I actually hear someone speaking inside my head; words that I could repeat aloud if I so choose. I often have to pay careful attention because my mind must keep up with the pace of the voice of the speaker. If I am distracted or do not pay careful attention, the words are not repeated by the sender but are lost to me. This can, on occasion, be quite disconcerting. There could be gaps in what I hear or the information is so abundant that my memory cannot recall all that was said.

The third means of receiving information is when I am in an altered state and allow the channeler to speak through me. Although it appears that my consciousness is not in this dimension, it seems that both my awareness of this world and the voice of the speaker are inside my head. Although the channeler is speaking through me, I have the ability to censor, block or alter what comes out of my mouth. When I return to this reality, I am able to remember only certain parts of what I spoke aloud.

The fourth means of channeling, which I call deep-trance channeling, is when my consciousness appears to be fully dormant. I am speaking aloud but I am totally unaware of what I am saying and have no ability to control what I say. After channeling, I come slowly back to my everyday third dimension level of consciousness and have no memory or only foggy memories of what was said through me.

Chapter 9

THE SPIRIT GUIDE

Every person receives guidance and assistance from individuals in the spirit world. The majority of us are not even aware that we are guided by the spirits. Very often communication from spirit guides comes as intuition or "thoughts from out of the blue". We often give ourselves credit for being so intelligent, so clever or so perceptive when actually the origin of our ideas was not from our own mind.

Both spirits and angels have the ability to communicate with us telepathically. That is, they can project thoughts or ideas into our minds. How we respond to those thoughts or ideas is totally up to us. This is because each human has been endowed with a free will. We are the masters of our own fate.

Each of us has at least one spirit guide that stays with us from the time we are born until the time we die. Some people have more than one guide. At times other spirits come to help us in specific situations.

Even though most people are oblivious to their spirit guide, there are some people, however, who have the ability to hear and communicate directly with their guide.

Those in the spirit world are at a higher level than those in the physical world. This means that spirits have the natural ability to see and understand more than humans do. They can see what we can do to improve our lives, what can be done to solve our problems and what lies ahead for us.

The intent, goal or purpose of the high-level spirits is to help humanity, individual by individual, so that all humankind can evolve to higher levels in their spiritual evolution.

There are people in our world that can communicate with their guide and are often able to share information that they receive from their guide to help other people.

I would like to tell you a little about my spirit guide and my relationship with him. First, however, I will begin by mentioning a few things I have learned from him regarding spirit guides in general. You will find some of what I will say here, in abbreviated form, in the question and answer section that follows.

We all have a spirit guide who, before our incarnation, agreed to guide us throughout our lifetime. Some of us have two or three, perhaps even more. At times, other spirits guide us for specific situations or periods of time. Like humans in the physical, spirits have emotions and personalities. They vary in their ability to provide guidance; that is, some guides are better than others. Some are very good and helpful in the information they transmit to us and, at the opposite end of the spectrum, some guides can be not so helpful, often even providing information that is incorrect, not understandable, or incomplete.

All of our guides communicate with us. It is we who do not hear them. Unlike most people, but like many other people, I am able to hear the voice of my guide within my head just as if a person were speaking to me. It seems that the majority of humans receive guidance that appears to them as intuition or thoughts from "out of the blue". Even then, many people do not recognize their intuition, but instead either misinterpret it or just ignore it. Usually intuition appears as your very first thought when you are focusing on a situation, especially in decision making. This first thought is very fleeting and often escapes before it is captured. The secret is to recognize your first thought, hold onto it, and then act on it.

Spirits have varying degrees of energy. This is what is meant by "levels" in world of spirits. The higher the level, the greater degree of accuracy in their communications. I will try to tell you everything I know about my guide but I will not reveal his name. This is not by my choice, but by his. If many others were to call on him, he says that this would drain his energy.

My guide is a very old soul; that is, he has had many, many incarnations in the physical both on Earth and in other star systems. He states that the earth is not his home base. We may therefore assume that he is of extraterrestrial origin. He views life in the physical as very difficult and says that he has no desire to reincarnate. He does at times, at his discretion, manifest himself to me visually also but not always. He has told me that he can manifest himself to me in whichever of his incarnation experiences he chooses. He has said he does not come to me in the visual form of his last lifetime but rather when he was on Earth in Biblical times.

He appears as a prominent personage in the Old Testament of the Bible. It is his preference to show himself as an old man with a white beard, dressed in a robe, wearing sandals and holding a crook in one of his hands; often walking on sand such as a beach or on cobblestones. A few times he has shown himself to me as a younger, strong, muscular healthy man. I do not know if that was his younger self in his Biblical lifetime or if it was he in another incarnation. I know nothing else of his other lives in the physical. He told me his name as a Biblical personality. Actually, since I am not well versed in Biblical characters, his identity was of little significance to me. Practically all I know about his life as portrayed in the Bible was told to me by my husband, who had a strong religious upbringing. He did indeed play a significant role in the Bible.

Since spirits have distinct personality characteristics just as do humans, I will attempt to tell you what I know about his personality. He is a gentle soul, kind and caring. He has quite a sense of humor, which can often be misinterpreted as what we might call a big ego. Yet he is modest and unassuming. He takes pleasure in helping those on our plateau. I say "others" because he has told me that he is the guide for other people in addition to me. He is quite down to earth and at times can be even rather earthy, even having a sharp tongue.

When I am communicating with him, I often question what he tells me and I dispute what I am told. When I am in the third form of channeling, as described in the previous section, I sometimes hold back and do not say aloud what he tells me, or I tone down what he says to make it sound more dignified or tactful. I sometimes cover up his earthiness. It seems that tact takes a backseat to truth in the information my guide provides. There is something almost like a childlike honesty in his communication.

He has told me that English is not his language and that on rare occasions it is difficult for him to understand what we are saying to him. To us his spoken English is quite good. His vocabulary is rather extensive and his speech is precise although his phraseology is sometimes slightly different from what we might use, almost bordering what one might think of as slightly old-fashioned. For example, he would often say "'tis" instead of "it's" or in answering a question that would evoke a "yes" answer, he would say "indeed" to mean "yes". He often says, "They are existing" rather than "They exist". Many people have told me that they particularly enjoy his down-to-earth type of speaking rather than the inspirational or lofty platitudes that are often channeled through other mediums.

When someone once asked him a question in English but with a thick foreign accent, my guide asked him to ask his question in Spanish, the questioner's native language. The man then asked the question in Spanish and the guide answered in English through me. I myself do not comprehend Spanish at all but his response was very clear to the questioner. The guide has also answered questions asked in Portuguese, Italian, Polish and Russian. When I asked him what language he was most comfortable speaking, my guide's response was "Tongues". He says that Tongues is a fantastic way of expressing oneself. It is something that is built into the system of everyone who has a brain.

It is interesting to note that some of what I know about him did not come from what he said to me or how I visually perceived him. Instead, it came from what members of our group told me after I had concluded a deep-trance channeling session. Although I knew he liked me, it made me feel good to hear group members repeat all the nice things he said about me and some of my specific traits that he liked. When I would channel, he would refer to me as "she" or "her" but never by my name. Using my name could have pulled me back into this reality. The group enjoyed my disputing him and his earthiness. His sense of humor often evoked laughter from the group.

We can make a parallel if we assume that all Earth people are in the second grade in school. To us the whole school is our teacher. Our teacher is the whole school. We cannot conceptualize beyond that. Some students are more intelligent and some are less intelligent. If we need help, we can ask a more intelligent classmate. Sometimes more intelligent students know the answers to your questions. Sometimes they do not. Even the more intelligent students can sometimes give you the wrong answers. We seek help from all our classmates. Then one day, a high school student enters our classroom and says he will help us with our work. To those of us in the second grade, the high school student appears as an intellectual giant who knows everything. We do not consider that there are others above the level of a high school student who knows more than he knows. All we know is that we have in our presence someone who can immediately assist us. Perhaps we are the second graders and the guide is the high school student.

In addition to my guide, I sometimes allow others from the astral world to speak through me. Years ago, when I would deep-trance channel in front of a group, my listeners told me that I was speaking in a thick Irish brogue. I have often been told that there are very slight but perceptible facial changes when I channel certain entities. For more information about interesting experiences with other non-physical entities, I suggest you read my first book in this series <u>Scattered Glimpses: A Mosaic.</u>

Chapter 10

KNOWLEDGE
PROVIDED BY THE
SPIRIT GUIDE

The major section of this book consists of information taken from the questions asked of the guide during the meetings of the Coral Springs Metaphysical Group over a period of several years, as Sondra was deep-trance channeling.

Please keep in mind that Sondra was not aware of the words that she spoke while in a trance. She admits that when she listened to the recordings afterward, many of the answers truly surprised her and would often fly in the face of what she thought she knew. It is quite likely that some of the content herein will surprise, shock or offend the readers as well; especially in the areas of religion, extraterrestrials and ancient history. If any of the content is not in accord with your belief system, please do not judge her for what is written. She is only the messenger. We find that there are on occasion some of the guide's responses may appear to contradict other responses or seem not to make any sense. We have included them anyway because sometimes understanding comes later.

Although Charles and our group members formulated the questions, by no means can they be considered experts in the areas of the content in this book. Therefore, to those who are more knowledgeable or enlightened in such areas, many of the questions will undoubtedly appear amateurish. On the other hand, to those who are less knowledgeable, many of the questions may be "off-the-wall", the work of delusional people.

We strongly stress that in no way are we trying to establish any kind of cult-like following. Our intent is simply to provide information for the readers to ponder and make their own decisions regarding the worth of the responses.

Please keep in mind that the information provided by the guide is from the perspective of someone who dwells in the world of spirits and the content reflects his experience, his knowledge and his viewpoint. Sometimes when giving information, he receives assistance from sources above the level where he is. He often confers with other entities in his realm. As a dweller in the astral realm, he still maintains his personality. This often comes through in the humor noted in some answers.

The group enjoys the manner in which the guide speaks to us. He speaks as one of us and is usually easily understood. He is different from most other channelers because he does not throw fluffy platitudes to us. He is very down to Earth.

Since the content has been organized under several topics, the same content may appear in two or even three sections if it is relevant to the topic. If the same information, or part of the information, appears in more than one topic, a letter in parentheses after the statement indicates that the statement has appeared prior to that point. On occasion a statement will be enclosed in brackets []. Those entries are editorial comments.

In regard to the questions that Charles asked which were prepared in advance, the sources of inspirations for those questions include the following: 1. Subjects which he thought he knew from his past learnings or experiences but wanted validation. 2. Questions for which he had no definite answers. 3. Questions which came to him during periods of meditation or in dreams. 4. Questions which developed from reading or watching television or You Tube programs, most notably the videos by David Wilcock and his associates.

A. DEATH: THE TRANSITION TO A
NEW LIFE IN THE SPIRIT WORLD

1. The process of dying

Going from the physical world to the spirit world is as easy as going from one room to another. People will be there to assist and bring you comfort. The living experience can be much more painful. The death process is not painful. It is what occurs before you die where the pain is. Life can be more painful. It has been to many others. Dying is as easy as falling asleep and then waking up in a different place. There is absolutely no pain in death.

Although dying is just like going through a door from one room to another, some people have more difficulty adjusting to life in the spirit world. In a lifetime the fear of death is predominate. Adjusting to the new life in the spirit world is not always an easy process just as in the physical world some babies have a more difficult time adjusting to the new life.

Your prayers may or may not be of benefit to that person. It may not be their wish. You are wishing for them what you wish to be. You can make their transition easier if you pray for peace. Most humans have a great fear of dying, but in reality the only basis for that fear is the unknown from my own experiences with many deaths there is no reason to fear dying.

Although the disposition of every single person varies, the transition from the physical world to the spirit world is probably easier if you are knowledgeable about the spirit world before you die; how people will accept their fate, because it will be familiar to you. We greet you depending on how you arrive. It is easier to show you your familiarities.

When you cross over to the spirit world you see what you want to see. Your spirit guide is there to meet you just when you come home. Preferably your family is there.

At the moment of death, a review of your whole lifetime flashes before you. It is a flashback; especially your moments of guilt come to mind. The mind is a wonderful, magnificent instrument. Everything you have done then, all of the sudden comes to your memory. That does not stay with you after you have crossed over to the spirit world.

It is not necessarily true that if people are in a state of mind where they expect to die soon or consciously want to die, their transition to the spirit world is easier. The same is true when a person has no fear of dying.

When death is imminent people sometimes wait for certain conditions to be right before they die; conditions such as loved relatives or friends being present at the time of departure. Human nature is able to greet and say goodbye and say hello to your old friends. You make the decision about when to go at the subconscious level but you are not aware at the conscious level.

The transition to the spirit world is not any different for those who have Alzheimer's disease than it is for others. They are not aware. They are in a different element.

There is truth to the belief that as you cross over to the world of spirits you should follow the white light.

I cannot explain at this moment why humans who see auras emanating around the physical bodies of people say that often before a person dies, sometimes days or even weeks before they die, the person has no aura when death is eminent. If there is no aura, then the person is going to die every living thing, whether they are animal, vegetable or whatever, everything that is alive, has this field of aura energy around them.

2. What we take with us when we cross over

When you die and discard your physical bodies, you do not maintain the same attitudes, emotions, and desires after crossing over to the world of spirits. If you are angry when you die, you will take over that same emotion for the moment. It is not lasting. It is for the moment. The attitudes, emotions, and desires that you have in the physical dissipate gradually when you enter the spirit world. Those that are based on physical appetites such as food, alcohol, drugs and sex cannot be satisfied in this world. This is not one of the concepts of hell but is torture.

If someone is jealous while in the physical world, they could take that jealousy with them after they enter the spirit world. Spirits can be jealous of other spirits, or angry.

Although some spirits maintain their religious beliefs after they crossover, most no longer have the same beliefs. Religion makes no sense in the spirit world. It is made up.

If a person does not think properly and has poor reasoning or judgment or is driven by emotions in decision making rather than logic, for the most part that person carries over those same attributes into the spirit world. As you are in the physical world, you will be pretty much the same in the spirit world.

If a person dislikes homosexuals simply because they are homosexual, that person continues to have that prejudicial attitude regarding humans after that person enters the spirit world. Your attitudes don't change. You just don't learn. If you can't learn while you're here, you are not going to learn while you're there. You have to come back again into another lifetime.

There are times that people who have mental or emotional disorders carry over those same disorders when they arrive on my plateau. They can overcome them on my plateau. Anything is possible. It depends upon the individual. It depends on the length of the mobility whether people that we call insane retain that insanity for a while when they cross over to the spirit world. Eventually with their residence in the astral world they overcome the insanity before their next incarnation. They can shed that.

A person's level of intelligence carries over from the physical world to the spirit world; that is, if you are stupid as a human you will be stupid as a spirit. 'Tis not true that the level of intelligence is carried over when we transition back to the physical world from the spirit world. The level of anxiety and fears and beliefs are not cultivated and do not turn over. They are dropped with the new life ahead. Some of us do not remember what we learned while in the physical after we transition to the spirit world. The transition to the spirit world varies with the individual. It is very difficult for me to tell each individual what they will retain in life in the spirit world.

When souls cross over to our world, some need long periods of rest while others need very little or practically none at all. When you pass over into the spirit world while in a coma or are heavily drugged with pain medication, sometimes some people are immediately alert and some are not. I cannot tell you how long it will take them to become alert because time is up to you. I cannot give you a specific answer.

Most people lose their religious beliefs when they enter the spirit world but the terrorists who have killed in the name of their religion still have the same attitudes but they don't have their religious beliefs. There is no such thing as religion in the spirit world and God didn't create any religions.

Those who have committed an atrocious crime, such as mass murderer suicide bombers, feel they were justified in doing and continue

31

to feel justified for what they did after they have crossed over into the spirit world. Why should they change? When you step on ants and see nothing wrong with stepping on ants, there is no such thing as right or wrong.

When a person dies and enters the spirit world that person is not forced to be confronted with all the memories of his recent lifetime if he does not want to revive those memories. Different flashbacks will come to aid him to progress to go forward. Memories are just flashbacks that are given at different moments. Do not fear flashbacks.

If a person is in severe pain when death occurs, the pain will not disappear immediately upon entering the spirit world. It lingers for a while. It is the same as why a person should not be cremated for a least a couple of days after death. It is similar to when a person feels pain where a severed leg once was. The pain can be felt in what some call the etheric body and the etheric body does not separate immediately. The etheric body is never needed after death.

3. Effects of the living on those who have crossed over

Those in the physical can impede the progress of those who have recently crossed over by excessively mourning them and by not letting go of their personal possessions. Sometimes those that are alive keep them earthbound by mourning them. It is best not to mourn them. Let them go. Let them be well. Let them follow their path. Let them go like a bird has to fly and your children have to grow. People who are alive do help in keeping those earthbound. They do help in a negative fashion. They help and do not let us go on. Those that are earthbound continue to be earthbound because of people that continue to call them. You will not let them go. You do not relieve them. You keep them for your own personal business. Sometimes they continue for many, many centuries to be earthbound.

If a person's possessions are disposed of very soon after they die, that can have a negative effect on that person as a spirit. If attachments are disposed of too soon that has a negative effect. You should hold onto the possessions until you are sure. On the other hand, if you hold onto them too long, that can sometimes cause the spirit to be earthbound.

You do not hold back those who have passed on when you think happy memories of them. Happy thoughts make us joyous. It is fine to have memories of happiness. Be grateful for your cherished memories and your moments of pleasure. You can help them by telling them to follow the light.

In some ways it is possible for humans to help earthbound spirits to make the transition to the spirit world. The best way is to give them comfort.

After a person dies is it not difficult for the spirit when humans say critical or harmful things about him that they never said while the person was in the physical. It makes it more difficult for the person who says negative things.

Elizabeth Kubler Ross was correct when she said that when a person's death is imminent, friends and relatives should not encourage that person to hold onto life but should give them permission to die. It is very kind to give to the dying person such permission. It is okay to eat the cherry on top with whip cream. In other words, it is not particularly good to encourage the person to hold on to life and to stick around if they don't want to.

When a candle is lit for a person who has died, it will help that person. I would recommend that you light candles only at the beginning to say goodbye and to say that you love them. If you light candles for them over a period of time, that could keep them earthbound. But why do you want to keep them earthbound? You light candles more for your own comfort than for helping the person who has departed.

4. Remaining earthbound after we cross over

After a person dies, there are sometimes occasions when at least part of that person's consciousness remains with the body at the gravesite. The part that remains earthbound is what we call a "ghost" as contrasted with a "spirit", that part that moves to my plateau. There are times that your consciousness does not dissolve.

People do not have to fully enter the spirit world immediately after they die or as you say "follow the light". They can remain under the sphere of the earth influence for a while before moving on. Each individual is different and there are many different individuals as you well see. There are many different flowers to make a bouquet. When it is time for individuals to leave the physical world, they can get trapped on that plateau if they remain longer than they should. I cannot say how long a ghost can stay before becoming trapped.

Spirits can become earthbound if they do not follow the light and go into the spirit world. You have so much confusion on your plateau and some cannot follow the light. It's like a jigsaw puzzle. It's up to you. There are many, many earthbound spirits who are confused and are not fully in my world. When a person passes, let them go in peace. Please do not hold them down. They want to leave in peace.

A strong willed person can take measures while they are alive that would assure that they do not become earthbound when they die. If you die and want to go directly into the spirit world and not be in the in-between world, you can prevent yourself from being earthbound by eating the right food; that is, think the right thoughts.

If you love to listen to music while you are in the physical, you will still maintain that love after you cross over to the spirit world. It means nothing. It is just giving you peace to give you the right word. Since music does not exist in the spirit world, your love of music might cause you to remain earthbound for a while before crossing over fully into the spirit world. If you love something, that is another reason why you might not follow the light right away.

Some spirits stay earthbound for a short time and others go directly to the spirit world when they die. It depends on the individual. Each individual is a different person. Some people take time to go. Some people when they are not breathing are still breathing. In other words, when you are dead you are not dead. You are still there. The soul does not put any pressure on the entity to go swiftly into the spirit world but allows them to remain earthbound as long as they want before they go over. In a simple way that is correct. They remain earthbound even though there is no pulse. They still hear. They do not talk.

There is a danger of a person fully entering the spirit world too rapidly after physical death. It is sometimes of greater benefit to the person to remain earthbound for a while before fully entering the spirit world. There is no requirement that after you die you must go directly fully into the spirit world. You can remain under the sphere of influence of the physical earth for a while.

5. Adjusting to the new life

There is no one factor that is more prevalent than others in determining how easily a person will adjust to the transition to the spirit world. Each individual is individual and the adjustment is individual.

There are many levels in the spirit world and when you cross over to that world, you reside at the level which matches your actions when you were in this world. I am at one of the higher levels in the spirit world.

If you were well-known but hated by many people because of your evil deeds while in the physical, that would that make your transition to the spirit world or your life in the spirit world more difficult. It would be more difficult for a negative personality to appear in our culture.

When a person crosses over to the spirit world, he will be able to recall all the events of his recent lifetime with clarity if he so chooses. He even recalls events that he could not recall while in the physical.

If you unexpectedly die instantly, such as by murder or in an accident, that has an effect on your entry and adjustment into the spirit world. When you go to sleep at night and you wake up alarmed, does that not have an effect on your feelings for the day? If you die after a long illness and are sort of expecting to die, it is sometimes easier to adjust to the spirit world than if you die unexpectedly.

When they enter the spirit world, people who were very religious have difficulty in accepting the fact that religion is manmade and does not exist in the spirit world but those in the spirit world eventually get over the idea of religion. There is no such thing as religion in the spirit world.

People who are very materialistic and emotionally attached to their possessions have more difficulty adjusting to life in the spirit world than people who are not materialistic. There are times that they are not wishing to let go and it is true that their transition becomes more difficult. Possessions mean nothing to you in the spirit world. Possessions are of no importance. They are not needed. I would absolutely advise you to try to not get too attached to physical things.

Those who have left the physical world but are still attracted to their possessions can be fully in the spirit world. You don't have to be an earthbound spirit. You could be an earthbound spirit or you could be fully in the spirit world.

People who hoard many physical objects because they are emotionally unable to dispose of them have difficulty adjusting to the transition to the spirit world. They are likely to become earthbound because of that. It is not good to hoard things because you are unable to dispose of them.

The transition from the physical world to the spirit will be easier for people who are interested in helping other people rather than those who have been selfishly materialistic. Helping others is very important.

6. Funerals and cremation

There is sometimes a danger if a person is cremated too soon after dying because there is a possibility that what some call the etheric body may not have fully separated from the physical body, thus causing the entity to feel pain. You must wait two or three days before being cremated. When a person is cremated, the soul evolves no differently than if the person were buried in the ground. If you are cremated it will absolutely not hurt the soul. Regarding whether people should be cremated or buried when they die, it is whatever they feel comfortable with. If they want to be burned, from earth you come, from earth you go back. Neither way has an effect on your spirit. When you are gone, you are gone.

There is neither a positive nor negative difference between being buried in the ground and being cremated except that you should not be cremated within two or three days because your etheric body feels the pain. When a person has a leg removed, for example, they can feel pain where the leg once was. Pain can be felt in the etheric body. It takes time for the etheric body to separate from the physical body.

When someone passes over, it is not important to have a funeral with a priest or rabbi or minister to assure the safe passing. You will not have any trouble adjusting to your transition to the spirit world if you don't have a minister giving prayers over you or have people praising you. It will actually make no difference because you will be in peace, in happiness, in calmness. Have no fear. Even though having a funeral or a memorial service does not help that soul to get on the other side more comfortably, it does help the people that are going to the funeral. When you come into this world, you come in alone. When you go out, you also go out alone. So it doesn't matter who is saying goodbye because those who are with you will always be with you.

7. Miscellaneous

When a person has what we refer to as a near death experience, some enter the spirit world and some do not. Each individual is individual. The NDE experiences are spontaneous, not preplanned. You cannot preplan.

Many religions teach you that when you die you go immediately to either heaven or to hell but they say nothing about going to the world of spirits. It's another way to have control. You have control with your religion. You make your own heaven, what you call heaven, and you make your own hell as you well know. Heaven and hell are states of judgment. When people arrive on this plateau we are here to greet them and console them. They will feel comfort and ease and happiness in arriving when they come on our plateau. This is not heaven. Heaven and hell are purely religious concepts. They are not actual places but I would say they are states of mind. We go on from there and we learn or we come back again into another physical lifetime. When we cease to exist in spirit form we go on or we reincarnate, or we go on from there.

A person's age at the time of passing into the spirit world has no effect on his transition to the spirit world or his life in the spirit world. It makes no difference how old you are when you enter into a new regime. Age does not matter.

When people die, their pets in the spirit world sometimes appear to help their transition to the spirit world. They are part of the family. It is a very great possibility that your [the Zechers'] dog that died twenty years ago will be there to greet you but your dog needs to rest.

When we pass over there will be no language. Spirits can read thoughts. A language isn't necessary.

When people die it is their predestined fate to die at that moment but their death could have been prolonged if their actions had been different. You can prolong your leaving if you don't want [at the subconscious level] to go and you are helping others. Angels help in your passing. They guide you there and help you cross over.

People die only when their higher self wants them to die. If there are catastrophic events such as war, typhoons, mass murders, and hundreds of people are killed, all of those people were meant to die at that time. A person's life cannot be cut short if that person's higher self does not want to leave the physical. When we reincarnate the length of our life is predestined at that time.

37

At the soul level, sometimes a husband chooses to die in order to allow his wife to go in a different direction. Sometimes the same is true of friends or other relatives.

After a person dies, there should be a waiting period before any actions are taken that might shock the departed soul that might bring them to the reality that they have died. You should be careful not to shock the departed souls that they are dead because they don't realize it in most cases. That is why in some religions they choose to cover the tombstone.

Some souls are immediately aware that they are in the spirit world but others do not realize they have crossed over even though they are communicating with Sondra. Sometimes souls are able to communicate immediately after they cross over but then must spend a long period of no communication before they begin communicating again. Sometimes those that pass over can aid you but then they have to move on.

When people cross over to the spirit world some people see clearly and are able to see themselves more accurately than they did when they were alive, and some never do.

When someone passes away they cannot leave their energies on a person so that that person who is still alive becomes them and acts just like them.

When people cross over from the physical world to the spirit world they sometimes wish they had not, but wish they had remained in the physical instead. Yet some spirits like me have no desire to come back into the physical. It is too laborious for me to come back. I do not want to follow orders. I have no need to come back. I am not required to come back. I have reached a level where I don't need to come back. It's like religion where you are being told what to do. There are some spirits who have reached a level where they don't need to reincarnate but choose to reincarnate to help mankind advance.

B. LIFE IN THE SPIRIT WORLD

1. Personality traits of the spirits

People in the spirit world have the same kinds of emotions as those in your world. Some are happy, sad, or grouchy. Jealousy exists in our realm, just as in your world when one human is envious of another. There are lazy spirits and there are ambitious spirits and spirits that are not aware. High energy spirits such as I are more ambitious.

Just as some humans have very strong will power but others have weak will power, the same is true of spirits. Some spirits are stronger willed than other spirits.

Like humans, some spirits are immature and playful and other spirits very serious with little sense of humor. I would say that as personalities there is not a whole lot of difference between the range of humans and the range of spirits, and the range of their mentality.

Those in my world sometimes have memory problems and forget things they would normally be expected to remember, just as do people in your world. Me, myself, no. I have no memory problems. Some do.

Entities on the physical plateau that have mental or emotional disorders carry over those same disorders when they arrive on our plateau. There are times they can they overcome them on our plateau. Anything is possible. It depends upon the individual. (A)

A person who has had severe emotional problems all his life and is unaware of the cause of the disturbance can learn the cause of those problems after entering the spirit world if they are not emotionally disturbed. Just like in the physical world, there are emotionally disturbed spirits also. When you go into the spirit you don't go into a state of perfection. In fact, if you are a nut you become a bigger nut.

Just as there are people in the physical whose thinking process is distorted, some entities in the spirit world do not think logically. We do not always think properly at the proper time.

Just as many humans can be quite egotistical and not much concerned for other people, the same is true after they enter the spirit world. One's crossing over does not mean there's going to be a change. There can be an awareness but that does not mean there's going to be a change. If one is a nincompoop one is going to remain such. If you are ignorant you will remain that way. You can grow after you cross over if you wish.

There are no rules or no such thing as right or wrong in our world but we energy beings can still be judgmental. 'Tis fun, you know, to be in judgment of nonsense.

Since time does not exist where we are, spirits generally have a greater degree of patience than those in your world. I do not experience boredom, not even when dealing with those in your world. I can become impatient at times.

Astrology exists in both the physical world and the astral world but spirits don't make use of it. The date of a person's entry into the astral world has an influence on his personality while as a spirit.

There is just as much variety among spirits as there is among humans. Spirits do not seek to have you put them on a pedestal or worship them. Humans' opinions are not necessary.

2. Spirits' Capabilities

Entities in the spirit world have differing amounts of energy; the more highly evolved souls, the greater the level of energy. Spirits or as I say, energy beings, can perceive the level of energy of other spirits. Jesus has a very high energy level. There are entities with a level of energy similar to that of Jesus, and much more. There are times we need to rest in order to restore our energy. We use our energy to help others.

The amounts of energy spirits possess determine the extent to which they can help people in your world. More highly evolved souls in the spirit world have a greater amount of energy than less evolved souls. Some have more energy and assistance as well. Jesus is called most often by humans and he has the energy for that. Others have similar amounts of energy to help you also.

It is true that spirits have differing amounts of energy and that some spirits have an extreme amount of energy like the various Christs that have appeared throughout history, including Jesus. A good sense of humor is an example of a personality characteristic of people that might be an indication of the level of energy level they will have when they enter the spirit world.

In the physical world there are children and adults but the same is not true in the spirit world. All are what you might say equal.

Depending on their level of energy, spirits have the ability to project thoughts into the minds of humans. They can protect you by using telepathy to put thoughts into your mind that you believe are your own thoughts if you allow it. It is up to the individual.

It is easier for spirits to show themselves to some people than it is for them to show themselves to other people; that is, spirits have to use more energy for some people to see them and less energy for others to see them. To teach, you have to use more energy for some people. I can get through to some people more easily than others. If they have no brains, how do I get through? It is the same as teaching.

Spirits can sometimes combine their energies so that they can create enough energy to create an apparition dense enough for humans who are not mediums to see. A spirit may not have enough energy to create an apparition that you can see but they can get other spirits to combine their energies. Then they can disappear or evaporate, just like you think you are seeing something for a moment and then look again and it is not visible to your eyes. That is not the same as what a medium can see. A medium can actually see the spirits in their true forms.

Time and space do not exist where I am. That means I can instantaneously be in the presence of or be in contact with any other entities that I so choose. Spirits can be in more than one place at the same time. Most of us can do that. Spirits can also be in different time periods simultaneously, past and future. Spirits are able to communicate with more than one person or spirit, on totally different matters, simultaneously. Do you not have two hands?

Since time does not exist in the spirit world, spirits are able to witness or become aware of the past thoughts and actions of humans. We can be aware of things you did in the past. The same is true about thoughts in the past. All spirits can do such, not just those in the higher level. As soon as someone adjusts to life in my world, they can see your thoughts and actions if they are interested. Those in our world have the ability to hear, see, and read the minds of those in your world as soon as they cross over. This is an ability that is given at birth. Be aware. They can read your minds if you wish that.

Since time does not exist in the spirit realm, spirits are able to view scenes from their life when they were in the physical, such as their home as it was when they were a child. If you were in the spirit would now, you could go back in time and actually visit or in some way feel your home as it was then.

Do not go backwards. Go ahead. That is a big issue.

If we wish, we are able to go back and witness or re-experience past events such as President Kennedy's assassination. You humans can do the same, more than with just your memory. Those in our world are often able to recall events of their most recent physical life more vividly and with greater clarity than they can with their memories while they are in the physical. Entities in the spirit world can recall events from many of their lifetimes in the physical if they so choose. That is why I am not coming back. I do not want to recall. They are not all pleasant.

If spirits want to see the house where they lived while in the physical, they can see that house as it was while they were living in it or they see it as it is now. They have a choice as to which way they want to see it. They can see whatever their wish is.

It makes no difference if it is in the near future or the far future for spirits to accurately predict events but, as I have said, since the element of time does not exist in our dimension, we are not able to predict the timing of future events.

When people cross over to the spirit world they see what they want to see. You can create your own personal world when in the spirit realm if you wish to. Most are so miserable and are so unhappy that they don't think clearly. You can create whatever you wish.

If creating your garden gives you pleasure you will be able to recreate that garden with your mind when you are in the spirit world. The garden will appear just as real to you when you are in the spirit world as it did while you were in the physical world.

There are animals in our world. Since in our world entities can create what they want with their mind, it is possible to create one of the person's animal pets that were on your plateau when they were here.

We in the spirit world are not interested in recalling events of past lives or virtually relive past events. Wouldn't that be a wonderful situation to go back and relive all our past times? If I were a notable murderer person, wouldn't that be wonderful? I do not think that is so. We learn a little from each lifetime. What would be the sensibility and possibility of observing past events. What will it achieve for me? I am not curious. I am not sensitive to the past. I am looking forward to helping you for your future and for what you can gain ahead. Your past is what you learned.

It is not easier for those in the spirit world to become knowledgeable about their previous incarnations than it is for those in the physical world to do so. Your memory is just as good as our memory. It is up to the individual and up to the memory to realize and recognize their past lives. It is not especially easier for spirits to know about their past lives. You don't remember your lives past and sometimes that is good.

When individuals are in our world they are at times better able to see and understand themselves more accurately than when they were in your world.

Entities from my realm can go to the Akashic plane of information. We can create miracles you know. Every ingredient of nature and of awareness is right, is true, and is real. Every word that is said is right even when it's wrong; even the wrong is correct. By studying the Akashic record for each individual, if you wish it to benefit your current life it will be of assistance to your current life.

People in our world can be knowledgeable about technologies they never knew during their lifetimes in the physical. Not all of us are advanced but we are aware. We have been knowledgeable about the future, have we not?

If a person has never had a physical incarnation in a certain star system, that person is still able to go to the spirit realm of that star system after he disincarnates.

If your grandfather were to reincarnate into the physical world as another personality, your other relatives in the spirit world would not still have contact with him as the personality of your grandfather. I do not believe that they would be aware of the new personality.

It is not important for spirits in our realm to be instrumental in exorcising evil spirits from places or people in your realm. It is more important for you to exorcise them.

Some spirit guides are more competent in helping humans than are other guides. Some people are better than others. It's like some people play the piano better than others. Some people mislead and we do too. Just because we passed on does not mean we are correct. Yes, as in life, we are not all guided properly.

Sometimes when a person passes over to the spirit world they are able to communicate with humans immediately and sometimes they have to wait a while until they are ready to do so. It is an individual answer.

In my world we don't have to touch. We don't have to smell. We can read each other's minds without any touching. Smell and touch are part of the physical world. We are not part of your world. We have the same senses but we use them in a different way.

Entities can be in the spirit world and also have one or more incarnations in the physical world.

Spirits sometimes want to be in the physical because humans experience sensations that spirits cannot. That is what happened many years ago when Gandhi's mind entered Charles' body and he could feel the sensations Gandhi felt. Sondra saw Gandhi and Charles could feel Gandhi's mind enter his body.

Spirits can cause a sleeping person to wake up. That is somewhat the reason Charles wakes up so many times during the nights. You can blame it on the spirits.

When a spirit sees humans, they can see them as they now are or they can see them as they were when both the spirit and the human were on this plateau together.

When humans grieve the loss of their loved ones, those spirits can feel any guilt or pain or sadness for those still here.

3. Spirits' connection with other spirits

Spirits feel more connected with each other than humans feel toward each other. They blend much more. They don't disagree as much. Spirits cooperate much more with each other than you do. They are eager to cooperate. They are not simple minded as you souls are.

When a person crosses over to the spirit world and encounters former friends and relatives, do they do not have the same type of relationship with them as they had when they were in the physical, such as a parent/child relationship. There is a new kind of connection. You won't consider your parents to be your parents in any way. Some friendships in the spirit world are carryovers from previous incarnations and some are not. Just as with humans, spirits like some spirits and dislike others.

On our plateau spirits can perceive the personality of the spirits we encounter. We can perceive different personalities. We can perceive past life personalities of the spirits we encounter but only past lives, not future lives. In our realm our emotions are open. We can see and feel each other. We do not hide feelings like you people on Earth. You look in the mirror and you lie.

Those in the spirit world do not necessarily choose which of their lifetime personalities they want other spirits to perceive. Spirits perceive other spirits in the personality of their most recent lifetime. Their recent lifetime comes in very forceful. It is stronger. Other spirits see me more as in my last lifetime than they do in previous lifetimes. We grow roots that keep growing. The roots grow from the same tree. There are all different roots. That means that other spirits can perceive me in previous lifetimes but the most prominent way they perceive me is in my latest lifetime or in my strongest lifetime. What I am saying is that my most recent lifetime is not necessarily my strongest.

On our plateau, we can choose which personality we wish to show to other spirits or mediums on your plateau. I like to show the best of my personalities. The personality now showing is the nicest. I'm the happiest. We all have different sides. We show what we want to show. Yes indeed, we can show different sides.

Entities in our world always know when another entity is lying to them or trying to deceive them. We do not always tell the truth. We know when we are deceiving. We lie to each other like you do but I and my group will always tell you the truth. A spirit does not hide from another spirit. Why would one wish to. What is there to hide? We don't have dirty bloomers.

There are times that when a spirit creates something with his mind, such as a reproduction of his physical home, that creation is perceivable by other spirits.

We in the spirit world need not verbalize. We can read each other. We just feel each other. We can see each other. We know each other without verbalizing. There are some spirits we like and some we dislike. Some we trust and some we distrust. We pick our own friends. We all are spirits and we all speak the same language. We do not need to speak verbally. We can adjust so emotionally. We are reading the mind of each other's soul. We all get together.

Spirits have names in the spirit world; that is, names by which other spirits can make contact with them or refer to them. We certainly do have identification as you well know. We can call a spirit by name. It is important I can call Jesus. Many of us call him all the time. Time and time again. We say it in vain. We say it in happiness. We say it in prayer. We call his name. Not just people calling on him but spirits also. He is in my world.

Spirits who have similar interests can band together to work toward a common goal. Once we are human we continue as a spirit to be human too and so we console each other and we correct each other and we argue with each other. When I come to your group to answer questions I sometimes have other spirits with me to help.

As in the physical world, there are leaders in the spirit world if we wish. We select those that we put on a pedestal if we wish to put a person or someone on a pedestal. We have no rules like you have on Earth. It is not completely true that there is no one in charge. The only person that is in charge is self. Each spirit is in charge. We have no rules.

All people, criminal types and good people, live on the same plane in my world. There are all phases of people on one plane. It is made so that they will unite. In the spirit world, people of the same type tend to stay together because they agree on the issues. I tend to associate myself with people similar to me as far as the level of evolution. Those that agree with me in answering your questions are giving me advice in helping me give advice to you.

4. Evolution of spirits

A soul that has learned or experienced all that can be learned or experienced on our plateau [i.e. in our world] can remain on our plateau or move to a different realm. We have different levels. At this time I am not able to tell you about levels above me. It is necessary to reach a certain level of perfection before those on our level can move on to a higher level. Entities not ready to reincarnate remain on our plateau or they can go on to another satellite. There are many different worlds out there. There are many different plateaus.

If you are no longer required to reincarnate, most energy beings remain on the astral plane indefinitely or eventually move to a higher realm or to a lower realm, wherever you wish, wherever you feel comfort and solace. A lower realm is other star systems. The earth is not the only place for us to arrive in.

When spirits reach a level that they no longer have a need to reincarnate they can then eventually reside in a level above the spirit world. There are many different levels above. The physical world is the bottom level, then the spirit world, then numerous worlds above the spirit world.

An entity can dwell both in the physical world and the astral world simultaneously. It is also possible that a soul can dwell in the astral realm and realms above that simultaneously. I myself am able to visit what some call the mental world. The mental world is a private world. Since this is a personal world, there are times that individuals do not communicate with others. That is very true. A soul can reside in the spirit realm and simultaneously have several physical incarnations.

In order for a spirit to serve as a guide for a human, a spirit must not necessarily have completed the required reincarnation cycle. No one is perfect. Serving as a guide to physical humans helps the personal growth or advancement of those on our plateau. Service to others helps us to achieve. We all feel better by serving others. Others have their own free will and don't always hear what we suggest.

In both your world and our world, individuals who have a good sense of humor are usually more highly evolved than those with very little sense of humor. Those who have more humor have more strength. Those with very little sense of humor are not as evolved.

There are no higher powers to which those in our realm are held accountable. Spirits are held accountable only to themselves, only to ourselves and the God within us. We are responsible

When a person who has had incarnations on several different planets dies, that spirit resides in the astral realm of the planet of his most recent lifetime.

There aren't any spirits in the earth's realm who have never incarnated. All spirits have had the education of being humanized. There are spirits who have reached a level where they no longer have the need to incarnate. They don't know what to do.

5. Spirits' connection with humans and other entities

Angels play a role in our plane of existence. They are there to guide and administer. Angels are with you also. In order to protect you, spirits can project thoughts into the minds of those who want to cause you harm. There is more overt communication with those on our plateau with angels than there is with them in your world. They hear you, too. They don't want to be known or seen but they do exist. Angels hear you when they want to hear you.

Spirits are able to communicate with entities in realms above or beyond the plateau on which they are. If they wish to communicate with us, we can confer with them. They are on a much higher realm and can see more than we do. Sometimes we can see more from the lower realms.

Spirits can communicate with animals in the physical world as well as with animals in the spirit realm. They can Influence animals too.

Highly evolved spirits can manifest themselves as physical human beings that anyone can see. They are not angels but they can manifest themselves for a brief moment with their energy. They wish for more energy.

Spirits are aware of the karma of those individuals in the physical dimension. Even though you may not be aware of your own karma, spirits are aware.

When a person is about to cross over to the spirit world, spirits know this in advance and are aware and ready to welcome and assist them.

Relationships don't always continue when souls transfer from the spirit world to the physical and thank God for that. Sometimes relationships can start where I am and can continue but don't always appear to be so. It is possible. Sometimes it is rejected.

On our plateau some spirits can learn from those in the physical. Although I have said that sometimes spirits can learn from humans, spirits would not become more knowledgeable if they became aware of the contents of this book that I have helped you write because they are already know the content.

In the spirit world there are times that an individual can like another person and other times dislike that person. Those in our world have reactions similar to those of individuals in the physical world. Is it not true in your world and in our realm we like and we dislike? I can like a person in your world but not like what he does or what the person is thinking of doing. Some are negative you know, and we do pick up your thoughts. You can keep your thoughts to yourself and not talk about them.

When spirits see the future of humans, that is always a definite future. It will occur but the time it will occur is not endured.

When people cross over to the spirit world and then discover that a trusted friend had been dishonest with them when they were together in the physical, spirits sometimes become vengeful toward those in the physical world. They are like humans. We don't forgive nor do we forget. We feel vengeful and sometimes we love to step on your tongues.

Some spirits seek to have humans worship them. They are not bad spirits, whatever worship means. I do not suggest that you do that. I do not suggest that you be easily manipulated. I think you should listen to your own inner self. Some spirits feel temptations, such as wanting to be put on a pedestal by humans but they do not give into them.

When a spirit manifests itself to someone in your dimension, that spirit can appear in whatever form he so chooses, similar to how the angels manifest themselves. A spirit could manifest itself as both a living object and an inanimate object. Like an angel, a spirit could manifest itself as lightning.

No spirit can read your mind. Your mind cannot be read. It does not exist but rather it is mental telepathy. When I said that spirits could read your mind, that was your emotions, not the actual words you were thinking because your word thinking can change. You can suggest and think and then come out with something completely different. There is a distinction between reading our minds and reading your thoughts.

Demons do not exist in the spirit world. They are only for humans. They cannot attach themselves to anyone or anything that does not want it. They are people or humans that are ignored. A person on Earth, through the use of their will, can avoid having demons attach themselves. You can absolutely be stronger than demons. You should not fear them because you are stronger. Even though they come across as being strong, they are really weak. They cause fear and that is control. So if you do not wish to be controlled you must set the demon free.

There are no parasites in the spirit realm that feed off of the negative energy created by humans. We don't allow it. We just reject it from the very beginning. We do not have that in our world.

Just as spirits assist humans, humans can be of assistance to spirits. They can do that by helping each other. Spirits are interested in making you happy, making you feel comfortable. The work of the spirits is to help humans. Therefore when humans help humans they are actually helping spirits.

I have said that I do not want to reveal my name to you because then you would call on me and that would drain my energy. Humans can drain a spirit's energy but they can also add to a spirit's energy by showing love and kindness and showing how well they are progressing. Only progress and be happy doing what you are doing and be of kindness and thoughtfulness and be well cherished. It is human interactions with other humans that elevate my level of energy. That is particularly why I am here to be of assistance to you. When I am helping you, I am also helping myself.

The actions of all human beings can be observed by the spirits. Everything you do can be observed. That doesn't necessarily mean that spirits want to observe you all the time. If you don't want spirits to know what you are doing, do what your wife says. Does she (Sondra) not say, "Stop. Go away. Leave."?

Humans are concerned about the conflict between the Cabal (the Luciferians) and the Alliance (the Elohim). That conflict has an effect in the spirit realm as well. It is affecting my world as well as the physical world.

Spirits perceive and communicate with nature spirits such as fairies, gnomes, elves and leprechauns. It just happens naturally.

6. Spirits' attitudes, emotions and desires

In regard to whether life in the spirit world easier or more pleasurable than it is in the physical world, it depends on the route you take. If you wish to take a difficult route, then life would be difficult. I have said that I do not want to reincarnate. That implies that I prefer my existence in the spirit world rather than in the physical world. Life in the spirit world can be more pleasant than life in the physical world. It's very simple and easier. On Earth you proceed to dominate each other as you well know. It's a possibility that many of the religions developed the concept of heaven because life is so much easier here. Only heaven knows that. I am not aware of such a place as hell. It is not on our map or chart, you know.

As in your world, more advanced souls at our level are less influenced by their emotions than are the less advanced souls. We have emotions and feelings too, you know, and we love to give advice. Like humans, spirits sometimes do or say things that they later regret. That is why pencils have erasers.

Although spirits do not experience physical pain, they can experience emotional pain. I myself do not experience physical pain because I am not in the physical but I experience emotional pain when people do not listen to me. It is painful when I am here to assist you and my assistance is ignored. So it does hurt, not me individually, but it is hurtful when you are not reaching your hand out for help and help is given for you.

If individuals were obsessed with sex while in the physical, after they cross over they take pleasure in observing the sexual activities of humans. They take pleasure in participating indeed. They wish for themselves to have sex.

There are differences among spirits.

When a spirit serves as a guide to a human, that is considered a noble endeavor. Other than serving as guides, there are many ways of serving. We travel and we do help. There is so much to be helped; to give you peace of mind. Many of you are here and suffer and are tortured inwardly. Work is a pleasure.

Spirits serving as a guide to a human sometimes feel relieved when the human crosses over and they don't have to guide the person anymore. Some of us don't always like you but we succeed in being there for you. You don't always like us either.

In your world some people are gregarious and enjoy being with others but there are also people who are not very sociable and prefer being alone or having very little contact with others. The same true in our world. I am one that is gregarious. I like to talk. I do not like to listen. There are also people in my world that tend to be loners and like being alone more. They are fearful people.

On our plateau we have combinations of thinkers, some more liberal and some more conservative in thinking. Some are more intelligent and some are just stupid. There is a wide range of intelligence among the entities in this world just as there is in your world.

There are people here who are nosy and like to pry into everyone else's business but spirits don't read minds for entertainment. They mean to be helpful.

After people cross over into our world, religion is eventually no longer important to them. Religion is manmade. We have no religion where we are. No spirit has any affinity with the religion they had when they were in the physical. It is left behind on Earth. Religion is rules. We are too intelligent to take rules or guidance from religion. When did religion start killing. Adam and Eve had no religion. Here they look back and smile and realize what a joke it was. So they lose their religious beliefs. Although religion does not exist in the spirit world, there are some spirits who do hold on to their religious beliefs from when they were humans.

If a person did not believe that there is such a thing as reincarnation, that person does not continue to hold that belief after they have crossed over to the spirit world. They wake up and say, "Here I am." If a person leaves the earth world and comes into our world, that is not what they think any more. It has dissolved in their thinking.

Just as in your world, entities in our world have different opinions about situations or how to answer a question, or what to do. We do not all agree. There varying opinions in our world regarding the social issues of Earth people, such as gay marriages in your world. We all have opinions which make no value. It is not necessary to have an opinion.

The use of numerology by humans is an effective device for providing answers, explanations or predictions. There is numerology in my realm also. We often make use of it. Numbers are important because they are fun and helpful to be fun. Doesn't a certain number hit you well sometimes? Can I just say "one one one one"? There is significant negativity in the number 666. It is not just something that religion has invented. Conversely, the number 7 is a very positive number.

If people like to travel and explore various cultures and places throughout the world, it is likely that they will still derive pleasure from doing that when they are in the spirit world. People who are inquisitive will remain inquisitive. People in the spirit world actually do like to visit places in the physical world.

When a person is in the spirit world, that person has no emotional attachments to the dates of birth or death from in the physical. The place where a person died has no significance or purpose after crossing over. It is just another place to be put at rest. It has no meaning. It is not where they have lived. The meaning of where they have lived is much more important than the place where they have perished.

In our realm we would define love as when we care about someone else more than we care about ourselves. That is true love.

Spirits do not become upset when the human spouse enters into a relationship with a new person. Since spirits are no longer confined to their physical being, they do not want to hold on to their physical spouse. In fact there are times that the spirit is relieved to have gotten rid of their spouse.

I said that spirits would not learn anything from this book because they already know what is in it. Yet Charles' grandfather said that the book we are writing was hogwash. It means he disagrees with me. He was a very religious man and did not believe in the hogwash you wrote about. He does not believe what I am saying even though he has been in the spirit world over eighty years. He believes in religion because he enjoyed religion. Even though there is no religion in the spirit world, people can sometimes still hold onto their religious beliefs. They will keep their religious beliefs even though religion does not exist. Don't you believe in things that do not exist? So why can't he?

When a baby is born it usually is a joyful experience to humans. The same true in the spirit world when a person transitions to our world. Spirits are indeed at times joyous to receive if they are pleasant people.

Spirits have basically the same kinds of emotions that you have but they are different from human emotions. They do not have fear, for example. In regard to personality types, some spirits are more creative than others. Spirits are psychic and they use their abilities all the time. Psychic plays a far greater role in the lives of the spirits that it does with humans.

We energy beings are not human. We were once sitting and suffering with illness and disease as you. We have no particular form, unless you see electricity. There are many shapes per individual. We can get any shape we want.

7. Spirits' activities

It possible for an individual to overcome physical addictions while in the spirit world if they realize that the addiction is an issue. Most of us do not realize that we have issues. It does not necessarily have to reoccur in a subsequent lifetime as karma.

In our world helping those on the physical plateau and helping those when they cross over is our work. I am aiding and assisting you. Is that not work? Not all are able to assist. On our plane assisting you is entertainment for us.

Spirits sometimes need rest to restore their energy. We do not sleep in a physical sense. We withdraw unto ourselves and do not communicate with others.

When there is a major disaster such as an earthquake or a tsunami in your world in which many people are killed, we are aware of what is to be and we are always there to welcome those who are coming into our world.

I have never heard of any places in the universe where spirits cannot or are forbidden to go. All systems are available to all. I have full freedom to go anywhere in the universe and can do that instantaneously.

When there are spirits in a house, electrical appliances can be activated by them. We cannot control this but have fun doing this nonsense. They can sometimes be activated even when they are not connected to an electrical outlet.

Spirits in our world can wreak havoc or manipulate objects in the physical world much the same as earthbound poltergeists do. In other words they don't have to be an earthbound spirit. They do it for harassment as you harass on your plateau.

Like earthbound spirits, spirits in our world have the ability, for example, to sit in a rocking chair and make the chair rock back and forth so that anyone could see it rocking without actually seeing the spirit.

If someone dies with unfinished business, they can try to finish it, or help a problem after they die but in most cases, they will just let it go.

Prayer plays a role in the spirit world much the same as it does in the physical world. It helps to a degree. We pray to ourselves, to the god that is within ourselves. I define prayer as wishing. I have said that even better than prayer is to visualize something. It is more productive than prayer, undoubtedly so.

8. Miscellaneous

A person's age at the time of passing into the spirit world has no effect on his transition to the spirit world or his life in the spirit world. It makes no difference how old you are when you enter into a new regime. Age does not matter. (A)

High energy evil entities exist in the spirit realm. A spirit at the same level as I am could be evil. If I don't agree with them they are evil. Evil is not knowledgeable. It is ignorance.

Since stars, planets and other celestial bodies exist in the physical world, they also exist in the spirit world. Astrology has influence in the spirit world as it does in your world. Astrology always existed and always was helpful. Those in my realm do not make use of astrology. It exists in my world but we don't use it. Not all of us are interested in stars or planets. It is actually effective in your world.

In regard to astrological influences, the date of a person's birth is important in the physical life. Spirits do not pay attention to astrology but the date of a person's entry into the world of spirits does have an effect or influence on the person while in the spirit world. Just as the date of your birth has an effect on you while in the physical world, the date that you die also has an influence on the personality when you are in the spirit world.

The aspect of life on our plateau that some entities find difficult is having to change the environment. Sometimes it is difficult, sometimes not; sometimes familiar and sometimes not. We don't always come back to America.

There no distinction between the past, present and future in the spirit realm. It is all together now. It is always now. As your wife has said many times, "How do you spell NOW? Turn it around and you have WON. You are living the present, past and future all at once. Since there is no such thing as time in our dimension, an action and the consequences of the action can occur simultaneously.

Life in the physical world on Earth is more difficult than on other planets but spirit life on Earth is not necessarily more difficult than spirit life on other planets. Each planet has its own spirit life as well as its own physical life. I can only answer from my past experience on Earth. I do not wish to come back. Now I reside in the spirit world of another planet, not in the spirit world of Earth.

From where I come there are male energies and female energies if you wish to call it so. It doesn't matter. We are all the same no matter what the gender is. The gender is a choice and there are many choices of gender. In the spirit world there is no such thing as gender but we can portray ourselves as either male or female or both.

Music exists not only in the physical world but also exists in the spirit world. We have a different kind of music, if you want to call it music.

Just as there are differences among the humanoid beings of the various star systems, there are also differences among the spirits of the various star systems.

I have said that the length of a person's life is predetermined but not cast in stone. Suicide is sometimes simply a means of fulfilling that predestination but not always.

The Luciferian agenda affects other worlds in addition to the earth. It affects the spirit world as well as the physical world. Luciferians are not only here. They are throughout the universe, throughout creation.

As there are group differences among the physical appearances of humanoid beings on other planets, there also group differences among the spirits of the various planets. We all have different minds or selections. Very few are the same. Some are more limited than others. It is like having a door in their minds. They shut their minds that they cannot do more.

When you re-enter the spirit world after an incarnation, you can choose which of your personalities to show but it takes time. When you first enter, your main focus is on your most recent incarnation.

Spirits inhabit the astral realm of the planet before they incarnate as humans on the planet.

C. EARTHBOUND SPIRITS, GHOSTS, POLTERGEISTS, DEMONS

1. The world of earthbound spirits

Earthbound spirits are people who have died but, for various reasons, do not go directly into the spirit word. Entities can remain earthbound for several reasons. A person can remain earthbound intentionally in order to conduct unfinished business. At times the person is lost and cannot find his way to the world of spirits. The emotions of Earth people often hold back the person from proceeding forward. Another reason for not going directly into the spirit world is that they do not know better. Their ignorance keeps them back.

When a person dies that person has a choice whether or not to remain earthbound. That decision is not made by forces beyond the person's control. That is made by the person himself. Some people want to come back again but they won't come back again after they have completed what they were here for.

When a person dies, it is sometimes more advantageous or desirable for that person to knowingly remain earthbound for a while before crossing over before entering the spirit world. At times it is possible that the person might want to oversee, for example, the work on a project he had been working on until it is completed by others. It depends upon the individual. It is not of advantage for a spirit to stay earthbound for a while when not needed. It is more hurtful to be where you are not wanted. In so doing is there a danger that the spirit will become trapped in the earthbound realm. It is best to follow the light as soon as you can and go into the spirit world.

Some spirits remain earthbound because they fear that they will go to hell if they follow the light, perhaps because of their religious upbringing. Who is to judge and what hell is? There is always fear. The unknown is always fearful. Fear could be a reason why they remain earthbound.

Some earthbound spirits are people that cannot leave the physical world because they are seeking your assistance on Earth and because you do not let them go and continue on their journey. They are in a very much confused state of mind and they will continue to be so until you let them go. Most of the time individuals are not aware that they are deceased but they will move on once they realize they have passed.

When we use the term ghost to refer to a spirit that is earthbound, that entity can be simultaneously in the spirit world. Sometimes it is only what can be referred to as the etheric body that is earthbound. Sometimes it is the full spirit. It can be both.

There are things that earthbound spirits can experience that a soul which has entered the spirit world cannot experience. Earthbound spirits are not fully in my realm. They do not wish to leave the earth. They sometimes wish to stay on the earth and cause problems. That spirit is partially in my world also.

Earthbound spirits do not hold themselves to the place where they are buried. They do not suffer on the grounds that you make for them to be sheltered. They do not suffer in the cemetery but that is where you place them. Where they are buried is not a place where they have selected. You do not have to fear cemeteries. They are often attracted to the place where they have died not to where they are buried.

If someone died many years ago and at that time their house was a small cabin and now it has been rebuilt as a large house, the earth bound spirit will see the house as the cabin it once was.

The spirits of children who experienced a tragic death are often likely to remain earthbound longer than other earthbound spirits and they are likely to show themselves to other children.

Sometimes earthbound spirits who have not fully crossed over into the spirit realm can foresee the future the same as those in the spirit world do and sometimes they don't. Everyone in the spirit world can see the future to some extent. Some are not interested in seeing the future.

People who live to a very old age and have no close friends or relatives are not necessarily less likely to remain earthbound than people who die in the prime of their lives. Even though they have no friends on Earth, they can remain earthbound before going on to the spirit world if they wish to be that way. They are not worth anything if they have no friends.

Those in the spirit world do not have gender but they can show themselves to humans as whichever gender they prefer. The same is often not true of those earthbound spirits who have not fully crossed over. They cannot show themselves with gender. They are just beings, neither male nor female.

Some spirits intentionally stay earthbound for a while knowing that they can go fully into the spirit world anytime the wish to do so.

2. Earthbound spirits' interaction with the human world

Earthbound spirits who have not yet fully crossed over to the spirit world can influence a person's thinking to help them. They can help them be fearful too. That earthbound spirit is not a ghost but has just not fully moved over yet. They are not fully dressed.

If a person can see earthbound spirits, they can see spirits from my world also. Earthbound spirits sometimes materialize to ask for help from those in the physical world. They not only do ask for help, they plead and they beg for help. They also materialize to control. That can be good and it can be bad.

The use of tarot cards can provide an entry for an earthbound spirit to communicate or in some way make its presence known to humans. They can be given positive energy. There could be danger in using tarot cards in regard to calling in negative spirits, depending on what they are used for. If they are wishing for control, it helps. It's like going to your psychic. Does she wish to control you or does she wish to harm you? Ouija boards are definitely more harmful than tarot cards.

Children's imaginary friends are not imaginary. They are usually earthbound spirits. They are real friends. They are playful usually, not destructive.

When earthbound spirits repeatedly do the same thing, such as moving the same object again and again, that action is usually to let people know of their presence.

Earthbound spirits tend to follow physical laws, such as turning a doorknob and pushing the door in order to enter a room. They need energy, a great deal of energy to do that. They like to move chairs also. Spirits in my world can just appear and we do need energy.

Earthbound spirits, even those which are not demons, can inflict physical injury, such as scratches, on a person.

Animals, especially dogs, have an innate ability to perceive the presence of earthbound spirits. Indeed they are aware and they are very sensitive. They are not touched like humans are touched or confused.

The room temperature drops when an earthbound spirit is present because it is easier for them to communicate in coolness. When it is cooler and not heated temperature, it is easier.

The pilot and the engineer the Eastern Airlines flight 401 that crashed in the Florida Everglades in 1972 appeared as earthbound entities on other airplanes which used parts that were salvaged from that crashed plane. The parts that were used in other airplanes attracted them to the airplane and they were seen on a number of airplanes that used those parts. They were shadows that were seen. The equipment was seen also.

There is usually a disturbance in electromagnetic energy in the vicinity of earthbound spirits. They can and will be measured by equipment that you have.

There are physical entryways to the earthbound spirit world for humans who have sensitivity to such.

When spirits attach themselves to a person, those spirits are able to experience the world through the senses of that person with all six senses.

The footsteps at nighttime that Sondra hears when there are no other humans present are earthbound spirits making their presence known. Spirits in my realm can also do this.

Spirits who remain earthbound for only a very short time can show themselves in a form other than that of the physical life they have just left in many ways such as butterflies, birds etc. Before they move fully into the spirit world they can show themselves not only as humans but also as animals or insects. If you see that butterfly, wave to it.

3. Ghosts

When it is time for individuals to leave your plateau, they can get trapped on this plateau if they remain longer than they should. They are referred to as ghosts in your language. I cannot say how long a soul can stay before becoming trapped. (A)

After a person dies, there are sometimes occasions when at least part of that person's consciousness remains with the body at the gravesite. The part that remains earthbound is what we call a "ghost" as contrasted with a "spirit", that part that moves to my plateau. There are times that your consciousness does not dissolve. (A)

Sometimes ghosts are people who have passed away but do not want to make the transition or cannot make the transition because you hold them back. Do not hold a deceased person back. Wish them well to go on.

Don't mourn. Let them go. Let them be free and you will be free too. If a person has committed suicide they are not at rest. They are hurting not only themselves but their inner being. There are many people in every one of you. There is not just one person. That is why you don't know which way to go. That is why you have to listen to your first thought.

The majority of ghosts are harmless to humans but if poltergeists can frighten you if they wish to frighten you. If you wish not to pay attention, then they will not frighten you.

I am a spirit not a ghost. Ghosts are people who are stranded and they cannot be moved. To be unstranded they have to release their thoughts, their garments, and their impressions. Release them. Please release them.

There are rules that ghosts must play by and a limit to how far they can go. No one will have control over you that you do not allow. The more education you have in this area, the better off you are. The more education you have in this area, the better off you are. The more you know that you are in control and that no one or nothing can control you unless you wish to be controlled, the better off you are. The wanting or not wanting comes from the unconscious level rather than the conscious level.

Ghostly spirits are not the cause of so many people committing suicide at Aokigahara located at the base of Mount Fuji in Japan. Japan has its own influence and has been inundated by much water. The concern there in Japan is the water, the overflow. There is very little truth in ghostly influence. They are committing suicide because they are mentally disturbed and they are in fear.

If a ghost passes through a person's body, that person can feel the energy pass through him even if the ghost is not seen. It is often like a cold energy.

There are ghosts who want to receive help from humans to free them from being earthbound. Ghosts can be aware that they are stuck between the physical world and the spirit world and that is frightening and fearful. It is a nightmare.

There are still many ghosts in the city of Pompeii Italy which was destroyed by a volcano in 79AD. Some people can sense their presence.

2000 years ago about 960 Jews in Masada Israel committed suicide rather than being captured by the invading Roman army. That area is haunted by the ghosts of those people today. It is another place where there are many ghosts.

There numerous earthbound spirits or ghosts in the abandoned buildings on the coastline of Antarctica.

4. Demons

A demon is a miserable negative energy. It is a scorpion that clamps onto you; a soul that wishes misery to join misery. A demon is a very negative earthbound spirit. All earthbound entities are not demons. The intent of demons is to harm humans, or frighten or control. Demons can be removed through exorcism.

Demons sometimes attach themselves to a person and then remain dormant until many years later when something arouses them. If a person becomes religious, that is not the cause of awakening the demon. Fear within the person is the action that will bring the action out. If you believe in demons, you will have demons. If you don't believe, then the demons will not harm you. Demons will only harm you only if you believe in them.

Demons that attach themselves to people usually performed nefarious deeds when they were in the physical world. They were negative and continue to be negative until they learn to be positive. They are bugs in the attic. Some are of alien origin. They are not fallen angels. They are amongst you also. Demons have gender even though in my world we don't have gender. They can be either male or female.

Demons can attach themselves to a person at any time. They sometimes attach themselves to the individual while they are still in the womb. There are different cycles that demons attach themselves. They attach themselves to specific organs sometimes. A person can be simultaneously possessed by multiple demons.

Demons are not created by Satan. They are a state of mind. Whether they exist or no longer exist depends on your mind. As I have said in the past, demons are negative energies. The source of those negative energies is a negative mind. You attract demons to yourselves by your thoughts.

Demons can attach themselves to objects and places as well as to people if you believe in demons. Demons exist but you can tell them to go away. Tell them to leave and go in peace. You don't have to listen to them. Demons cannot force anyone to do anything they don't want to do.

Demons can show themselves to humans in whatever form they choose. That is how demons are demons because they deceive you. They don't show their faces because it is pleasure for them when they are scaring the person more. They are devious. They are controlling. They wish to control. They are evil. Anything evil that wishes to control should not control. Some demons have been physical humans before becoming demons; some have not.

At times it is possible that people can sense the presence of demons in other people. Demons have names but they do not want their names to be known. Most demons are idiots.

Demons do not exist in the spirit world. They are only for humans. They cannot attach themselves to anyone or anything that does not want it. They are people or humans that are ignored. A person on Earth, through the use of their will, can avoid having demons attach themselves. You can absolutely be stronger than demons. You should not fear them because you are stronger. Even though they come across as being strong, they are really weak. They cause fear and that is control. So if you do not wish to be controlled you must set the demon free. (B)

Although I have said that there is no such being as the devil, the origin of the concept of the devil is actually demons that manifest themselves with forms that resemble what humans portray as the devil.

5. Poltergeists

Poltergeists are ghosts that have enough energy to make noises and make objects move. They can do anything they wish to scare the hell out of you. Some poltergeists can be negative and others not negative. They can be negative when they wish to have control. They are there to control and have their way. Poltergeists can be evil entities or just children or pranksters. They sometimes make things move just to get your attention because they need help from you.

Poltergeists get their energy to move physical objects and cause various kinds of havoc and damage in your world by drawing on their own anger or other strong emotions. They can become energized to the point that they can be heard or move physical objects. Their energy is so strong in what they want to say to you. They want to say it over and over and repeat it over and over. They want you to hear them. They want you to listen to them. They want to control you. You do not wish for any other entity to control you. You do not want to be controlled. Fear or other negative emotions of people make it easier for poltergeists to perform their activities. If they do not control, they get angry.

Poltergeists can attach themselves places as well as to people. 'Tis possible but not probable that places, such as a house, prison or hospital serve as entrances for multiple poltergeists to enter the physical world. Poltergeists which haunt a place can make things, such as blood, appear in the physical world. If they wish, they can actually make things appear.

Poltergeists can frequently be the victims of a violent death such as a murder or tragic accident.

A poltergeist's actions do not directly result in the death of a person but sometimes rather indirectly. They can cause fear when one is not aware.

Poltergeists sometimes show themselves when they are making objects move. Some people can actually see the spirit and the results of the spirit's actions. Their voices can be heard by people, not just by those who mediums. You would be able to hear a poltergeist's voice if you wished to but you do not wish to.

It is possible but rare for poltergeists to follow people when they move from one home to another rather than remaining in the original home. They do not always want to harm and hinder. They more often remain in the place but they can move.

Teenagers often provide an easier entryway for poltergeists or demons than do other people because teenagers are more easily influenced. Some of those that are in adulthood can be easily influenced also.

Babies can become poltergeists when they die.

6. Negative Spirits

Malevolent spirits can attach themselves to a person and influence them to perform evil deeds. It depends on what you consider evil. Do you kill unless you want to kill? It is your willingness to do many things. You can't be forced by malevolent spirits.

Evil earthbound spirits can lie dormant for long periods of time and then become active when someone disturbs their resting place or comes in the vicinity of where they are. That is enabling.

The use of Ouija boards can definitely unleash evil spirits that can take possession of a person or bring about negative happenings.

Animals can be possessed by evil spirits and they can be earthbound and not cross over.

It is easier for a spirit to enter a person when that person is not in control. The danger in taking drugs or alcohol is more than just a physical danger. It is it dangerous for a person to imbibe large quantities of alcohol or to take mind altering drugs because doing so makes it easier for negative spirits to influence or attach themselves to people when they are in a weakened condition.

It is not easier for an evil entity to take possession of that person who has been hypnotized. They cannot take over when a person does not wish to be taken. They cannot take over one who does not wish to be controlled. The same can be said about a person who is influenced by drugs. The drugs will take over. Taking drugs does not make it easier for an evil spirit to take over a person if the person does not wish to be so. The wishing or not wishing does not have to be at the conscious level. [This seems to contradict the previous statement.]

An evil spirit can take over a person and make the person's facial features appear different or endow the person with supernatural strength.

There are certain specific words or phrases, which when spoken, have the power to remove negative spirits. "No" is one such word. There are also certain specific words or phrases that can be uttered to bring about change that the speaker desires. Your phraseology is very important. An example of one phrase to get a spirit to go away is "Leave in peace." That has power.

Depending on the energy of a person, ancient Egyptian mummies or artifacts from their tombs can bring negative energy to people. If conditions are right they can affect people. It is nonsense to believe that the mummy can take possession of a person. The influence depends on the weakness of the individual that you are referring to.

There are books that exist that give effective instructions for conjuring up evil spirits. There is always a book for anything. If a person follows the instructions in a book and it is their desire, which is nonsense, they can actually conjure up an evil spirit. There are those that seek out nonsense.

There is power in the use of the pentagram to evoke evil forces if the user believes in it. If the user believes in it, it will be for the user. The user that is doubtful should not be a user.

Diabolical entities that attack or attach themselves to humans sometimes can be something other than disembodied Earth humans. Dark forces that affect humans can emanate from anywhere in the universe, not just from Earth.

A single diabolical entity can simultaneously manifest itself as multiple diabolical entities. I also can manifest myself as different entities simultaneously but not diabolical.

7. Haunting

Objects, such as a car, can be possessed or haunted by earthbound spirits. There are all kinds of spirits and people. Some are evil. It depends from which end of the road we wish to see them.

There are places that are haunted by earthbound spirits. It is very easy for spirits to attach themselves to people if they are weak. Spirits can attach themselves to weak people and cause them to perform destructive deeds. When a place is haunted by earthbound spirits, people often become depressed and withdrawn or frightened. It can affect the person's personality.

If an earthbound spirit haunts a house and then that house is torn down and replaced by a new house, that entity can haunt the new house. The entity will haunt the earth until it finds peace. It is often the land, rather than the building, to which the entity is attracted. The land is essential. The building doesn't really matter.

It is possible but not probable that the presence of a specific person living in a home is the only reason that an earthbound entity haunts a house.

8. Exorcism and cleansing

Even though it is nonsense, religious articles or religious scriptures read aloud are useful in exorcisms of poltergeists and demons. It does work. A means of exorcizing an evil spirit is to pick up a cross and hold it close to you. That will work even though you don't believe in the cross. The same is true even if the user is doubtful of its potential. It does have power. In exorcism you don't necessarily have to believe in something in order for it to become effective.

Evoking the name of Jesus Christ can help exorcise an evil spirit who possesses a person. It is absolutely effective in cleansing a place, and powerful. If you were to use that name, or any other name that has power, it would have the same effect as a priest using it.

Sage is actually functional for the cleansing of a house from earthbound spirits. Water itself is also good for cleansing. It does not have to be holy water. What makes it holy?

It is not important for spirits in our realm to be instrumental in exorcising evil spirits from places or people in your realm. It is more important for you to exorcise them. (B)

Demons can be exorcised trough the rituals of the Catholic Church. This church is very strong and so it can be done. It can be helped. It depends upon the belief. Do not put the Catholic Church in the Jewish church. I am not saying that if you are Jewish and have an attached demon, that you should not have a Catholic priest exorcise the demon. It really doesn't matter.

9. Miscellaneous

When a person has a near death experience, there is an increased likelihood that the person will pick up a spirit attachment. That is at times because the person does not have full control. It is easier for a spirit to attach under those circumstances. Sometimes that attachment will remain with the person after the near death experience, sometimes not, either way.

Ordinary cameras can sometimes photograph earthbound spirits that the human eyes cannot see. Ordinary sound recorders pick up sounds from them that humans cannot hear. Thermal imaging cameras are definitely an effective means of detecting earthbound spirits.

It is important for you to enlighten earthbound spirits and encourage them to move on, more than for those on our side to do so.

When a spirit becomes earthbound, souls from our side who love them come forth and help that spirit go forth to our side. There is always help and comfort from us to aid them cross over. Some are greater than others. It is like relatives. Some are better and some are not.

D. COMMUNICATION AND INFLUENCE FROM SPIRITS AND OTHER UNSEEN SOURCES

1. Spirit influence and assistance

All people have a spirit guide who stays with them throughout their entire life. Some even have two or three. At times other guides will come for specific occasions. We will stay with a person as much as needed and we will guide as much as needed. What you call a person's good luck often comes from the influence of a very attentive spirit guide. What we call intuition is often the influence of spirit guides. It should be taken seriously and must be followed through. Remember your first thought when confronted with an issue to be solved. That thought can be called intuition or your psychic thought.

Those in the spirit realm can bring protection to humans directly or they can also act as intermediaries between humans and angels or other higher level entities.

Most of the time persons engaged in intellectual activity are assisted by one or several spirits. People are sometimes assisted by other people just like on this plateau. Some of us need assistance, good or bad. On our plateau we at times get assistance of other spirits.

When you know people on Earth who have transitioned into the spirit world, they often keep in contact with you and they want to help you. Some wish to help you and care about you. Some are not able to but some are able to. You can tell who the helpers are and who just want to go on their own voyage.

All modern communication technologies were inspired to humans by spirits who previously experienced embodiment on more advanced worlds. It was all here before you simple souls appeared. My good friend Plato had all of these advanced capabilities like your electricity.

Angels do not choose whom they protect. The same true regarding spirits and the humans for whom they serve as guides. A guide has no choice for whom they want to be a guide.

Spirits sometimes seek to harm people in the physical world who wronged them while they were together in the physical. The harm can be real. We try to show you we do not forget. We do not forgive either. So be careful. Sometimes the mere facts can make a person deranged. Spirits can have malevolent influence over people in both the physical world and the spirit world. On our plateau a spirit can be hurtful to another. They can be misleading to the living and to the passed on. Some of us are tricky.

Spirits sometimes show themselves as another person you know, not in order to fool you but to help you interpret things. Sometimes you see us from the corners of your eyes. Spirits can show themselves as another person to manipulate you.

Some people have said that they feel more energized after a channeling session with me. I would say that they are picking up energy from me. The source of being more energized is being relieved and freed. We are here to aid and help others. If you wish to state it that way, you will be stronger and more assertive to go ahead full force with kindness.

All prayers are not responded to equally by spirits and angels. There is less reaction to some prayers because of the actions or lack of action of the person asking for assistance. I have to report to you to please do not ask anyone to pray for you. Do your own prayers because someone weaker may be doing the praying. You don't need that. You need your own force to pray for yourself.

Spirits can send healing energy to humans. One of America's greatest healing ministers, Kathryn Kohlman, asked Sondra to join her as a healing partner because Sondra was a great healer. Kathryn is with her now. She adores Sondra. She says she loves her so. She was going to help her. She is always with her. She is so kind and she wanted to go into the ministry with Sondra but she couldn't make it. She was sorry she couldn't see Sondra that last day. Sondra does have amazing healing powers. Let her use it on herself. She is a very strong healer. Remember all the people she knocked down by just touching their foreheads when she was with Kathryn.

Projecting thoughts into a person's mind is a major means by which spirits help humans. If you can, it is possible to open up your mind that is so closed that you will not be able to determine. There ways that spirits can assist humans other than by telepathically projecting thoughts into their minds. They can send healing if your mind is open. You can get or send whatever you wish to. It depends upon the person that is collecting or receiving. It depends upon the individual human whether or not they get the help.

2. Spirit communications

Angels and spirits can project thoughts into the minds of humans. Humans also have the potential for that ability.

Although it may seem that more high energy entities in our world that channel to humans are of male energy rather than of female energy, both are equal. It does not matter what gender we select. We have no gender here, neither male nor female. We have fun either way. When we show ourselves to others we can show as either male or female.

Spirits are not more likely to manifest themselves to humans in the same gender they were in their most recent lifetime in the physical. Gender is not an issue.

Some souls are immediately aware that they are in the spirit world but others do not realize they have crossed over even though they are communicating with Sondra. Sometimes souls are able to communicate immediately after they cross over but then must spend a long period of no communication before they begin communicating again. There are times that your consciousness does not dissolve. Sometimes those that pass over can aid you but then they have to move on. (A)

When you sleep and travel to the spirit realm, you sometimes meet directly with your spirit guides. Spirits on my side enter your dreams if they wish to. People can receive information from extraterrestrials when they in the dream state.

Individuals who are in a coma or vegetative state can communicate actively in our realm.

Some spirits channel in rhyme because that is their way to express themselves. We at the beginning spoke in rhyme.

When a soul is on an interplanetary or interstellar sojourn between physical incarnations on Earth, the entity is often unable or reluctant to communicate to mediums in this world.

The orbs that often appear in photographs are people that have messages. They are entities probably from our world. In our world we have so many plateaus. We have a star system. We don't have just one system like your Earth system.

There are writers of poetry or prose who have transitioned who still want to write and are looking for someone to write or receive their words. You can get in touch with them. If you are interested, you can think of them and call them but not all will answer. Keep thinking of it and it will come to you and it will bring you comfort and aid.

Several nights ago a very polite man came to your wife in spirit and gave her some advice. Unlike other spirits, he gave her his name. He said his name was Peter. It was Peter from the Bible who came to her. Very often people from the Bible come to her.

The questions that Charles asks me are sometimes sent to his mind by nonphysical entities, but he can take credit for the origin of some of the questions. Some of the questions come into his mind from other sources and some he creates from his own mind. He has a wonderful mind.

Gandhi is Charles' friend. He gives him guidance at times by projecting thoughts into his mind. He has tried over and over and over to help him but Charles did not listen. Now he hears him easily. Gandhi did not share his spirit with Charles. He shared his mind. Charles could feel his thinking. There is a distinction between sharing one's spirit with you and sharing one's mind with you.

3. Influence and assistance from other entities

Angels, spirits and physical extraterrestrials can influence your thinking by putting thoughts into the minds of humans; thoughts that you think are our own, especially when you can't make up your mind. Mental telepathy occurs very frequently. Humans usually think that those thoughts are their own thoughts. If you were to meet me or other extraterrestrials in the physical, we could project thoughts into your mind without saying anything aloud as just spirits and angels do. This would be easy. Your minds are wonderful attractions.

Extraterrestrials that are in the physical can telepathically send thoughts to a person in order to influence the person's thinking if you allow it. It doesn't mean that you have to listen or have to do what they say. It is the exercise of your will that determines whether or not you obey. Extraterrestrials do not have to be within a few feet of you to influence your thinking. The thoughts that they put into your head are generally helpful thoughts but it doesn't mean that they are always correct. They might be sincere but wrong.

People are sometimes considered to be insane but are actually being influenced by malevolent extraterrestrials. In addition to malevolent extraterrestrials they can also be influenced by malevolent spirits and be considered insane.

Extraterrestrials can remotely influence a human to act violently through activating a virus in their DNA. They can do this by putting their minds into it. Sometimes when a person acts violently it is really because of outside influence rather than the person himself.

When spirit guides serve you, there are sometimes situations where they call on angels for assistance. Sometimes there is more than one spirit. Sometimes there are two or three or four of us. I myself would call on angels in situations to help someone.

Angels channel information to humans as the spirits do. Angels are more apparent. Sometimes they show themselves and other times they don't show themselves for all. Mediums can tell the difference of an angel and a spirit. Angels are dear souls. Spirits are not always that. Angels are always honest, truthful and sincere but spirits are not always.

Angels manifest themselves as physical human beings that anyone can see. They often manifest themselves to humans as butterflies or dragonflies. They wish to show themselves to you as what you picture as beautiful. They can be anything that flies. The butterflies that often appear to people after a loved one has died are sometimes manifestations of angels or some sort of communication from the one who has just passed over. They should be cherished.

Entities from realms other than that of the angels or our plateau can communicate directly with humans. Some are able to and some humans are very stubborn. They don't listen.

There are individuals in the physical world that channel entities from realms above the spirit realm. That would be above what some might call the mental world.

It is possible for humans to tell the difference between angels and spirits manifesting themselves as physical humans. If they wish and they seek an answer, yes, they can tell the difference. Most of the time, is it not what we wish or we ask for advice. Someone negative can also respond and give negative advice.

Animal totems that are said to hover over each person's head are a reality. They are part of a composition a build-up of strength to help the individual gain strength.

Conscious entities are present at the time of conception ready to aid in the process of bringing life to the human body. However, you each have your own free will. The free will will make its own choice.

Some science-fiction authors are influenced by something other than their imagination: either past life memories or some outside source. Science fiction authors are often influenced by outside sources and they will become more known. The better science fiction writers will be those of the future. Gene Rodenberry, author of the television program Star Trek, received information from extraterrestrials that influenced his writings. His thinking was influenced partly by extraterrestrials and partly by his imagination. The part that was influenced by extraterrestrials was real. It actually existed.

Throughout history the majority of great scientists have been influenced by extraterrestrials. Their creations were not necessarily emanating from their own minds but their minds are being influenced by the external and being controlled. Thomas Edison, for example, received a lot of his information from other sources. He had information on what we call electricity. He channeled the information from extraterrestrials.

Although some people believe that there was extraterrestrial or angel involvement in aiding the Americans in the fight against the British in the War of 1812 in regard to the manipulation of weather conditions, that is ridiculous. However, angels and extraterrestrials were always there to help the Americans.

The Illuminati exert a strong influence on the Hollywood entertainment industry. They own the music industry. They have a strong influence on the media also, all of it. They control it. They control your political situation. I would like to think that they are more influential on one political party rather than the other. There will be a third party. The third party will arise as an offshoot of one of the current parties.

It is ridiculous that casting spells will be more effective if devices such as a lock of their hair or a voodoo doll are used. Spells cannot be cast if the affected person does not believe that spells can be cast on them. You can always avoid what you may relate as a spell. You yourself may be pointing the gun and remember where the trigger finger is. It can backfire.

The messages that Brad Johnson channels from an entity named Adronis from the star system Sirius are credible. People know people and take people's advice and they do not take their own advice. It is always good to listen to the messages that he channels but the advice of jumping off the bridge isn't always right. The messages from Adronis are not always accurate.

The people of Dogon tribe in Mali, Africa are descendants of the inhabitants of the Sirius B star system. They are strange people. They love to play around.

When a person prays for assistance, it always helps if more than one person prays for the assistance. It can be heard. It is a stronger signal for the request. When everyone cries out for rain, more rain will come.

Years ago Alan Turing played a pivotal role in cracking intercepted coded messages of the Nazis because he received assistance from extraterrestrials. Srinivasa Ramanujan, the brilliant Indian mathematician also received assistance from extraterrestrials. The people from India understand very well what you mean because they are very intelligent.

There is an intergalactic council of nine gods that oversees or dictates the course of humanity on Earth. They are advising me now on how to answer your questions. They are working in conjunction with the Illuminati. Everyone in the group works together. They do not work against each other. They all agree. This group of nine extraterrestrials are overseeing or protecting the development of humanity.

Nefarious non-physical entities did not influence David Berkowitz to commit murders as the Son of Sam. He is mentally deranged. It was not outside influence. He is at this time in a mental institution. He is mentally ill.

Angels and spirits can respond to your prayers. You will make your own choices and you will do your own decisions. You are responsible for each one of yourselves. You are in control of yourselves. I, as a spirit, can answer your prayers. I do not wish you to know my identity because I do not wish to be called like Jesus is, forever hearing his name being called. You pray to yourselves; that is, to the God within you.

A form of geometry is being used in the creation of crop circles throughout the world. Geometry can be used as a key to communications between humans and higher dimensions. Life is all numbers. The extraterrestrials that create the crop circles are trying to communicate to you. There is meaning in the designs of the crop circles. You should be trying to interpret those meanings and you can use them for your own pleasure.

There are both non-physical sources and non-human physical sources that are influencing or controlling humanity.

4. Influence and assistance from objects

Physical objects such as a statue of St. Jude placed on the dashboard of your car or a mezuzah placed at the doorway of your home or amulets are not imbued with special powers, such as for protection or healing. It is only for comfort to those who believe. A person can imbue any object of their choice with the power to bring them good luck if they believe it will do so. Sondra has done that many times. If, for example, you are attracted to a particular gemstone, that can bring you good luck.

Some people use symbols, incantations or physical objects such as voodoo dolls to bring harm to people or put a curse on them. Do it if it makes you feel better to put a pin in someone's behind. It is much better to be able to forgive. A person who wishes to do that to someone might receive it themselves. If you think evil about a person or wish them harm it will go back to you. When you point an arrow and aim at a person with your arrow, that arrow will boomerang. You cannot either physically or emotionally harm another person. It is your thoughts that hurt you. If you had a doll that represented another person and stuck a pin in it, the thoughts or actions only hurt those that have it. The one that has the evil thoughts will have the evil. No one can hurt anyone. You only hurt yourselves with your thoughts. Your thoughts are very important and very useful. Think positive and be positive.

In using a pendulum to douse answers to questions evoking a yes or no response, the force to move the pendulum come from within one's self. The pendulum gives you comfort. We as individuals when we are on this earth make things happen. We do things to make things happen. We walk away from things to make them not happen. We plan and do whatever we perceive ourselves as I have mentioned. We go for the brass ring and pull it if we wish it. How many are fearful in going for chances. The force that causes automatic writing is mental. It is the same force that causes the pendulum to operate.

Holding a crystal can enable a person to receive communication from spirits more clearly. It depends upon the person. It doesn't matter what type of crystal.

When the human believes in them, gemstones play a role in assisting them. Gemstones can absolutely communicate to humans and they can help protect them.

5. Humans seeking and providing assistance

If you want something to occur, you can think it, say it aloud, visualize it, or pray for it. Saying it aloud will bring it to you. Visualizing will definitely help. It is the best way, better than praying. Praying is asking an outside source for help. Visualizing is going to the god within you for help.

The best way to pray is whatever feels comfortable for you, whatever makes you feel complete, and whatever makes you feel good and resourceful. You needn't pray aloud but praying aloud can help. You can keep your thoughts within you. Praying is thoughts. When we pray to God or whomever we wish to pray to, we are asking for help. Most of the times when we need to ask, we are pleading for help. When you pray you say that you are praying to God but you are actually like broadcasting out to any entity that wants to pick it up. There are many gods. You always think of prayer as something going directly to God but sometimes it is an angel that will hear you or a spirit that will pick up that broadcast. You can be helped from various sources. That is what God is if you wish to call it God. Maybe an angel is what you call God and maybe God is one's self; the god within you. I have said that you can pray to yourselves, meaning the god within yourself. Kneeling on your knees when you pray does not make your prayers more effective although it may help you feel better. Likewise promising to do or stop doing something in return will not help your prayers but it will help you feel better. You answer your prayers. Your soul connection brings the energy. It makes you feel better when you feel there is a mommy or a daddy watching over you that can fulfill your dreams. Is that not true? In reality you are self-dependent. It's like the Theosophists who believe that thoughts can be manifested into reality. Prayers are thoughts.

Through meditation and prayer a smaller group of people can have an influence on the thinking and behavior of a much larger group of people. For example, if a thousand people pray for world peace, the possibility of word peace will increase. The positive nature of people will help

Talking lovingly to household plants and other forms of vegetation can help them to grow more healthy. A plant or anything that is perfection will blossom. Likewise, talking lovingly to inanimate objects, such as your car, can have a positive effect on them or their functioning. Talk positively. It is very necessary for a person to think positive and be positive. It is very important for your existence, not only for you and what ails you.

The use of numerology by humans is an effective device for providing answers, explanations or predictions. There is numerology in my realm also. We often make use of it. Numbers are important because they are fun and helpful to be fun. Doesn't a certain number hit you well sometimes? Can I just say "one one one one". There is significant negativity in the number 666. It is not just something that religion has invented. Conversely, the number 7 is a very positive number. (B)

6. Miscellaneous

With all of what you call the laws of science, such as the Law of Gravity, you can say that conscious entities, whether they are angels or some other kind of entities, see that those laws occur are implemented.

There is power in sound. There is power to raise your level of consciousness in the Aum chant. The same is true of the Buddhist chant Nam-mythoi-renge-kayo. It would be of your benefit to practice these sounds in a group situation. In speaking to me the sound of your voices are able to project and tell me about your future as you speak.

What appear to be weird, unrealistic dreams can be just the meaningless products of your minds. That depends on your dream. They are not necessarily some sort of coded or disguised information that comes from your higher self.

There are no such things as random events. Outcomes of everything that occurs are the direct result of specific actions or the influence of conscious entities That is, is there no such a thing a toss of the coin but rather it is the way we toss the coin. Everything that occurs is the result of specific actions. There is no such thing as random results. It is already achieved who is going to win the lottery.

When a person sends thoughts or energy to another person the receiver does not who it is coming from but it is of no importance who is sending the message.

It is possible for both angels and extraterrestrials to project some form of consciousness into inanimate objects. Spirits can do the same and so can highly advanced humans.

Spirits can access the Akashic records plane of information and some psychics on Earth are able to access that information also. Some can and some cannot. Edgar Cayce went to the Akashic records. The information in the Akashic records is not infallible, not always correct. It is left up to interpretation. It is left up to how people exercise their will. Information about time cannot be accurate because there is no such thing as time except in the physical realm.

On several occasions at nighttime your wife has seen you asleep in bed next to her and, at the same time, she sees you walking in the room. That is not because you are having an out-of-body experience. That is not your etheric body she sees. Instead she is seeing your twin which has not yet been born. The twin is the image of you.

The utterance of certain specific words can evoke supernatural powers or results and they can annoy. In addition to calling out for Jesus, whether it be for good or bad, there are certain phrases that when you say them will cause things to happen simply by the utterances of those phrases. It will only happen to those that cause it.

A thought pattern can become an entity and then go to a person or place.

Some people subconsciously block any projections of thoughts into their minds by unseen entities. You have the ability to block the reception of anyone unseen sending thoughts to you.

Imagining that a specific spirit is in your presence wouldn't necessarily encourage that spirit to be with you but you may feel more comfortable in doing so.

There are no factors which can influence the selection of winning lottery numbers. The winning numbers are by chance. You can pray and pray and pray for the winning numbers and it will not have an effect. Winning lottery numbers cannot be foretold. They are totally random and unpredictable. I may predict a number or two but that would be all I can give to you.

You should heed the prophecies presented by Mark Taylor on You Tube. You should listen because they are somewhat accurate

The original Star Trek television series is more than just pure fiction. Some extraterrestrial reality is portrayed in the episodes. Some of the things you see in the original episodes are true.

When hypnotized some people can channel information by an omniscient intelligence but they often disregard it. In other words, theoretically you could be hypnotized and then channel information from a higher level source even though you can't do it when you are conscious. It doesn't mean that it would be correct.

Some science fiction movies are very close to reality and have

77

been made for the purpose of gradually educating people about extraterrestrials. The intent of some of the science fiction movies is to get you to gradually accept extraterrestrials. Some science fiction movies, such as 2001 A Space Odyssey, are designed by the Cabal to educate you about reality for the purpose of their having influence over you. Arthur Clark, the author of 2001 a Space Odyssey, received information through telepathy. His thoughts were not necessarily his own thoughts just as your thoughts are not necessarily your own thoughts even though you think they are. He was guided by angels, extraterrestrials or spirits.

It is true, as sometimes mass murderers have said, that they were driven to kill because of voices they have heard in their head. Sometimes mass murders hear another entity, an evil spirit, and other times it is because of the individual's psychological disorders.

There are non-human entities that thrive on the negative emotions of humans but it depends upon the human. There is no entity that can be stronger than you. In other words somebody can't cast a punishment on you unless you accept it.

E. MY GUIDE

1. Incarnations

If I were to tell my names in one or more of my incarnations, you would probably have heard of those personalities. I was more than one of the major personages portrayed in the Old Testament of your Bible. Indeed I am him, her, them. I was also incarnate at the time of Jesus. Jesus was a dear friend. John the Baptist started trouble in our realm. I was incarnated there at that time. It was difficult times. You wouldn't recognize the clothes I wore.

When I was there at the time of Sodom and Gomorrah, we had long black hair, curls. It was beautiful black. I was several significant personalities in the Bible and so was Charles.

My current personality, the one I show your wife, is not the same as my last life. Indeed not. I have been here sooo many times before, so many times. It took me a while to learn what I needed to learn. I do not remember all my previous lifetimes and thank God for that. Some I wish I remembered. Some I don't. I remember drowning in Ireland. I didn't like that. I don't wish to tell you my names in my incarnations for fear you would be calling me.

I no longer need to reincarnate. I do not wish to come back to the nonsense you people put on yourselves. I decided not to come back. The community agrees. They are those who make regulations above and beyond our plateau. They help us. It seems I am a trouble maker. I have lived on Earth many times before. I do not wish to return. I am administering a good deed by working and helping and assisting those that need assistance and pleasure. That is why I am here with my friends to assist you. I have had other physical lifetimes on other planets in your star system as well as Earth.

Since I no longer have a need to reincarnate, that does not mean that I will remain on the astral plane forever. I will move eventually beyond the spirit world.

When I incarnated in other star systems my physical bodies always needed air, water and food. They were different from human bodies. Since I have had incarnations in other star systems you could consider me an extraterrestrial if you wish and a human also. As with humans, in other star systems our bodies were always carbon based. It was easier for you to see through a carbon based body. You have not seen me but my form is different from the human form. Indeed, very different. To me humans look like birds without wings. I can identify myself with a physical form that does not resemble you. I do not always see myself as a physical human being but rather as something else. In my lifetimes in other systems I did not look like human beings. I am not as ugly as you are. I can display a human form to your wife because I have had Earth incarnations. I can also display myself in other forms. I do not wish to offend you but you all look so strange. Where I am from, my physical appearance is not the same as the appearance of Earth people. We do not have male or female. There is no such thing as division into sexes. We have more fun than you have. We are able to please ourselves. We don't rely on others to please us. I would say that we are what you might call hermaphrodite. Some would be like a starfish where you cut of part of and a new entity appears. There are other ways of reproduction. I prefer my own physical appearance over yours.

2. Personal characteristics

It is appropriate to say that I am of a high level of energy in the astral world. I consider myself to be more advanced than most people because I've been to your earth many, many times and I'm not coming back. I do enjoy coming and being in your presence and giving advice.

I did not have the same level of intelligence or awareness when I was in the physical as I have now. I arrived at this level of understanding by the view. I am now on a very high view. I can oversee much. It comes automatically at my level. It was not easy you know.

Those in our world sometimes have memory problems and forget things they would normally be expected to remember, just as do people in our world but me, myself, no. I have no memory problems but some do.

English is not my language and that is why I often I ask if I have said things correctly. There are many languages. We don't have to speak in Tongues. Probably my best language is Tongues.

Using spoken language, I have shown you that I have a good sense of humor. Just look at me and you will see how I am able to show you a sense of humor on your plateau without spoken language. They sense my sense of humor. I had a good sense of humor in my previous lifetime.

In your world some people are gregarious and enjoy being with others but there are also people who are not very sociable and prefer being alone or having very little contact with others. The same true in our world. I am one that is gregarious. I like to talk. I do not like to listen. There are also people in my world that tend to be loners and like being alone more. They are fearful people. (B)

If you were able to see me in the physical form of our native planet you would be fearful of my appearance. Not fearful, hysterical. I like my natural appearance better than my human appearance. The reason I show myself to your wife as I was when I was incarnate as a human is so that she will accept me more. She will also recognize me more. She loves the sandals I wear. That is the incarnation I choose to show myself to her. That was one of the incarnations as a character in your Bible.

3. As a guide and channeler

Since I have had many lifetimes in the physical, I have a choice in which personality I will use in your work as a guide. Since spirits have had physical incarnations as both male and female, they can portray themselves as either male or female to humans. I portray myself as a male to you but in some other situations to some other people I portray myself as a female. As you well know, my talk on gender is not always accurate. You have noticed that sometimes a woman can be speaking to me and I will say "sir" because I really don't see the gender distinction as you do.

I serve as a guide for several people and I can communicate with them simultaneously at times and sometimes collectively. Simultaneously we reach out and they can hear us.

I am a guide to other people as well as to your wife. We are very busy with her too, you know. And we are enjoying the pleasure of aiding and assisting. I was led to becoming her guide because she is so sweet, such a nice person. She is very kind and thoughtful. We enjoy working with her. She has a good sense of humor.

When I answer your questions, I often have a favorite group of friends assisting me. Some are not here with me now. They don't always agree with me. I am so always right. I have others assisting me but they don't know any better. When you ask me questions, most often I give an answer immediately but sometimes I pause for a while before answering because I am conferring with others. I am asking for advice from others who can help and give me advice to help you to become more successful.

Sometimes it is true that there are questions or topics that I am not permitted to answer or talk about by those in charge. There are areas of knowledge or information that I am forbidden or otherwise unable to access, either directly or indirectly. We are gathered here to explain to you. A simple answer and direct is most important.

I understand your questions not so much by your words but rather by the vibrations of your voice. When I answer you, it is sometimes difficult for me to formulate the responses in your language for you to be able to understand what I am saying. Your vibrations tell me much more than your words. Indeed, the voices, the feeling of the body, the feeling within, we know. We pick it up by the vibrations of your voice. When I answer you it is sometimes difficult, especially for those who do not speak Tongues but I am reading peoples' minds if you want to call it that.

When you ask me questions I receive information from both levels above me and from the angels. It depends on how I administer the answer. There are times I consult with others from my realm.

Although I said that those in my world can take any form they choose, from some of my answers to previous questions it appears that I often visualize myself as a physical human because I wish to adapt myself as an equal to you when I address you.

From my own experiences the most important piece of advice that I could give to the people of Earth is to not look for an enemy. You fight each other and argue with each other and slaughter each other. You disagree with each other.

Very often when I come to your meetings I begin by saying that it was a long journey. I have also said that in the world of spirits there is no such thing as time or space. By a long journey it means that transferring from where I am to where you are takes a lot of my energy. I am not talking about distance. I am talking about the amount of energy. When you travel does it not take energy for you? Even though there is no time or space, it takes energy. I have to get dressed for you. That is indeed a pleasure for me. I am an extraterrestrial. When I say I have to get dressed that means that I have to put myself in an Earth human being form rather than my native state. You hear me but cannot see me. Your wife sees me only as an Earthling not as an extraterrestrial.

The high degree of accuracy of my predictions is based on considering the past actions of people but there are also occasions where I actually foresee the future as it definitely will occur. The future is very bright and not alarming but full of gaiety.

When I am in your group answering questions, it is my pleasure to be here and be of use to aid you and comfort you as best as possible. It is a pleasure that we get from your world to come here and help you as far as comfort is concerned. We do receive pleasure when we give pleasure. My pleasure in my existence is to be able to help others that need help and to give peace of mind and I want so much to love and care for you and find peace. When I as well as you am helping others, we are really helping ourselves. A good way to help ourselves evolve to a higher level is to help others.

I cannot predict alternate futures clearly. It not possible to predict alternate futures as well as what will actually occur in the future. For example I have said that Trump will be reelected as president. An alternate future would be that a Democrat would be elected. I would not have the ability to tell you what would likely occur during the term of a Democrat president.

4. Contacts with other sources of information

I have contact with human-like beings in other star systems. They are all the same or similar, just different systems.

According to the Blavatsky materials, there are entities which we call the masters who dwell in the higher realms. We indeed have contact with them but we do not necessarily get advice from them, just their thoughts.

I can visit the plateau above my plateau much the same as you visit my plateau when you sleep. I get help and guidance from those above me. We get interference and annoyance but sometimes they are correct. It is still interfering.

When I have said that when helping humans I sometimes confer with my elders, I am referring to entities that are superior to my thinking. They are spirits who are more intelligent and have more insight.

I am in the spirit world and have evolved to the point that I no longer need to reincarnate. I will eventually no longer have a need to be in the spirit world and will evolve to a higher level to what some people call the mental world. I communicate with those above the spirit world.

5. Miscellaneous

Although I have told you many things about myself, I have told your group that I do not want to reveal my identity to you. That is because if many people were to call on me, that would be a drain on my energy level. That is one of many reasons. I do not have the energy that Jesus and Hitler have to be called on. Jesus has so much energy that he can be called on and that doesn't sap his energy. Hitler is an extremely negative energy. His name was negative. The person was not negative. They made him into a negative. In the spirit world where I am, the entity that was Hitler has a great deal of energy.

I have written things that could be available for you to read. I had several incarnations during the Biblical era and had something to do with a few things that are written in your Bible, but I take no credit.

A long time ago I said I would help your wife write a second book. The questions you are asking and the answers I am giving are a means to the development of the book to which I was referring. I promised her I would stand by her and I do because she is kind.

I show myself differently to various other spirits depending on which lifetime I was associated with them in the physical. Do not we all have different appearances for different people? Some make us happy and some make us sad. Some make us hide. I do not want to be with them.

I do not have a companion. I do not need a companion. I need my strength and myself. Here on this plateau we do not have companions. That is not necessary. We are all strong.

There are multiple spirit worlds just as there are multiple physical worlds. Spirits such as I can instantaneously travel from one spirit world to another. My origin is not on this earth. Thank goodness for that. That is why it takes me a lot of energy to travel to you, from one spirit world to another.

The spirit world that is my home consists of entities that were once physical entities on my home planet and it also contains entities whose origin was in other star systems. We are all here and we help each other. Each physical world has its own spirit world. Spirits from different worlds can be in the same spirit world.

I have not traveled in the physical form from one place to another in the universe through wormholes. I have traveled only in the spirit form and wormholes are not needed when travelling from one place to another in the spirit world.

I do not like Earth. I prefer physical life on other planets rather than Earth. It is too regimented here. There are too many rules on Earth. You have too much religion and too much nonsense on Earth. Earth is one of the most difficult planets for physical life. That is from my own experience too.

F. JESUS AND OTHER PERSONALITIES IN THE SPIRIT WORLD

1. Jesus the man

What is written about Jesus is closer to reality as portrayed in the Koran than it is in the Bible. He was a very different kind of man than what is portrayed. He was not blond haired with blue eyes. He did not exist that way. Many of you may not like it but Jesus was black, as black as his curly hair would allow him to be, a lovely man indeed. His family pronounced his name as Yaho. There were many different languages there but that was the Aramaic pronunciation. Jesus is not fictitious. He is in the spirit world with me.

Joseph was Jesus' father and Joseph was completely human. He was very human, as you well know. Look at his lifestyle. He had nine children before he had Jesus but not with the same wife. He had a great influence on the education and upbringing of Jesus. He took Jesus to many different countries throughout the known world at that time.

Jesus traveled to far off lands such as Egypt, Persia or India for the purpose of study in his lifetime. All those places are so close and Jesus visited them. He was a very bright man you know. I dare not say anything negative about him.

While in the physical Jesus was what you might call in today's terminology a psychic. Indeed, all of you are psychic in many different areas. We all are psychic. He was also a medium to a point but his feelings were more to what you call psychic as he was able to see the future of people who could get well.

Jesus the man was a man that was caring and loving and giving. Jesus the man was a healer. The people who agreed with him and saw him and selected him to be a healer, he healed.

Jesus actually died on the cross. He voluntarily gave up his life. He was aware of what was about to happen. He was not ready to argue or fight. He was under restraint and overrun by his enemies and his friends too. He voluntarily incarnated knowing that he would serve as the Christ and be crucified. He wanted to help humanity. He loved people. He loved to be of assistance. He loved to help others. Jesus the man spent most of his lifetime preparing to be the Christ but it was not intentional. It was his growth. He did not want to be of the status that he later became in life. Jesus was a split soul, meaning that Jesus the man was in that body and then the Christ entered also. When the Christ spirit entered, there were two spirits in the same body.

Both Jesus the man and Jesus the Christ performed miracles. A lot of the information in the Bible about the miracles is imaginary. He healed the sick but he did not raise the dead. He did not change water into wine but he did calm the stormy sea and he did cast out demons. Although exaggerated, he did feed thousands of people with just a few loaves of bread and two fish His catching a fish with a gold coin in its mouth is just a story.

Jesus married and had children. He enjoyed his life. He had a good time when he was here. I am not going to say if Mary Magdalene was his wife. There are an increasing number of children born today who can do things that far exceed the abilities of other children. We call them star children. Jesus was a star child. So was Mohammad. So was Confucius. So is your wife.

Spirits, like angels, can create miracles. Jesus was a healer in his lifetime and he is now in the spirit world. Jesus heals people on Earth. Jesus the man will always bring comfort to you. He was a kind giving man. He will give comfort to you. You do not have to be Christian for Jesus to answer your prayers. Jesus was not Christian. He was a Jew. He will answer Jews' prayers also.

Jesus the man dwells in the spirit world where I am but the Christ spirit has withdrawn. Jesus is a very powerful spirit. His role is to help people. There are other spirits who can help people as he does. Jesus is a good soul, a kind soul. When you call him, he is there for you. He will help Jews, Moslems, Hindus or everyone, not just Christians.

When a fire broke out in Notre Dame Cathedral in Paris, an item called the Crown of Thorns was rescued. That item was not actually the crown of thorns that was placed on the head of Jesus at the time of his crucifixion. They say it was, but it really wasn't the crown of thorns.

2 Jesus the Christ

Jesus did not perform all of the miracles attributed to him but Jesus the Christ did perform miracles. Jesus the Christ performed wonderful miracles and a great amount of happiness and security. It was not the

Jesus that is my friend. It was Jesus the Christ. Jesus that you call the Christ Almighty was a powerful one that was able to make peace within you.

What we call the Christ or the Christ Spirit is a soul that has evolved to the point of completion. Throughout history there have been many Christ spirits, many spirits. Christs are highly evolved spirits that have helped mankind to evolve. Jesus and Buddha and other such people are considered Christs. There will be future Christs. There are Christs sitting here now. The Christ spirit is one that gives hope and peace.

Jesus is going to make a second coming as they predict in the Bible. It is Jesus reincarnated in the physical. Even though I have said that religion is manmade and that religion does not exist in the spirit world where I am, I have said that Jesus is going to make a second coming. Jesus the man will be reincarnated. Jesus in my world now will reincarnate and he will also be a high level savior. He and Moses will appear at the same time.

3. Jesus' Birth, Crucifixion and Resurrection

A good deal of the information about the birth of Jesus in your Bible is more fiction than fact. The physical birth of my friend Jesus is very simple. There are many accounts of that birth. There were no palm trees there in the desert, I assure you. Palm Sunday did not exist. He was not born with Christmas trees around him. There were no pine trees in that part of the country. There were palm trees. December 25 was not the actual date of Jesus' birth. He was not born in a stable and they weren't riding on donkeys for example. He was born in a luxurious home. Joseph was quite a wealthy man. There was not an unusually bright star about the time of Jesus' birth. He was in a comfortable family and Joseph loved his son, all his children. He was a good father. Both Joseph and Mary influenced Jesus. Joseph went with Jesus to India to study while Mary was busy with the children. She kept a kosher household.

Mary was Jesus' mother but Joseph was not his biological father. A human being was his father, but not Joseph. Joseph married Mary in order to protect her.

When Jesus arose from the grave, as the Christian scriptures say, and people saw him, they saw what they wanted to see. The plasma of his body rising, the ethereal body, could be seen. Those in the medical field could tell you about plasmas.

The shroud of Turin was actually something that was used to

cover Jesus' body. The shroud that covered my dear friend was very uncomfortable you know. It was not made for him but was used on him. It was very annoying for him.

There is some truth in what Tom Harpur says about the Pagan roots of Christianity (i.e. such as the details about Jesus birth, miracles and crucifixion) as being based on ancient Egyptian traditions. Is there not some fact of truth in every story we hear and then we embellish the truth? The account of Jesus as being born of a virgin is modeled after older traditions. If you wish to call Joseph a virgin, that would be nice. Virgin birth actually exists but not in this case, for other children followed. Am I not correct?

Jesus actually physically died at the crucifixion even though there are a lot of rumors. Stories are made up, like there are about Donald Trump.

4. Jesus and the archangel Michael, John the Baptist and the disciples

There is a special bond between Jesus and the archangel Michael; the choices and love that they have very deep within themselves. They are very loving. The archangel Michael played a significant role in the ministry of Jesus. He is here to bring peace. At times Michael influenced Jesus' thinking. Jesus was not the incarnation of the Archangel Michael. Michael is not in my realm. There is a difference between Christ and Jesus. Jesus was too busy being himself. He was Jesus and he became the Christ which is very powerful and very noble and very dear and very loving.

There was a soul connection between Jesus and John the Baptist but they are two different entities. Jesus was a dear friend. John started trouble in our realm. I was incarnated there at that time. It was difficult times. You wouldn't recognize the clothes I wore.

Jesus' disciples do healing from the other side as Jesus does now but there is no comparison as to the work that dear Jesus does. The disciples' healing does not have the same empowerment.

5. Jesus in the spirit world

Jesus is a very gentle man. He is here with us in the spirit world and is shocked at what is happening on Earth with his name. He had no idea he would be worshipped like this. He is very grateful. He is a nice guy. He is right here tapping on my shoulder. He speaks Hebrew, you know. There are others of the same stature as Jesus. More highly evolved souls in the spirit world have a greater amount of energy than less evolved souls. Some have more energy and assistance as well. Jesus is called most often and he has the energy for that. There are spirits in my world at as high a level as that of Jesus. Jesus is not above all others. There are some others at his level. Jesus was a person who walked the planet of the earth who healed. He was a wonderful person: a kind, giving person. Your scriptures say that he was the only begotten son of God. We are all begotten sons of God.

If you say "Help me Jesus." it brings on the assistance of angels or Mohammad or any other name. It is not necessarily the Jesus that is in my realm in your very limited realm. Jesus will answer your prayers but you could also ask for Mohammad or others.

Jesus resides in the realm where I am. He channels information to many humans the same way that I channel to humans.

6. Jesus and reincarnation

Jesus dwells currently in both the spirit world and the physical world and has simultaneous multiple incarnations on Earth. Many parts of his heart and his soul have reincarnated and have been here many a year. Jesus is both on my plateau and on your plateau.

It is true, as many Christians believe, that Jesus will be there to greet them when they cross over. Jesus actually greets some souls when they cross over if the soul very strongly wishes so.

There is some truth in his book *Lives of the Master* in which Glen Sanderfur talks about the previous incarnations that Jesus had according to Edgar Cayce. Jesus did have many incarnations.

7. Other personalities in the spirit world

The readings given by Edgar Cayce provide knowledge you should consider somewhat important. He, like me, has lived many times but he wishes to reincarnate again. He has not reincarnated at this time. He was the reincarnation of Ra Ta, the ancient Egyptian high priest.

The writings of Zachariah Sitchin are substantially factual. He will smack me in my face if I do not tell you he is factual. That's what he wants me to say.

The entity Seth who channeled information through Jane Roberts several years ago is on my plane. He is a lovely kind gentleman, appreciative to be remembered.

Plato is a friend of mine. He is a friend to everyone, a lovely man. He is at a knowledgeable level. He is with his friend who is also his teacher, and very bonded to his friend. By friend I mean Socrates. They were very close you know and Socrates did suffer quite a bit. It is true that they gave him hemlock.

Since his arrival in my world Adolf Hitler has experienced what other people who have done evil things have experienced. At this point in time he is not sleeping. He is aware. He is no longer in control. You can step on him. A person's place in my world is where people of a similar level of consciousness are. I am not saying or advocating that Hitler was wrong or that he was bad. He was doing his thing. He was playing a predestined role. It wasn't him. He was giving the orders but he was being given orders too, playing a role in Earth's history. He himself was not necessarily evil. He doesn't want me to say it but he was given orders to do what he did. He was not knowledgeable. He was a simple man. Extraterrestrials helped him.

Leonardo DaVinci received information from extraterrestrials. He is with me in my world now. There are many hidden messages in his works of art. He has reincarnated since then, not as a scientist but he has reincarnated in many different volumes. You got information from his drawings about how to invent the helicopter. You could say that Leonardo DaVinci provided your scientists or engineers with some of the information.

The boy that Pythagoras adopted and who provided much information regarding mathematics, religion and philosophy was a star child. It is from this source that Pythagoras developed his knowledge of mathematics.

Mahatma Gandhi is in my realm and has not reincarnated. He exerts influence on, or provides assistance to the people of Earth. He is Charles's friend.

A spirit entity name Ra channeled material called "The Law of One" to three people. That material is valid.

G. REINCARNATION

1. Reincarnation in human evolution

Life in the physical is a necessary experience for all souls in the spirit realm. All souls have to go through this at least once. We all must suffer to be in the physical. I would say a high number of lifetimes for a soul to have reincarnated on Earth to be six hundred. That's a good number. People do not learn. So they come back again. I cannot estimate the average range of the number of years between incarnations into the physical because we do not have the element of time here.

There are some spirits who have not yet experienced a physical incarnation but most have. Some are not long-lived so they will come back and recapture. There are people on Earth who are now experiencing their first incarnation as a human. There are some spirits who do not wish to incarnate. There are some who no longer have the need to reincarnate.

When to reincarnate or whether to reincarnate is completely up to the decision of the individual. We do have a little push. We do have some say. Basically it is the decision of the individual involved. When a spirit reincarnates that is the result of the spirit's desire to do so. If they want to do it, it is by choice. Before a person reincarnates, that person chooses his parents just as you selected your parents. That choice is usually related to karma. Not just one parent but both parents are a significant factor in the choice.

The necessity for physical incarnations of Earth humans or spirits will never cease to exist. It will be over and over and over. Reincarnation is a continuing process forever. Reincarnation existed and will always exist. Humans cannot escape the reincarnation process. Humans must reach a level of evolution before they are no longer required to reincarnate. All spirits that have chosen to be part of the reincarnation cycle must remain in that cycle until they have reached a level that entitles them to forego future incarnations. Future incarnations are not available until we decide in which direction we should proceed.

Souls who no longer need to reincarnate remain where they are or they can move on to a higher level. We move on to different levels like you people. We embrace more. There is more to do.

Spirits sometimes choose to reincarnate after they have reached the status that reincarnation is no longer needed for them. I have said that I have reached the status where I no longer have the need to reincarnate. There are some spirits who choose to reincarnate to help humanity.

When souls cross over to the spirit world they can come back immediately or they can stay on this side to relax before coming back. Souls can do whatever they are comfortable in doing. Every individual soul is very different.

People have different lifetime experiences in all of the human races. There are absolutely no differences among the different races.

If someone in my realm is very annoying to other spirits, that person still has the need to reincarnate. What is annoying to one may not be annoying to others. That person will grow when he is aware and more knowledgeable. When one loses the fear of losing knowledge then one cannot grow.

With each incarnation a person does not necessarily advance forward in his evolution. Sometimes the clock stops. Your current incarnation is not necessarily your most highly evolved. It is not likely that you could go back in history and reincarnate to a prior time.

It is not unusual for a person to be the reincarnation an ancestor. This is absolutely true. In some cases it happens rather frequently. Charles is the reincarnation of one of his ancestors. Children usually have had previous incarnations with their parents although there might have been a different combination of relationships.

People who die at a very young age are likely to reincarnate more rapidly than people who die when they are older. If a person dies young, they can come back in a very short amount of time. Miscarried children reincarnate.

When a person excels in a profession, such as science or medicine, it is difficult to say if that person likely to enter the same field in subsequent lifetimes because everyone is different. Everyone has a different answer. Everyone has a different opinion. For example, Charles felt a strong compulsion at the age of six in this lifetime to be a teacher and he followed through on that. That came from his having been a teacher in previous lifetimes. But in another previous lifetime he was a physician. He finds that hard to believe because he absolutely abhors anything having to do with body operations, blood and things like that. That is because he had a very unpleasant experience as a physician at that time.

The great majority of people have no conscious recollections of their past lives even though many people seem to express curiosity about them. The loss of memory of previous lifetimes is built into the reincarnation process.

When a fetus is aborted, the same soul will manifest itself in a child again. The same would apply when a baby is born dead.

People do not always incarnate in a linear time manner. Sometimes they incarnate backwards in time. That is what I meant when I said you could time travel to the past but you could not change history but only change yourselves. It would be possible for you, for whatever particular reason, that you could reincarnate in the past if you so choose.

2. Incarnation in places other than the earth

When you retire from Earth, the soul can inhabit other planets in other forms. Most souls have a particular star system into which they prefer to incarnate. They tend to go back to the same star system. It is not incorrect to assume that they can from time to time incarnate in a different star system. They only incarnate in the same star system because they are familiar and feel at home. They feel safe in the same system. They will learn to go to other systems. Many times it is easier for a soul to create over and over in one system than going to different systems because sometimes you are not well mentally. In other words we are not allowed to use the word dumb.

Earth is the most difficult planet on which to incarnate. The souls on Earth are not the most intelligent souls in the universe. The physical beings on Earth are less evolved than the physical beings on other planets. The more advanced souls incarnate elsewhere rather than on Earth. Souls do not have to reincarnate on Earth. They reincarnate where they are more comfortable. It is the people on Earth that make it the most difficult planet for physical life. They reincarnate on Earth because of their level of stupidity. So all you Earthlings, be aware of how limited you are.

Many souls must have interplanetary sojourns in spirit form for specific purposes before they are able to reincarnate. Each planet in our solar system serves for a different purpose in the evolution of the soul. The earth's moon is a wonderful place for such decisions. If a soul wishes to go, there are so many atmospheres and options for a soul to select. There are specific lessons that the moon is noted for, as the earth is needed for certain lessons. Many of you don't want to leave the earth and are fearful of leaving the earth.

Highly advanced entities that were once on your plateau can eventually evolve to the state in which they can become a cosmic entity. That is at a much higher level. Souls can evolve into planets, stars or other heavenly bodies. These are very highly advanced souls. It's hard to believe that all the billions of stars out there are souls. That's why we wish upon a star. Do we not? Planets and stars have a level of consciousness that is far above the level of that of humans. Humans have the potential of someday becoming a star but first must become more knowledgeable. Indeed if you are good in school, you will become a star. I will not tangle with a star because they are more knowledgeable.

3. Entering a new life experience

Before spirit entities reincarnate they choose to be knowledgeable about the physical world they are about to enter. It is not a shock. They have some feeling about the new life they are about to enter. They have comfort as to where they are going to reincarnate. When they see their past relatives and friends they have more comfort.

Your attitudes, emotions and desires can change from one incarnation to another as a result of your experiences in the spirit world between lifetimes.

Sometimes the knowledge you gain in a lifetime can be taken to the next lifetime. What you call knowledge is sometimes actually stupidity.

Certain incarnation event destinies are determined between lives and then the outcomes of those destinies are determined by the use of your free will during the physical lifetime experience. Your free will can be used at any time. When you get to a corner, you make up your mind whether you want to proceed straight ahead or go left or right.

At times the length of a person's life is predetermined before birth and the person can achieve what they wish after birth. The length of time is predetermined but is not cast in stone. Although the length of a person's life is determined before birth it could be shorter or longer depending on their actions. The length of a person's life is the life they want, how long they want to live.

People sometimes make the choice at the soul level to have a particular disease or physical problem so that they can advance more rapidly in their spiritual evolution.

There are times that people who have mental or emotional disorders carry over those same disorders when they arrive on my plateau. They can overcome them on my plateau. Anything is possible. It depends upon the individual. It depends on the length of the mobility whether people that we call insane retain that insanity for a while when they cross over to the spirit world. Eventually with their residence in the astral world they overcome the insanity before their next incarnation. They can shed that. (AB)

It is usually true that if a person has severe mental or emotional disorders in a lifetime they are likely to have similar disorders in the next incarnation. Such disorders can be overcome in the spirit world before the next incarnation, but usually not.

The extent of an individual's ability to remember things increases somewhat from lifetime to lifetime. In some cases indeed and in some cases it does not succeed. What you call déjà vu.

Homosexuality can but does not necessarily occur when a person reincarnates in the opposite gender from that of the previous life. It's what the person chooses at the subconscious level. It depends on how many times they have been male or female.

If you become knowledgeable in a certain field of study in this lifetime, some of that knowledge can become easily retrievable in future lifetimes but only if it interests you. If you were a physician in this lifetime, you will remember some details but not all. The learning of that content will come more easily if you had learned it in a previous lifetime, more easily or more acceptable; more of interest to you. You may not do well with it but you will be interested.

If a man has an intense attraction to fishing or hunting, for example, that interest didn't necessarily emanate from previous lifetime activities.

If you are studious or observant and learn a lot while in the physical, you will somewhat retain that information when in the spirit form. If you remember, that information will be easily accessible in future lifetimes.

If you have an addiction, such as for gambling, you could be predisposed to have that same addiction in future lifetimes. It depends on the mentality of the person, on the strength of one's soul.

Birthmarks are often vestiges of fatal wounds in previous incarnations.

Every person has the life they selected. They are in charge of their life. The route they choose to take is before they reincarnate. Life for some humans is more difficult but for others it is very easy. The same is true of those in the spirit world.

4. Multiple incarnations and split souls

A soul can reside in the spirit realm and simultaneously have several physical incarnations (B)

Some souls have multiple simultaneous incarnations because they want to progress more rapidly. It is especially true when a new era on Earth is approaching. In time a new era on Earth will approach. Some souls choose to have several lives, several goings on, several interests. They advance more rapidly when they have several simultaneous incarnations, very much so. You have choices to do as such if you wish.

A soul can have multiple simultaneous incarnations in several different star systems. It doesn't matter whether it's on Earth or a different star system. The soul can have a physical entity on Earth and a physical entity on other planets at the same time.

Individuals that have multiple simultaneous incarnations sometimes have some special bonding or recognition if they come into contact with each other. Some are not so happy about it. The contact may not be happy or good. They may dislike the others profusely.

Many lives come into the existence when we reincarnate but the soul has always been there. Sometimes in many instances it would be what we call a split soul. We come into this life with so much confusion because of the split soul. We remember a lot of things from the other existences. We don't remember them but we are confused by them.

5. Before a new incarnation

At times there are some individuals who have the choice before entering the physical life of having some kind of preview of the new life in the physical that they are about to enter. When you choose to reincarnate, you somewhat, sometimes have a plan for your new life. Some people do and some people don't.

Before a soul reincarnates there are flickers of memories of lifetimes before the most recent lifetime that are brought to mind. We recall but don't recall completely. In our lifetime we don't forget but we remember what we want to, just as you do.

People cannot come into their next lifetime more intelligent than in this lifetime but they can choose to be less intelligent. They always wish to be more intelligent, a little brighter but once a cook, always a cook.

Before an incarnation the spirit of every newborn human baby is imbued with the language or dialect of its future parents; like English, Tagalog, French, and Mandarin etc. Upon arrival they have already decided the language.

When people are born deaf or blind or in some way deformed, the reason for that condition is not necessarily something they have chosen at the spirit level. It could be the result of karma or something that was chosen for their own advancement. It is very similar with animals.

You have a choice to never reincarnate with certain people again but you know that what we choose will happen. You will reincarnate again and again until you learn not to come back. You have much learning to achieve.

When abortions are performed on fetuses, that does not cause problems in the spirit world. Spirits always know in advance if an abortion will occur.

Before an entity reincarnates into the physical world, the entity first ascends from the astral world to a place where they lose their astral body before descending back into the astral world and then back the physical world.

6. Relationships

Relationships don't always continue when souls transfer from the spirit world to the physical and thank God for that. Sometimes relationships can start where I am and can continue but don't always appear to be so. It is possible. Sometimes it is rejected. (B)

When people are in the spirit world heaven forbid that they tend to associate mostly with people they were close to in previous incarnations. People like you may not want to associate with people in your lifetime. You may not like people here, so why take them with you into the next lifetime.

When individuals reincarnate into a race different from that of the previous lifetime, they are not necessarily more likely to feel greater affinity to people of that race rather than to people of other races. It depends on the individual and the amount of prejudice in that individual.

People whom you consider to be your enemies are in reality often friends who, prior to reincarnation, agreed to help you with certain lessons that you needed to learn. When we dislike a person it is easy to look into a mirror and see ourselves. Our enemies are often our friends at the soul level. Our enemies are often ourselves because we are our own worst enemies as you well know.

Charles was predestined to meet up with his wife Sondra in this lifetime. It was a match that was made a long time ago.

There is a connection between a person's physical ancestry and his reincarnations. Sometimes people tend to reincarnate with members of their own families over and over again. It is an unending process.

7. Miscellaneous

Note: Information regarding the reincarnation of animals is in Section U of this book.

After a soul has had several difficult or unpleasant incarnations, they sometimes choose to have a pleasurable incarnation of enjoyment but they do not get it. They have to learn. They are on the earth plateau to learn. Make sure you learn while you are there. The learning while you're there is much easier.

Individuals sometimes choose to reincarnate for the purpose of working toward a noble goal for the betterment of others or mankind. That is one way to become successful if you wish.

When a soul reincarnates, sometimes there are physical characteristics or features that carry over from one lifetime to another. There are certain physical features that could be similar. There are different markings like your cat will have. There are different markings on humans that may appear. Birthmarks may be a carryover from a previous incarnation where the person was fatally wounded. If you had a very wide nose in one incarnation, for example, there is a possibility that you could have a wide nose in another incarnation.

More Atlanteans are currently reincarnated in the yellow race than in other races. That is why that race is so bright. The yellow race will inherit the earth.

It doesn't matter if Individuals have transgender operations. I cannot say if they are working against their predetermined plan for that incarnation. Each Individual is individual. I'm not sure that the purpose of the changing of one's sexual habits will change a person.

An increasing number of people are covering themselves almost entirely with tattoos giving them a reptile like appearance. This is connected with their physical forms in previous lifetimes. That is another way to cover up who they truly are. On other planets humanoid forms are not all like you. Some are covered in feathers, scales, and things like that but they are all basically the same inside as I myself am. When people tend to cover their whole bodies with tattoos it is a hidden memory of a previous incarnation on a different planet, another way of what they consider art work.

The current Delhi lama is the reincarnation of the previous Delhi lama, like your kings and queens, a blood inheritance.

The study of reincarnation evidence that Ian Stevenson made from the University of Virginia was very accurate.

It appears that some people love or bond with animals more than they can do so with other humans but that is not because they have recently transitioned from the animal kingdom to the human kingdom. An animal does not talk back to you. They are so grateful when you feed them and care for them. Some people love animals more because they don't talk back to you.

Jesus taught reincarnation even though very little is said about it in the Bible. He was taught many thoughts. Jesus was a brilliant man. Jesus knew the answer. He was quite an intuitive. He was a healer. When some books were chosen to be in the Bible and some books were not chosen, some books were intentionally kept out so the Church could have more control. It was not completely understood what reincarnation is. Jesus taught reincarnation. Jesus the man, not Jesus the Christ, is with me in my world. He is a very powerful and energetic soul.

H. KARMA

When most of you think of karma the first thing that usually comes into mind is paying back for the wrongs you have done but karma is much more than that. It is simply a case of cause and effect. Even if you think of karma as being either negative or positive, karma is not judgmental. It is simply the reaction for every action that is taken. All actions, thoughts and spoken words have consequences.

An entity's entire karma is not part of his being in every incarnation or dimension he is in. Part of it will be. In this incarnation you do not have to experience the effects of all of your karma. Karma is what your future is to be. It is nothing threatening or nothing to be afraid of. It is the dealing of cards; which hand you are given and how you play your hand of cards.

When people reincarnate they do not always bring all their karma with them into their new lifetime. Sometimes they bring only selected aspects of their karma that they will focus on that lifetime.

Before reincarnating a person does not have a choice regarding which aspects of his karma should be avoided in the new lifetime. He brings all of the karma from all of previous lifetimes together into the new incarnation at times. Each one is individual. He can bring it all in or sometimes not bring all his karma in. [This appears to contradict the previous entry.]

Karma does not relate only to the physical world but also some aspects of karma can be played out in the astral realm. We can learn and grow just as much in our world as in your world and such is taking place.

An individual can still have what some of you might refer to as karmic debts and still have much to learn and yet not be required to ever reincarnate. In my realm there are some entities that do not need to reincarnate. In my opinion they still have a lot to learn and karmic debts to pay back.

In no circumstances can individuals be absolved of paying back what you might think of as karmic debts and the slate swept clean, so to speak. There is no way of getting around it. There is no such thing as what some call a state of grace.

A person's will power can be so strong that it can be used to override or negate the effects of predetermined karma in a lifetime. Even if something is predetermined, it can be changed. You can override it by the use of your will.

There is a point in an individual's evolution where they become aware of the karmic cause of why seemingly negative things occurred to them while in the physical. This does not occur until after they are in the spirit world. Then you will be able to make the connection between things that seemed negative and their karmic cause. You will understand that you are not being, as you say in your life, punished.

If a person commits a crime and consequently sentenced to a term in prison, his karma is not affected differently than if he had not been apprehended and imprisoned while in the physical. If a person commits a wrong and is punished while in the physical that does not affect his karma differently than if he had not been punished.

People are sometimes confronted with problems or negative situations that are not the result of their actions either in this lifetime or in previous lifetimes or decisions made between lifetimes. These happenings are neither the result of karma nor the result of decisions made between lifetimes. They are learning opportunities presented to the individual.

Spirits are aware of the karma of those individuals in the physical dimension, even though you may not be aware of your own karma, spirits are aware. (B)

It is not possible for an advanced soul to remove someone's negative karma but they can help remove it. Remove is the same as forgive. However, it is possible to take on the negative karma of another entity.

The language a person speaks can influence or reflect his character, personality or karma in your world of existence because you people have likes and dislikes.

Like people, some groups especially like nations or other large groups of people have group karma somewhat. Some do and some do not. Natural weather disasters sometimes fulfill that karma but that was not the case with the island of Haiti. Karma does not play a role in the numerous natural disasters that have affected the country of Haiti. Ignorance and not being knowledgeable has affected Haiti. Making their homes out of straw but they will learn and they are wonderful people. The Haitians are misunderstood people. It has nothing to do with karma of things that occurred in the past. They are kind people. They are gracious people. They have not been educated. Natural weather conditions had nothing to do with the karma of the people of Haiti or with Rio.

It was the karma of many of those in the black race to become slaves and so it was with the Jewish people. They were mishandled as well as your Jewish people. Anyone who was put into a position where they were slaves, that was their karma to become so. The United States now experiencing what some may call negative national karma payback because of its history with slavery. It could be said that karma has a domino effect and is a process that never ends. You are paying back. Slavery still exists. It should be abolished because you all have the same blood. You have the same sweat. You have the same tears. You are the same.

An individual is not held accountable in a karmic sense for the actions of his ancestors. Each individual is responsible for himself. Each individual has an individual will, either he will or he won't.

At times animals have soul groups, much the same as humans do. They feel as we do and at times karma plays a role in their world. Both humans and animals have karma. In a way, there is karma in the mineral and vegetable kingdoms.

If you wish, at the subconscious level, a long painful death, such as from cancer, can help resolve karmic debts.

If a person is born blind or in some way what we might call physically defective, that is not always the result of karma. It is not the result of mistakes by the intelligent entities that created you. It can be an opportunity to teach you to grow faster, to gain further results.

When a person is born malformed, conjoined or crippled in some way and then doctors are able to fix the problem, the doctors have absolutely not interfered with their karma.

There is a cosmic system of justice. If someone wrongs you or behaves evilly in this life, they will be eventually punished or get their "just desserts". It goes on and on. Do not force anyone.

There is no such a thing as harmless lies; that is, lies that appear to have absolutely no consequences in a person's lifetime or future lifetimes. On the person creating these fabrications, there is no difference. If a person repeatedly tells many lies about himself that have no negative impact on other people, those lies do have a negative impact on his karma. If a person's actions are the result of demonic possession, those actions do not affect the karma of that person.

Karma plays a role in my realm, the astral realm, and it plays a role in the realms above that.

Extraterrestrials have karma. There is a mixture similar to your color. Color goes on and on and on and karma goes on and on and on.

If you just don't know any better, you will still have to pay back for that. If you are a slow learner, you will learn.

If you bring harm to others because of your ignorance, that has a different effect on your karma than if you were knowledgeable and intentionally caused them harm. Even though the results are the same your karma is different.

If a person is harmed by another person, the person that is harmed is done so because it is the result of his karma or whatever you choose to blame it on. They will be affected by whatever negativity they chose for someone else. If you are harmed by someone that is not always because of something you have done wrong in the past. No one is above you. You are the one that makes your choices.

If a person laughs when another person experiences physical injuries or suffering or misfortune, simply the act of laughing can create karma to cause the person who laughed to have similar misfortunes or suffering in a future lifetime. For example if they laugh when they see someone being hit by a car and their body is smashed, merely having laughed will affect their karma. It shows how sick they are. They will have to pay some similar retribution in a future lifetime for having laughed. Their face will not smile any more.

All conscious entities have karma. That is true of angels and nature spirits as well as celestial bodies including planets and stars.

Although many people feel that stealing something from another person is wrong but stealing from a large impersonal company such as large stores is less wrong, that is not correct. Stealing is stealing. Your karma is not affected differently.

I. RELIGION

1. Religion as viewed by the spirits

After people cross over into our world, religion is eventually no longer important to them. Religion is manmade. We have no religion where we are. After a while no spirit has any affinity with the religion they had when they were in the physical. It is left behind on Earth. Religion is rules. We are too intelligent to take rules or guidance from religion. When did religion start killing. Adam and Eve had no religion. Here they look back and smile and realize what a joke it was. So they lose their religious beliefs.

Although religion does not exist in the spirit world, there are some spirits who do hold on to their religious beliefs from when they were humans. Charles' grandfather was a born again Christian minister who died before Charles was born. His reaction to the book we are writing was "Hogwash". (B)

All entities in the spirit realm, for the most part, do not have attitudes similar to mine regarding religion. Not all of us, but most, think religion is nonsense. We are not religious and do not have any religion or any rules. Religion is rules.

People lose their religious beliefs when they enter the spirit world but the terrorists who have killed in the name of their religion still have the same attitudes but they don't have their religious beliefs. There is no such thing as religion in the spirit world and God didn't create any religions. There is no basis in reality for what some religions call purgatory. Is not life purgatory? (A)

There will come a time when religion will no longer play a significant role in the lives of those in your world. 'Tis coming so soon. Religion is manmade for different benefits of man. Some are needed and some are not; like you have a police force where you are and we do not.

The Bible was written by man. I do not know what or who God is. Man has been behind everything that has been created. I am God. You are God. We all are God.

The meaning of the Trinity: The Father, the Son and the Holy Spirit is nonsense. That is religion; you know, religious belief only, man made. The Holy Spirit is something that is manmade for comfort. It is important for one to believe in one's faith.

From the point of view of those in the spirit realm, there such no such thing as sin. That is purely a religious concept. That is so ridiculous. That is manmade. What is sin?

2. The Bible

Some of the ancient history portrayed in the Bible, including that of the Great Flood, is a recounting of earlier Sumerian legends. All is recounting of interesting stories. Some happened and some did not happen. Some of what is in the Bible is taken from earlier civilizations and embellished.

Even though I have said that much of the material in the New Testament of the Bible is not entirely factual, Christianity did nevertheless did serve the purpose of helping to raise the level of consciousness of the believers. In that aspect Christianity was a positive thing for those that got benefit. Although Christianity is one of the great hoaxes played on mankind, it is also true, so they tell me, that the creation of Christianity was part of a master plan to raise the level of consciousness of humans. It keeps people together.

Some of the prophets in the Bible were people who received information from extraterrestrials. Those that didn't receive information from extraterrestrials got information from the spirit world. Others accessed their information directly from the Akashic records.

In the Christian Bible, Judas was portrayed as having betrayed Jesus in a way that would result in Jesus' crucifixion. However, in reality he was greatly misunderstood. Judas was not the enemy of Jesus. Judas was not a good friend of Jesus. He was just a friend. His role was predestined

The creator of Adam also created a first wife, before Eve, for him named Lilith. The Biblical story was a story. We make up stories to please ourselves.

Adam and Eve were your mother and father. Adam and Eve come from people who make up names. The Garden of Eden was a name you derived for a peaceful habitat for people a "Pleasantville" in your dimension. Wherever we place it, it will survive. Everybody wishes it was a specific place on the planet. There were several places, different Gardens of Eden in China, in Japan, in Italy. Everyone has their own Garden of Eden.

The original purpose of male circumcision was to identify those men who were descendants of Adam or the superhuman race created, at least in part, by aliens. It was to be part of a tribe purely identification reasons. They were not knowledgeable at that time about health reasons. This was for purely identification reasons.

There was a connection between Moses and King Akhenaton in ancient Egypt. Moses was a member of the royal family if you wish to put it that way. I say yes, but if you wish to put it another way, I say no. It was because of the religious beliefs in one god and trying to change the religion of ancient Egypt that all traces of King Akhenaton were removed by the Egyptians after his death. Moses took that belief in one god when they left Egypt.

In your Bible there is an account of people trying to build a tower called the Tower of Babel that would reach heaven. This was what they believed was a star gate. There is no such tower. Your Bible says that this is how the proliferation of languages came about and that God made it impossible for them to build the tower because he had them all speak different languages. That is just a story.

Noah played a significant role in aiding the evolution of human beings. He was actually an extraterrestrial who worked with embryos. The ark was a UFO spaceship and the animals were not animals but they were the embryos or the DNA of animals and in that way they were able to put all the animals into the spaceship. That's how they got the thousands of animals into the ark. There are no physical remains that archeologists will ever find because it never existed as such. Noah in the Bible and humans who lived on Earth before him had physical features different from ours, such as webbed fingers. He was not the founder of city of Zion which later became the city of Jerusalem.

When the Israelites were crossing the desert they were able to eat many, many different foods and seeds that they grew. The desert is not all desert. There are plants in the desert. A device called the Manna Machine described in the Jewish Kabala did not actually exist. It did not provide an algae type of food for the Jews when they wandered in the dessert. It did not take the Israelites forty years to cross the desert but it did take them time. It was not as long as was interpreted to you. They intentionally prolonged their stay in the desert, one reason for which was to amass a large army for battling the various Canaanite groups in the reconquest of the land of Canaan. The pillar of fire that guided the Jews through the desert was something in the sky guiding them manipulated by extraterrestrials.

In the Biblical account of the Israelites crossing the Jordan River on the way to the Promised Land, the river was always dry, all full of pebbles underneath the sea.

My dear friend Moses was black, a cheerful man who was very humorous. He had black skin, dark curly hair that was a little on the kinky side but he liked it long. I must admit he was a little bit sexy. He was a Jew. He was more than an ordinary human. He was an extraterrestrial hybrid. I knew him. He was such a nice man. The ten plagues of Egypt in the Bible in his time were actually the result of a sequence of events of natural causes.

The Ark of the Covenant existed in Egypt before Moses led the Israelites out of Egypt. There were other Arks that remained in Egypt. The Ark of the Covenant in the Bible produced energy. There is an Ark of the Covenant. It still exists today. Indeed, it will comfort you and you need to have that. It is hearsay that it is in Israel. It contained alien technology, energy producing technology. There were several Arks of the Covenant. They were all used as weapons. In Biblical times, the Philistines stole the Ark of the Covenant and then suffered the serious consequences of its effects. After the return of the Ark of the Covenant from the Philistines, many people, perhaps as many as seventy, actually died when they looked at it. The technology encased within the Ark of the Covenant was instrumental in bringing down the walls of Jericho. It was amplified sound waves of the blowing of the trumpets that caused the walls to fall. Loud noises can jar anything. The Biblical account of this event is accurate for the most part, and you know how interpretations get misconstrued. The ancient temple of Solomon did not house the Ark of the Covenant.

In the fall of the walls of Jericho in your Bible, the walls did not just crumble. They liquefied and fell like mud. The sound of the walls was horrendous. Just the sound will be horrendous. The stones became liquefied and melted because of the sound. The sounds were caused by trumpets attacking the wall. Sounds can absolutely melt walls.

The origin of the historical significance of the Stone of Scone that is placed under the throne of the British monarchy is nonsense. It is not the pillow that Jacob slept on in the Bible. Jacob took his pillow with him and it has since disintegrated. The stone is of meaningless significance.

Solomon's ring was believed to have magic powers. Magic powers? Nonsense!

The people who call themselves the Lemba in Zimbabwe are actually descendants of one of what are called the lost tribes of Israel. They are the priestly tribe of the Cohens. They are black and they are slaves.

I do not know if the most cherished object in Christianity, the Holy Grail, did exist. If it did, I did not see it. It does not exist today. Religion is what the intellects taught you.

The Essenes did not originate on Atlantis. They originated at the time of the Jews.

What happened to Lot's wife is a made up story in your Bible.

Many of the current world affairs are foretold in the prophecies of very long ago. It is repeated. It is a reoccurrence of the past. Your current world situation regarding the forces of good and evil are foretold in the scriptures of various religions. The parts from the prophets in your Bible seem to be that that situation is occurring at this moment.

There is a parallel between our current political situation involving the Clintons, President Obama and President Trump and King Ahab and Jezebel in your Bible Somewhat of a replay that occurred a long time ago. And the Jezebel certainly does exist. The reappearance of Jezebel is currently a female [Hilary Clinton].

Jesus taught reincarnation even though very little is said about it in the Bible. He was taught many thoughts. Jesus was a brilliant man. Jesus knew the answer. He was quite an intuitive. He was a healer. When some books were chosen to be in the Bible and some books were not chosen, some books were intentionally kept out so the Church could have more control. It was not completely understood what reincarnation is. Jesus taught reincarnation. Jesus the man, not Jesus the Christ, is with me in my world. He is a very powerful and energetic soul. (F)

The origin of the enmity between the Arabs and the Jews was not related to opposing extraterrestrials. It was created from sibling rivalry, similar to what any sibling rivalry would be. They did it themselves. The enmity began on Earth before Abraham. It is competition, which is stronger.

In the Biblical story of Adam and Eve, the being in the Garden of Eden represented as a serpent was not a negative extraterrestrial. The serpent was a positive force. For some reason, people are fearful of the serpent but the serpent is very useful and helpful. You should not consider the serpent as a negative.

The prophecies in your Bible and in the scriptures of other religions are essentially accurate although perhaps misinterpreted.

The Biblical concept or portrayal of the appearance of the devil was based on the appearance of reptilian extraterrestrials who desired to harm the human race. Although there is no such thing as the devil it was portrayed [as such] because of extraterrestrials.

The physical description of Noah as described in the Book of Enoch found in the Dead Sea Scrolls is indeed accurate. Noah in the Bible was a first generation human hybrid. He could be considered a Christ if you wish. There have been many Christs and there will be many more. The development of modern humanity was definitely influenced by Noah.

3. Extraterrestrials in the Bible

Many events portrayed in the Old Testament of the Bible are actually a recounting of encounters with entities from other worlds. Some are precisely that situation. Some are true but not all. Many of the events portrayed in the Bible actually did occur or were allegories and there are other events that could be termed as made up stories. Events did occur but were interpreted in a different way. Jonah being in the big fish? Ridiculous! It's interpreted differently. Your interpretation is very different. It is possible that he was in an extraterrestrial submarine. Some of the people in the Bible were actually extraterrestrial beings disguised as humans with the intent of the betterment of humankind. The same space people are involved here now as were in Biblical times. They are not all welcomed and some are evil.

Many of the world's great religions today came about as the result of encounters with extraterrestrials, causing many of the confusions. It could be said that Jehovah was an extraterrestrial. Jehovah gave the Ten Commandments directly to Moses. Jehovah still guides the Jews in modern times. He is here now. I am telling some of your questions for him to aid me in guiding you. In answering your questions now, I have assistance from Jehovah.

The following events portrayed in the Bible involved the use of aliens or their technology: Moses receiving the Ten Commandments, Ezekiel's account of a wheel within a wheel, Enoch's ascension into the heavens, the walls of Jericho that crumbled (The power of sound will crumble anything.), Jonah in the belly of a big fish. The Israelites crossing the Red Sea and the manna provided to the Jews in the wilderness were natural occurrences.

The Nephilim were often considered as the race of giants that existed in Biblical times and Goliath was one of them. They were extraterrestrial in origin. They were not the offspring of fallen angels. They were not fallen angels. On some occasions, but not all, the accounts of angels in various cultures, including the Bible, were references to extraterrestrial beings.

The cause of the Great Flood that is mentioned in your Bible and in the lore of other ancient civilizations throughout the world was the accumulation of weather that had formed. It was not an accident. It was precisely planned by alien intelligence to be helpful. The Flood was caused by the Anunnaki to purge the earth. It was not to rid of any specific species. It was a great cleansing. It was engineered by the Anunnaki. At the time of the Flood were there cultures throughout the world that survived by going underground. It was safer to be underground than above ground, as it will be in the future. Underground will be more positive for you.

The origin of some of the rites and rituals of the Catholic Church is connected with ancient extraterrestrial encounters with humans and some of the rituals of the Jewish religion started with extraterrestrials. All religions were initiated or in some way connected with extraterrestrials.

The current Delhi lama is the reincarnation of the previous Delhi lama, like your kings and queens, a blood inheritance. (G)

The information that was given to Joseph Smith, the founder of the Mormon religion, which is used for the basis of the Mormon religion was not given to him by an angel but by some other intelligent non-physical entity. He was a brilliant man.

4. Islam

The Prophet Mohammad dwells in the spirit realm. He is among those of very high energy. He reacts to what is happening with the radical element of Islam with humor and fear. There are some instances where we want control and he wants control and we fear that he will get control. He is mainly a positive creation but everything positive does have a negative. I do not see a time in the future when the radical movement will cease. It is not showing any recession there but it is growing to amount in abundance. Your fear of what will happen in the future has no basis. The fear is still there but it is not taken in the abundance that it should be.

What is generally portrayed or known about the life of Mohammad is more consistent with reality than what is generally portrayed or known about the life of Jesus. Mohammad is more cherished than people are aware. What you generally believe about the life of Jesus is not always true but what is publicized or known about the life of Mohammad is more accurate. The murdering of those whom the Moslems call infidels in the current movement of Jihadism is not fulfilling the intent of Mohammad. It is not what Mohammad wants. It is ridiculous. They are killers.

The cause for the recent rise in radical Islam is that they blame the Jews. Many of the current radical Moslems are reincarnated Nazis. That is why they are reacting in such ignorance. It is the same hatred of the Jews that the Nazis had. The same entities have reincarnated against the Jews.

The radical Muslim movement is making a good point of its generation and more radicals will prove with time. It will still be here in twenty years and it will progress to be more of a threat. This will not come to an end soon. It was always there. At the present time, it is a very serious situation with Syria. Eventually there will be an end to the threat. Fifty years from now there will be more peace on Earth after more destruction.

The angel Gabriel did not dictate the Koran to Mohammad. The Koran is manmade. There were non-physical conscious entities involved in the writing of the Koran like spirits or angels or extraterrestrials but it was not the angel Gabriel.

5. Catholicism and the Vatican

The Vatican secretly accepts the fact that they believe in the possibility that extraterrestrials may exist on Earth. There are secret files in the Vatican that support the existence of UFO's and extraterrestrials, files and rows of books. That is why we are here. I am saying that the Catholic Church does know it but they're keeping it secret. They do not want to make you aware and scare you. Aware and scare! That is not the main reason they are keeping it a secret. The main reason is control.

At this moment there is hidden information about extraterrestrials hidden in the underground vaults in the Vatican. The government wants it quiet. They want control. Information about other surprising topics will also be revealed.

The Vatican will release hidden materials in their library that will astonish the world but they have it closed at this moment. The materials that will be released involve extraterrestrials. They are afraid you will think they are ill. The Papacy has information about alien life on Earth. There was always some sort of question about alien life on Earth. There are also documents that have been left thousands and thousands of years ago about aliens on Earth. Those documents that they have in the library were taken when Rome burned the library at Alexandria in Egypt. They actually took the ancient documents from even before the time of Atlantis to store them in the library in the Vatican. They knew they would be well protected.

When the Romans destroyed the ancient library at Alexandria Egypt, great numbers of the manuscripts were saved and taken to Rome and kept in the Vatican. They are still there. There are numerous artifacts and creations by extraterrestrials stored in the library of the Vatican. You will find out soon. That includes a lot of ancient written manuscripts. There are also artifacts from Earth civilizations prior to the time of Atlantis.

There was once a Catholic pope who was a woman disguised as a man and who was later referred to as Pope Joan. She was quite a lesbian. That person is still in the spirit world, not reincarnated.

A major crisis or scandal is occurring in the Catholic Church. That scandal will be the cause of the demise of the papacy. It is on its way out. Pope Francis will be the last Pope.

It was solely because of his health and age, as he stated, that Pope Benedict resigned. Anything that would cause health problems would be the reason he was resigning. It was only for health reasons and for gallbladder. It was because of differences of opinion and that can cause a gallbladder problem. That is why he resigned but he is there and will be of assistance. He is a dear, darling person, kind and genuine.

There is no connection between the Catholic Inquisition many centuries ago in which great numbers of infidels were killed and the current radical Moslem movement in which the infidels are killed. They are disassociated occurrences. It is not the same group reincarnating. They are similar but not the same but I have said that the current group of Moslem terrorists is the reincarnation of the Nazis. That is a fact.

When people reportedly have seen the Virgin Mary that is often the manifestation of an angel instead. Our angels are gathered all over the place. They are there to assist you and help you. The entity seen by the three children in Fatima Portugal in 1917 was Mary the mother of Jesus. She came down and sometimes she visits other planets too. She is very loving.

There is a great shake up in the Vatican now. The shake-up will be related to the disclosure of ancient manuscripts about extraterrestrials at the Vatican library as well as by corruption and sexual scandals. They won't expose all immediately but it is on its way out. The Vatican knows a lot about extraterrestrials but it is being controlled as most of the issues are controlled by your government. The Vatican is keeping that to themselves so the Church can have control over people because if they found out about extraterrestrials that would diminish the power of the Church.

The Jesuits exerted great influence over the Catholic Church so that they could promote the concept of confession and then somewhat used the information heard in the confessions to work in the favor of the Illuminati. The priests would listen to the confessions and then pass on the information to the enemy.

There are major shake-ups in religions coming soon. They are here now. Wait until the Catholic Church collapses. It will collapse, you know.

There is a gateway to other worlds at the Vatican. Mount Graham International Observatory in Arizona is a star gate used by the Vatican for contact with extraterrestrials. There are many places like that, as sincere as that. Not only one place. The Vatican is always secretly researching space. They are always secretly doing things. They are secretly in control. The observatory in Arizona is actually a star gate or wormhole that you can go into and end up somewhere else in the universe. The Vatican is making use of it but no one controls it. Representatives from the Vatican can go into it and end up somewhere else in the universe.

6. Christs and antichrists

Although you usually tend to think as Christs as part of religious dogma, they could be defined as souls who have incarnated for the purpose of helping to raise the level of human consciousness. There have been many Christs throughout history in different colors [races]. There will be more Christs in the future.

In every circuit there is always one that we look up to. We pick our different religions and they are all the same. I have said that there have been many Christs throughout history and that the Jewish Christ was the most despised. Many of the religions began because of the appearance of a Christ on Earth. You will believe anything on Earth that is given to you.

The Christ consciousness is from your soul. Jesus was not the last Christ to appear on Earth. There have been more recent ones. There are many. There are many different religions, many different races, and many different cultures. All of the religions are started from a Christ-like. There is not one that is more upholding than any other. Jesus was the most controversial. If you were a different color or in a different country, it would be someone else.

Just as various antichrists have appeared throughout history, various Christs have also appeared. The Buddha was a Christ. Krishna was a Christ. There were many Christs but the Jewish Christ was disliked most of all. He is a friend of mine. All my friends are of different faiths. We are all one and we all have the same beliefs. We are all equal, the same. Religion only exists in the physical world but it is necessary for controlling. It is controlling and it is a comfort to others that wish to be controlled. Religions will cease to exist within the next couple of centuries.

The first two anti-Christs that Nostradamus predicted were Napoleon and Hitler. The third anti-Christ is still baking in the oven. In other words, he has not been born yet but is about to come into the physical. It is shown that he comes from another country.

7. Miscellaneous

Various religions existed among Earth people before the time of the Great Flood. Ridiculous religions! There were religions at the time of Atlantis. There was always something to make you fear and be controlled. There are many kinds of gods. There could be evil gods, too. Sometimes in the past, Earth people saw extraterrestrials as gods.

When people speak in Tongues on your plateau it is the same language I speak. There are times they don't know what they mean. The inspiration for speaking in Tongues comes from the mind, the brain, you know. It is a fantastic way of expressing oneself. It is something that is built into the system of everyone who has a brain. When people speak in Tongues they are actually channeling non-physical entities. In the charismatic church services, where they speak in Tongues, they are actually allowing an extraterrestrial to speak through them which they themselves do not understand. I have said that my most comfortable language is Tongues.

Many religions teach you that when you die you go immediately to either heaven or to hell but they say nothing about going to the world of spirits. It's another way to have control. You have control with your religion. You make your own heaven, what you call heaven, and you make your own hell as you well know. Heaven and hell are states of judgment. When people arrive on this plateau we are here to greet them and console them. They will feel comfort and ease and happiness in arriving when they come on our plateau. This is not heaven. Heaven and hell is purely a religious concept. They are not actual places but I would say they are states of mind. We go on from there and we learn or we come back again into another physical lifetime. When we cease to exist in spirit form we go on or we reincarnate, or we go on from there. (A)

The acceleration of the demise of religion to some extent can be attributed to what we refer to as the New Age movement that was purportedly begun by Helena Blavatsky and the Theosophical movement which followed. She is here with us. She doesn't want me to say a thing against her. They would wish to be a major factor in pushing religion aside. She channeled information from both those in our dimension and the angels. Some of the angels try to help us or me. We have been able to help many people on Earth.

The devil exists only in the eyes of the beholder. There is a person Lucifer but that is not an evil person. If you are looking for an evil person, that is not an evil person. The entity that you refer to as Satan was instrumental, in a way, in giving you the tools for civilization. Lucifer and Satan refer to the same entity. The names are interchangeable. People like to give names out and determine whether they are good or bad or evil. Lucifer's intent was to bring both good and evil. It depends on what side of the street you are on. It depends how you view things, whether it is good or bad or evil. He brought knowledge to mankind that he shouldn't have given. Lucifer was not competing with higher authorities. Lucifer was competing with Lucifer. Did you not have conflict within yourself? Lucifer was involved in the creation or the development of Earth humanity. Many of you are here as friends of Lucifer. This was in accord with the universal plan of evolution. There were other angels in a similar process with you. As I have said in the past, Lucifer is not a negative entity.

If you wish, it is important to give special respect to cemeteries as "hallowed ground" All Earth is full of cemeteries. Every place you step on, there is a burial and even in your ocean you have burial grounds. You do not have to treat cemeteries any different from any other area of Earth.

That is not where we go. It is for you a comfort to go to where you believe the person is buried. It is all in your heads.

Throughout history a number of men have had stigmatas appear on the palms of their hands and on their foreheads which were believed to represent the wounds made in the crucifixion of Jesus but they actually represented disease.

Religions do not exist in any star systems in addition to yours because religion is manmade.

Although many religions condemn gay marriages as being against the word of God, those marriages can be considered as natural as a marriage between a man and a woman. A gay marriage is loving a person's soul. It is not what you appear to think as loving a gay. No condemnation should be made of gay. It was always there and not always of visual service. Religions condemn gay marriages because religion is manmade. It is for the purpose of controlling and having children.

In the near future I see major changes taking place in the churches of many religions, not just the Catholic. In a way the Cabal exerts influence over your churches. The churches are being controlled by forces that are not necessarily beneficial to humans. They are not necessary because there is too much negativity. I see the churches going in a more positive direction. They will become more meaningful.

The current Delhi lama is the reincarnation of the previous Delhi lama, like your kings and queens, a blood inheritance. (G)

The time will come when Christians, Jews and Moslems will exist peacefully without confrontations or warfare but in your lifetime you will still have wars. Religion causes wars. Religion is very good for those who are not knowledgeable. It is a safety guard. It is very strong for those that are not knowledgeable. They take advantage of religion. There will be religion after many, many, many failures and many deaths. Religion will no longer exist centuries from now. It will slowly dissolve and it is coming about showing you now very slightly how it is dissolving. The big churches that you perceive will become less and less. Fighting over religion is ridiculous. It does not matter what you believe. It's all one.

The cause of anti-Semitism is often the result of extraterrestrials having spliced some of their own DNA into the DNA of humans. You have mixes like you have races. The [most] mixed race of all is the Eurasians.

The rise of anti-Semitism in this country and the world has risen dramatically especially when you have congresswomen that make nasty remarks about the Jews and Israel and are really not rebuffed by other politicians if the same things were said about other minorities. The future of this sudden rise of anti-Semitism is that you always need someone to hate. You never point guns at yourselves. You always point at someone else that doesn't look good to you.

Although I have said that there is no such being as the devil, the origin of the concept of the devil is actually demons that manifest themselves with forms that resemble what humans picture as the devil. (C)

J. ANGELS

1. Manifestations

Angels manifest themselves as physical human beings that anyone can see. Like spirits, angels do not have gender but they can portray themselves as whichever gender they choose. They often manifest themselves to humans as butterflies or dragonflies. They wish to show themselves to you as what you picture as beautiful. They can be anything that flies. It is very interesting. The butterflies that often appear to people after a loved one has died are sometimes manifestations of angels or some sort of communication from the one who has just passed over. They should be cherished. (D)

Angels sometimes manifest themselves as your pets that remain with you. They sometimes manifest themselves as extraterrestrials. They can manifest themselves as bolts of lightning, flies, or butterflies.

When people reportedly have seen the Virgin Mary, that is often the manifestation of an angel instead. Our angels are gathered all over the place. They are there to assist you and help you. The entity seen by the three children in Fatima Portugal in 1917 was Mary the mother of Jesus. She came down and sometimes she visits other planets too. She is very loving. (I)

In the answer to one of your previous questions, I used a term *extraterrestrial angels.* That means that the beings were extraterrestrials but were thought to be angels. Frequently in the Bible they were extraterrestrials manifesting themselves as angels. Extraterrestrials and angels are always two distinct types of entities. They appear separately.

2. Characteristics and abilities

The nature of angels is such that they are programmed to help others. They are interested in assisting, abiding and helping those that need it. They help the spirits as well as humans. Angels are there and they are there to guide and administer, as you well know. Angels are with you.

Angels have the capability to create, much the same way as spirits do with their minds. They do not have to verbally communicate. It is not necessary. Angels can create physical things. They can manifest easily whatever they wish.

Angels can manipulate physical laws when they assist humans in the physical world. They sometimes manipulate the weather or physical laws, such as gravity, to prevent physical harm to humans. For example, they can slow down the pull of gravity on a falling object. Special humans too can do the same if they wish to. You can have different things occur but not like an angel. An angel will act immediately. We all have the power to use it. Do not ask your neighbors but you are the ones with the power. When I say that, I mean that the God within you is your connection. You don't need to go to another entity.

Angels have the ability to help you change your attitudes, emotions or desires. They are here to help you. If you seek their help they can absolutely help you change your desires. They care. By caring they love you. They mean well among you. At times angels will be there with you but whether you will be there with them is another question. Indeed they will help you if you need help. You must ask for their influence but sometimes they take the initiative to do so. Angels can help you change your wants without your asking for such when it is your best interests. If you are having difficulty doing something angels will sometimes assist you even if you don't ask for assistance.

I have said that angels can help you change your desires if you ask for such. If they wish, homosexuals can become heterosexuals if they call on angels to help them change their orientation. It makes no difference if they have vanilla or if they have chocolate ice cream. Angels can help them change their desire if they need to. It is not always necessary. Whatever they like is fine.

Angels have free will, attitudes, emotions and desires such as you have. Even a butterfly knows when to fly away. They are here to assist you. I have said that angels are here to assist you whether they like you or not. They might not like what you do. It is your actions that they do not like.

In addition to working with humans and spirits angels also work with animals. They do not work with the vegetable kingdom. The nature spirits take care of the vegetable kingdom.

The extent of the ability of angels depends on what kind of angel they are. They are just like people. Some people are more competent than others. The same is true of spirits and the same is true of angels. That is true of everything.

3. Assistance to humans

Just as you have a spirit guide who stays with you through your physical life, you also have a specific angel to help and protect you. Some of you are fortunate to have more than one angel. Some of you need more than one angel. The angel you have is related to the month and day you were born. They are there to greet you and assist you.

The construction, growth and maintenance of your physical bodies are controlled by numerous entities from other realms related to the angelic or other kingdoms. Not one type but many types. Your heart does not beat automatically. Several of us are involved in that situation.

Angels help you when you pray to God to answer your prayers. They come to your aid. They are there to embrace you, to help you, to teach you. They are there for you to benefit and they will be very beneficial for you. That is why it is always so nice to have an angel by my side and that is why some people react like an angel. They are so good and positive because they are angels.

When you wish to seek help from someone in the spirit world or from the angels it makes no difference whether you just think what you want or whether you say it out loud. Spirits and angels can read your mind. You can be silent or say it out loud.

Angels can exercise their free will to assist people without having received instructions from a higher level to do so. They do receive instructions or messages but whether they give you the message or whether you take the message is up to you. When you pray to God or what you think is God, it is the angels who answer your prayers. Spirits where I am also respond to your prayers. When you pray, it is not just Big Daddy up there in the sky who directly helps you. It can be spirits or other non-physical entities and also, it can be yourself. By yourself, I mean the God that is within you. In other words it is your higher self or your soul. That is the important one. You should go within yourself first, even in preference to praying. Go along with your first thought, which is not easy to connect. It is hard to catch on to that first thought.

Angels can influence the thoughts of those people who want to bring harm to a person. Spirits also can influence the thoughts of someone who wants to harm you. That is a form of protection. If a person is about to do something that will bring harm to himself, it is sometimes likely that an angel will project thoughts to him that will get him to change his mind about doing it. Spirits can also project thoughts into a person's mind. They can change a key. I myself have helped people by projecting thoughts into their minds to protect themselves against themselves. I certainly try to help if they will accept my help. My help would be for the betterment of them.

When they are helpful you often view extraterrestrials as angels.

When you want to do something that will harm yourself, angels have the ability to influence or change your desires. They do want so much to protect you. They do love you and care for you. Your angels are there to protect you. They have influence over your will. You take it for granted and think that you changed your mind. That is not true. You are being influenced. Changing your mind is not always a bad idea.

What you refer to as luck can be the result of assistance or protection from the angels or spirits. If you think about what luck is, it's the right thing if that you feel good. For some people when everything seems to go right and everything seems to go smooth and there is not much problem in their lives it is rarely possible that it is because of assistance from spirits and angels. But it is in the cards.

Although you have free will, angels can cause you to change your mind when you are about to do something that would be harmful to yourself or to others. They will be able to help you. They can absolutely influence your free will.

Although you have free will, when you consciously do something that will harm yourselves angels sometimes intervene to stop you from doing so. Angels do not override your free will but they influence it by often projecting thoughts into your head.

4. Communication

Angels channel information to humans as the spirits do. Angels are more apparent. Sometimes they show themselves and other times they don't show themselves for all. Mediums can tell the difference of an angel and a spirit. Angels are dear souls. Spirits are not always that. Angels are always honest, truthful and sincere but spirits are not always. (D)

There is more overt communication with those on our plateau with angels than there is with them in your world. They hear you, too. They don't want to be known or seen but they do exist. Angels hear you when they want to hear you. (B)

Humans have certain angels assigned to them. Sometimes it would do you good to know the names of the angels assigned to you but sometimes they want to be mysterious. They don't want to be named. They don't want to be called or pressured. In other words, don't wake them up. It is important to show your gratitude to the angels. The same is true of showing gratitude to the spirits. Just broadcast it your request and the angels will help. Even though you may not be consciously aware of your spirit guides or angels, it will make you feel better and it does not hurt to express your gratitude to them.

5. Evolution

Angels evolve through the mineral kingdom, the vegetable kingdom and the animal kingdom as do humans. They go through the same process of evolution as do humans. Birds and flying insects can evolve into angels. They are part of the evolutionary path of angels but the type of bird or insect does not necessarily determine what type of angel will evolve. There is not a direct line. Let's say, that a duck will become this kind of angel or that a canary will become that kind of angel but flying animals will become angels. I have said that butterflies become angels; but angels, in the reverse, can often manifest themselves as butterflies in your world. You have two kinds of butterflies; butterflies that have not yet become angels and butterflies that are angels manifesting themselves as butterflies.

Angels will always remain angels. They do not evolve beyond the angel state. There is potential for humans to eventually evolve to a level above that of the angels.

Those in the human or spirit kingdom will never evolve into the angelic kingdom. The two kingdoms are always separate. No one from the human kingdom or from the spirit kingdom can ever become an angel. Humans can evolve to a state that they are like angels but they will not be angels. We refer to them as what is commonly called the "masters". Some of us are not able to reach that plateau. Some can and will. Very few can and will reach the "angel state". There is potential for humans to eventually evolve to a level above that of the angels. Don't we call people who are kind an angel?

Nature spirits (such as fairies, elves, leprechauns etc.) are not on

123

the same line of evolution as angels. Leprechauns and fairies are very immature and childish.

Angels were created before the creations of humans. That's who created humans. The angels came first.

When I use the term "new angels", that means that angels are continuously in the process of coming into existence. They are trying so hard to be of assistance. They want to help or make you successful. A new angel is one who is learning to be bright and have experience.

6. Specific angels and types of angels

There is a special bond between Jesus and the archangel Michael; the choices and love that they have very deep within themselves. They are very loving. At times Michael influenced Jesus' thinking. Jesus was not the incarnation of the Archangel Michael. Michael is not in my realm. There is a difference between Christ and Jesus. Jesus was too busy being himself. He was Jesus and he became the Christ which is very powerful and very noble and very dear and very loving. (I)

The account of the fallen angels known as the Watchers portrayed in the Book of Enoch is basically accurate but they were extraterrestrials who intermingled with Earth women and men and bore offspring. Their offspring were sometimes giants. The angels described as the Watchers passed on knowledge to humans. Their role was for humans to be aware. The Incan god Viracocha was one of the angels described as the Watchers in the book of Enoch.

The devil exists only in the eyes of the beholder. There is a person Lucifer but that is not an evil person. If you are looking for an evil person, that is not an evil person. The entity that you refer to as Satan was instrumental, in a way, in giving you the tools for civilization. Lucifer and Satan refer to the same entity. The names are interchangeable. People like to give names out and determine whether they are good or bad or evil. Lucifer's intent was to bring both good and evil. It depends on what side of the street you are on. It depends how you view things, whether it is good or bad or evil. He brought knowledge to mankind that he shouldn't have given. Lucifer was not competing with higher authorities. Lucifer was competing with Lucifer. Did you not have conflict within yourself? Lucifer was involved in the creation or the development of Earth humanity. Many of you are here as friends of Lucifer. This was in accord with the universal plan of evolution. There were other angels in a similar process with you. As I have said in the past, Lucifer is not a negative entity. (I)

The angel Gabriel did not dictate the Koran to Mohammad. There were non-physical conscious entities involved in the writing of the Koran like spirits or angels or extraterrestrials but it was not the angel Gabriel. (I)

There are many different species of angels that play different roles. Angels work for the good of mankind. You can ask them to do something that is harmful to you or contrary to your karma but that is not always given. It is always possible that they might give you what you want that is harmful to you or contrary to your karma.

The form that the Seraphim angels often show themselves is similar to serpents with wings. They actually have wings and they can fly away with their wings. We refer to their arms as wings

There have been times when I have said that Lucifer was an angel and at other times and other times I said he was an extraterrestrial human. I am saying that Lucifer was an angel who manifested himself as a human. His intentions were to benefit the human race on Earth. He manifested himself as an extremely tall human on the planet Saturn and then manifested himself on Earth. He is walking around among you. He is a creation of artificial intelligence like the robots. Lucifer was created by your thoughts.

7. Miscellaneous

Events that you consider to be miracles are the work of angels. There are times when that is so. Spirits in my realm can also cause miracles if they wish. We wish to work for you. Humans can sometimes perform miracles without the assistance of angels. If I gave you a million dollars, would I not be an angel.

When they're not guiding you angels are resting. They always find work to do. They are always busy.

Angels and archangels are not bonded only to Earth. They help others. They travel.

Color exists in the non-physical world. Angels actually do radiate colors. When I look at people and look at their auras, the different colors reveal to me the different situations.

All non-physical beings, angels, nature spirits etc., are manifestations of souls.

The writings of Doreen Virtue regarding angels are accurate for her.

Angels are everywhere. There is no border like you have with Mexico. There is no specific angel watching over specific countries. All the angels are watching over all the countries. They are not assigned to specific countries.

Like humans, angels also have free will. They hardly ever make wrong decisions in their dealings with people. It is very improbable.

K. THE EVOLUTION OF HUMANS

1. The soul and its evolution

The soul is the only permanent thing that distinguishes one individual from another. The soul is very important and that makes the difference between each individual of mankind. Our souls are dynamic and forever changing by the information that is fed to them through the physical or spiritual form. All human souls part of a greater soul.

The soul is a complete being. The physical body is used to receive information for the soul and then the physical body passes away. Then the spirit form passes information to the soul. The spirit form eventually passes away and just the soul exists. The physical body is just temporary and the spirit form is just temporary. There is indeed a big difference between the spirit and the soul. The spirit form intervenes between the physical body and the soul. The soul is more controlling than the spirit. The evolution of a soul does not reach a limit. It just goes on evolving endlessly. There is no end to an answer. You will eventually evolve to the God level if you wish, if it makes you feel better. That is a personal thing.

The physical body is not a permanent part of the soul. Likewise the spirit is also not a permanent part of the soul. There will be a time when humanity will evolve where there will not be physical bodies and there will not be spirit bodies. I myself will eventually evolve where I will not be a spirit. Originally we were the soul and the soul created the physical body so the physical body could have input into the development of the soul. The physical body is like an instrument to make the soul grow and to help you achieve to get where you are going. The same is true of the spirit form where I am, to give input to the development of the soul. The soul is our real self. The physical body is not our real self and the spirit is not our real self. The brain is not the real self just part of the physical body. There will come a time where we will evolve to the point where we will not even need a mind.

New souls are still continuing to come into existence. The soul begins its evolution in the mineral kingdom through the vegetable and animal kingdoms and finally to the human kingdom. Elements of the soul are right from the beginning. The soul begins in the transition from the vegetable kingdom to the animal kingdom, when it's procreating.

The soul is the individual but there are different levels to which the soul can progress. The soul begins developing its consciousness while in the mineral kingdom, and then evolves into the vegetable kingdom, the animal kingdom and the human kingdom. Animals evolve into humans and then you go into the spirit world. Then there are many levels above the spirit world to which the soul could eventually evolve. This could take eons since in reality there is no such thing as time you don't have to worry about rushing. You can just take your time, if you want to call it that. It is very difficult for anyone to understand the nature of God.

I have said that the soul is there in the beginning and that minerals have souls. I have also said that souls begin with the transition from the vegetable kingdom to the animal kingdom. This means that elements or fragments of a soul are in the mineral kingdom and the vegetable kingdom and then those elements coalesce with upon the entry into the animal kingdom. All souls eventually evolve to the state of completion or perfection. They come back again, again and again. Souls are not totally dissolved. They just have to start over again. They start over from the mineral or the vegetable kingdom. There comes a time after many incarnations that a soul is deemed irredeemable and must start all over again in the evolutional process. Some souls are so un-evolved that they have to start all over. A soul can be destroyed if you let it. When a soul is destroyed it is not true that a soul has to start development over again from the mineral kingdom. A soul can be totally obliterated. [Note the apparent contradiction here.]

All souls were not created at the same time. Old souls are souls that have had many lifetimes. Since old souls are people who have had many previous incarnations, you tend to think of them as being wiser and more evolved than the others. That is not always correct. Sometimes they are old souls simply because they have been slow learners. They are slow learners because they block things out that they think are unimportant. Sometimes the unimportant may be the vessel to the most important. If you pay attention to things that may not seem important you might not be such a slow learner and you might not have to have further lifetimes. Actually listen a little more. Some old souls never learn. They are sitting among you. Just because you are an old soul does not mean that you are more highly evolved than newer souls. Some new souls, a young angel can deal with you in a more positive way, a more intelligent, knowledgeable way. Some souls evolve more rapidly on the spirit plateau. Your school is learning. You are repeating. Some repeat and repeat. New souls in your language "purple" They are very advanced souls, the indigo children. Listen to them.

There are human beings without souls. They are among you. They are your neighbor. It is true, as Edgar Cayce, America's most noted psychic, said that sometimes the soul does not enter a body until a long time has passed after a person was born, sometimes years later. A functioning human body can exist without being part of a soul. He told of a child who did not have a soul until the age of nineteen. That child did not wake up until the age of nineteen. That is when the soul entered the physical body.

Some souls have multiple simultaneous incarnations because they want to progress more rapidly. It is especially true when a new era on Earth is approaching. In time a new era on Earth will approach. Some souls choose to have several lives, several goings on, several interests. They advance more rapidly when they have several simultaneous incarnations. Very much so! You have choices to do as such if you wish. It depends upon the individual soul whether it can have multiple simultaneous incarnations. Souls are more likely to have multiple simultaneous incarnations when a major shift of Earth energy is about to occur. Right now you have more multiple simultaneous incarnations than in the past that we are aware of. (G)

Life in the physical is a necessary experience for all souls in the spirit realm. All souls have to go through this at least once. We all must suffer to be in the physical. I would say a high number of lifetimes for a soul to have reincarnated on Earth to be six hundred. That's a good number. People do not learn. So they come back again. I cannot estimate the average range of the number of years between incarnations into the physical because we do not have the element of time here. (G)

When people commit suicide they are disappointed with the life that they have created. Their soul will not rest because it was not a natural planned incident. They are uncomfortable and suicide is not always a comfortable but easy way out. If you wish to regard it as a severe detriment to an individual's evolution, please do because with suicide you hurt others around you. You make them feel guilty and responsible. You create your own fears. You must be aware of your fears because your fears become your reality.

'Tis true in many aspects that a soul can, through agreement with another soul, willingly leave the body permanently and return to the spirit realm so that another soul can take over that body until it dies in order to perform a specific predetermined role. It's what we call walk-ins, a change of personality. It is a change of who they were and no longer wish to be. This can happen and that's how evil gets into progress. It can be good or evil. Walk-ins are not always souls who incarnate for beneficial purposes. They have all different purposes. Just because someone is a walk-in does not mean they are here for good purposes. Walk-ins sometimes incarnate simply to complete an unfinished task from a previous incarnation. Souls that walk out often leave simply because they have completed the task for which they incarnated. Sometimes they have not. Souls that walk out run out. They go out on their own accord. Sometimes they just don't like the life they are living and just want to get out of it.

A split soul is half a walk-in and half not. An individual can be two personalities at the same time, the original and the new personality. Many of us are split personalities, if you wish to term it as such.

The noblest of souls' purposes in both my world and yours is to be of service to others. It is noble to always be helping others as I am here helping you. My helping you is aiding my own evolution. If it is not I, it will be others who will do the same, as your glorious Ruth [Charles' mother] wants to do.

Soul mate is an interesting made-up word. The soul is a heart. The soul should be strong enough to survive by itself and it doesn't need a mate.

All souls are part of a greater soul, similar to the way that a soul can have multiple simultaneous incarnations. Therefore we could say that all souls are connected and that each soul's actions have an effect on other souls. Sometimes those in the spirit world are part of this. Not all times but sometimes. It's like a hierarchy of souls. We have groups here amongst us. They are waiting to answer your questions.

What we call the Christ or the Christ Spirit is a soul that has evolved to the point of completion. Throughout history there have been many Christ spirits. Many spirits! Christs are highly evolved spirits that have helped mankind to evolve. Jesus and Buddha and other such people are considered Christs. There will be future Christs. There are Christs sitting here now. The Christ spirit is one that gives hope and peace. (F)

At times, it is absolutely true that the soul suffers when a fetus is intentionally aborted. That implies that there are times that abortion could be a negative act. There are different factions in your thinking. Some want abortions and some don't. My view of abortion is that I wish to be loved. I wish to exist as long as I wish to exist. I don't know how to interpret what I am saying but this is what I'm told to tell you. It is not my personal opinion.

I remember well when many eons ago major Earth changes took place in which the great majority of humans died. Some souls were accepted into the earth's spirit world and some scattered as you people have scattered. We scattered too. We are like dust in the wind. We go in different directions. I dwell in the spirit world of my home planet. Yet I can visit other spirit worlds.

DNA can be used to trace our ancestry lineage and for soul lineage or ancestry. Ancestry can be related in souls. We are all related. It does not matter what the color or kind is. We are all one. The spirit or the soul does not change when the DNA of humans is modified. The spirit stays the same as does the soul. Emotions such as fear over a long period of time cannot truly change your DNA. Blood is blood. Blood is thicker than water. Bursts of energy from the sun can change a person's DNA somewhat to a degree.

You can learn to expand your consciousness to a higher level if you learn to relax. Do not consider worry an issue and do not fret. Learn to relax your mind and be calm. Learn to meditate. To meditate is to listen to God. The key thing is listening.

Your thinking your feelings, your personality dwell within the structure of the earth. They live within your soul.

Humans go through the process of mineral, vegetable and animal before becoming human. Angels are first flying insects or birds. They follow the same path as mineral and vegetable but then they branch off from humans at that point. (J)

If you listen too much of the current popular music such as hip-hop or rap that can lower your level of Intelligence. You can increase your level of what you call spirituality or evolution by listening to classical music if that calms you. I don't wish to listen to a drum banging in my ear.

More highly evolved humans are less fearful than other humans. One with knowledge would be less fearful.

DNA is part of the soul as well as part of the physical body.

131

2. Humans before Homosapiens

In your ancient past there were once several types of human or humanoid beings on Earth at the same time, including Neanderthals and Homosapiens etc. The human race, both the Neanderthals and the Homosapiens, first appeared Earth in Africa. The Neanderthal humans and Homosapiens did not coexist peacefully but there was no warfare between them. They had different opinions. They were of equal intelligence. The Homosapiens outlasted the Neanderthals because it was a time for them to change. Every neighborhood changes.

The Ice Age affected the development and physical appearance of the Neanderthals. The skin color changed. That was primarily the many colors you have endured. The volcanic ash of approximately 39,000 years ago had an effect on the demise of the Neanderthals. If you were being burnt by the ashes wouldn't you say that you would be disappearing? The climate had an effect on the development of the races today. The races were created by climatic conditions.

There was only one human race before the Great Flood. We were all here together and we all separated different ways. When we separated we became different races. Until then we were all one. It goes back many, many years even before I was born. Atmosphere changed the color of the skin. The current races are one race that went to different atmospheres or, as you well know, climate. They are becoming more similar. They are blending and blending.

There was a time when reptilian physical characteristics were prevalent in a large portion of Earth people. There still such people on Earth living underground.

The early physical humans communicated by telepathy. Spoken language gradually evolved and became their means of communication. Telepathy is much easier when we would read other people's minds and actions. Then there was originally just one spoken language rather than the proliferation of languages that exist in the world today. The proliferation of languages was caused by people going to different climates. Then we separated and went different ways. Language was given by those that were able to communicate by sounds and grunts and sounds of pleasure. We speak many languages on Earth. Your grunts are closest to the original language

There is a significant degree of accuracy in the writings of Damon T.

Berry in his work called *The Knowledge of the Forever Time*. Interesting. It would be worthwhile to read it. It is only his words but there is a lot of truth with his words.

The many prehistoric drawings of humans with birdlike heads throughout the world show that such beings did exist on Earth at one time. They were drawings of Earth inhabitants.

The American Indians were originally just one race of people that went in different directions and then separated into various tribes. They originated in Asia and then migrated to Alaska and then to South America. The American Indians are the physical descendants of the Atlanteans. They look closer to the Atlanteans than do the other races.

Some early Earth hominids were only three feet tall. They still exist on Earth today and live together in enclaves mostly underground.

The Atlanteans were not physically different from you to the point that you could easily see that they were not like modern humans. They were beautiful human beings. They did not resemble one of the current races more than the others. They covered many races, not only one race. There were different human races, such as those now on Earth, at the time of Atlantis. The American Indians were the closest to what many Atlanteans looked like. They had brown skin and they were beautiful souls.

The physical characteristics of the Lemurians were different from Homosapiens. The early Lemurians were hermaphrodites, quite different from physical human beings. Before that they reproduced like starfish, cut off a part of them. There were physical humans on Earth before the Lemurians. Some of their bodies were as dense as your bodies are now. Some were lighter.

Humans and members of the simian family such as monkeys or apes have a similar common ancient ancestor from which both groups descended.

3. Extraterrestrial involvement and the Anunnaki

Extraterrestrial intervention in the development of the human race came from many star systems. There are many inhabitants in your system. Your Earthly beings are so simple. There wasn't one single system that had more influence. Your distant ancestors were given increased intelligence or intellectual ability by modification of their DNA by extraterrestrial beings. This is still going on today. Aliens introduced their DNA to the then developing human race in order to jumpstart it to make it evolve more rapidly which is why there are missing links. Extraterrestrial beings have created genetically modified both humans and animals on Earth. The Pleiadians have had considerable involvement on Earth perhaps more so than those of any other star systems but that is my opinion.

The Anunnaki are people on a different planet, what some call the tenth planet in your solar system. It is part of your solar system. They can be visualized. The Anunnaki also inhabited Mars in the distant past.

There were some humanoid beings that were indigenous to your planet before the intervention of extraterrestrials, before the Anunnaki came and changed them. The Anunnaki designed the human body to look like them. They modified the bodies of the then existing Earth beings by infusing their DNA into them. That is how they made them to look more like them. When your Bible said "Then God said, Let us make mankind in <u>our</u> image, in <u>our</u> likeness." that was actually in reference to the Anunnaki creating humans in their image. Both the human mind as well as the human body has been expanded with the infusion of DNA of the Anunnaki, more the body than the mind. The Anunnaki continue to play a role protective of mankind on Earth. They are in control.

The Anunnaki created modifications of human beings for the purpose of being workers for mining the gold which they needed. The Anunnaki did take part in the creation of human beings, and they enjoyed it too. They had a mixture of animals. May I add that you can attribute your beings, the way you look now, to the Anunnaki if you wish?

The various types of humanoids such as the Neanderthal man, the Cro-Magnons etc. were created by the Anunnaki as prototypes that led to the development of the modern Homosapiens. They were models of humans created as an aid and consistency to continue. The Anunnaki are very much involved in the creation of the next humanoid species after the Homosapiens that some people refer to as the Homonoeticus. The Anunnaki were involved in the development of both the Neanderthals and the Homosapiens. The cause of the apparent leap in human consciousness from the Neanderthal man to the Homosapiens was an awakening. It was an infusion of the Anunnaki DNA into the Neanderthal man. It was because of the Anunnaki that the Neanderthals died out and the Homosapiens survived. The Neanderthals weren't able to evolve to the level that Homosapiens are able to evolve. However, there still full-breed Neanderthals on the earth today hidden enclaves in the caves in southern

Spain. Today there is a mixture. Many of you are like part Neanderthal and that is why you are so odd. The Atlanteans were Homosapiens like you are now, not Neanderthals. Time has passed on and you must continue to grow. Now with, the Homonoeticus, Homosapiens will eventually be eliminated.

The Great Flood was engineered by the Anunnaki to purge the earth. It was not to rid it of any specific species. It was a great cleansing.

The Anunnaki used a spaceship to travel from their home planet to Earth. They did not use any type of vortex or wormhole to travel here. They are here.

All humans were at least once in their existence a hybrid; that is, a mixture of their original Earth being and an extraterrestrial being. Some humans have become hybrids on repeated occasions. That process is continuing to occur at the present time. Indeed among you.

There is interbreeding between extraterrestrials and humans. If an extraterrestrial should interbreed with a human, that child will not look completely different from a human. He would not be likely to have any noticeable physical extraterrestrial features. It would skip a generation. It is recessive and occurs in alternate generations.

Noah played a significant role in aiding the evolution of human beings. He was actually an extraterrestrial who worked with embryos. The ark was a UFO spaceship and the animals were not animals but they were the embryos or the DNA of animals and in that way they were able to put all the animals into the spaceship. That's how they got the thousands of animals into the ark. There are no physical remains that archeologists will ever find because it never existed as such. Noah in the Bible and humans who lived on Earth before him had physical features different from ours, such as webbed fingers. He was not the founder of city of Zion which later became the city of Jerusalem. (I)

As a result of extraterrestrial involvement, you humans are designer babies in both body and mind. That transition began hundreds of thousands of years ago. This is what is occurring now. So you will have blue-eyed babies and blond hair. You will have bug eyes. Hundreds of thousands of years ago extraterrestrials designed the human race by manipulation of DNA.

Humans are constantly being rehybridized. In other words, their DNA is being modified by extraterrestrials. New human hybrids usually resemble the rest of the humans more physically than psychologically.

Psychologically they are a little different from the rest of the humans but physically they look similar. There are some humans alive on Earth today who are not hybrids but are original Earth beings. Their DNA has not been tampered with by extraterrestrials.

Extraterrestrials can imbue some of their own attitudes and desires into the DNA of humans to make humans more like them. Extraterrestrials mess around with your DNA. Opposing groups of extraterrestrials have spliced some of their own DNA into different groups of humans in the past. The imbued DNA passed on from generation to generation. That is a major cause of the wide political division in your politics today. The division between the Democrats and the Republicans goes way back in history and it started with opposing extraterrestrial groups.

4. Humans in the future

Star children are the forerunners of a new race of humans that will eventually replace Homosapiens. Isn't such happening at this moment? Humanity is evolving to a higher level through the entry of star children being born on Earth. That is the new race that is often referred to as the Homonoeticus if you wish to give it a label. The new race will be more evolved. They will be able to see the future without talking. They will be what you would call psychic. When the Chinese government recently made a study of more than 100,000 children with unusual abilities, they were they what we call "star Children". Star children are very bright, intelligent and wise. They are more highly evolved souls than most souls with much confusion. Jesus was a star child. So was Mohammad. So was Confucius. So is your wife.

The Millennials and those born after the year 2000 are more advanced than the baby boomers. They are also very, very clearly intuitive or as you will, if I may, psychic. As time proceeds a greater percentage of the population will be more psychic than at present.

Indigo children, as you have named such, are brilliant, intelligent and very superior, you know. They are very bright, a bit mystical. They are aware of the past and they are aware of the future. Many of you are mystical children. Indigo children are an increasing percentage of all the babies being born today. They are much smarter than you. Most of you use less than twenty percent of your brain. As humans evolve, you will be using a greater part of your brain.

Human kind is getting more in touch with the psychic capabilities that we have had right along. You are going to get to the stage where people cannot lie to each other or when you can tell when we are being lied to. You can do that now by just looking at who you are looking at. Most of us are liars. We even lie to ourselves. Well, maybe not lie, fib.

The genetic manipulation of human DNA to create a more advanced human being by your scientists will become a reality in the near future. It is already in progress definitely and they are experimenting and this also will come to light in a very short time. The danger in what they will create is another person. It is not being developed for negativity. It is being developed to be used in a harmless way but everything harmless turns out with some negativity.

Humans will be more like the Grays thousands of years from now. Humans are gradually evolving into Grays in a different way, if you wish to call it that. You can assume that you will look somewhat more like the Grays. I will see you there then.

Humans will eventually communicate through telepathy rather than by spoken language. Some already do. Some people do not speak. In the very far future perhaps telepathy will be used, for your many different nations do not have to but they will be able to draw pictures.

At some point in the future women will become the dominant gender. Your wife will. Women will take more leadership roles in different areas of the world. Do not fear if it will be in the relative near or distant future.

Marriage will become less significant or popular within the next several generations. It will be less important. Your laws will change. Your bylines will change. People will change. A smaller percentage of the population will be married. Only those who produce will be married. By produce I mean bearing children.

The average life span of a human being will increase by more than twenty years within the next few centuries. It is doing that now. Humans will be living more than one hundred twenty years.

The time will come when you will be able to control tornados by using your technology. You will use your mind. Your mind is a wonderful asset and is not being able to be used to control. An example of this would be that you and your wife once knew a person who could make clouds disappear using her mind.

There is a reason for you to be inspired by the message in the *Celestine Prophecies* that you will all evolve into a spiritual state and that you will no longer be separated in matter. We are all evolved in one matter. We are all given by one god and that lies deep within ourselves.

As humans evolve to a higher density, you will be able to see things such as ghosts or cloaked UFO's that are currently beyond our range of perception. Some of the people in this room now can do that. People are all psychic. Everyone is psychic to a different degree. Some are more psychic much more than others.

5 The Ascension

The Golden Age that is referred to in the Hindu religion and in the prophesies of many other religions is about to occur. It is an individual thing. Some humans will enter that Golden Age and some won't. It is a delightful way of putting it to look forward to something. That is related to what is called the ascension where some will remain and some will move away.

Many ancient religions throughout the world have prophesized there will be an ascension of humanity. A forthcoming solar flash will initiate that ascension to push the earth from the third density to the fourth density. It will not occur in the lifetimes of anyone alive today. That was not the third secret that was given to the children at Fatima Portugal in 1917. The secret was pertaining to health.

After the forthcoming ascension to the fourth density that has been prophesized in various religions, all Earth humans will be in light bodies. Life in the fourth density will be much more peaceful than in the current third density. People will not kill each other. The light beings that remain on Earth will be able to manifest whatever they want, much the same as spirits now do with just their thoughts. They can think it and use their will to decide what to do with it. They can create it with just their mind. They do not have to take any physical action. Those who do not qualify for ascension will be reincarnated in the physical third density as they are now but on other planets. There are other planets that exist now and we will be travelling from planet to planet.

You are absolutely going through the process of Ascension beginning right now, going from the third density to the fourth density. Not only the earth but the entire solar system is moving from the third density to the fourth density. That could be referred to as a different dimension. In this case densities and dimensions would be synonymous. When you are in the fourth density you will all be at a higher vibrational and humans will have greater abilities. You will not have to speak different languages. You will read each other's thoughts. That is telepathy. You can communicate with people just by directing your thinking at them. People who often experience the spontaneous viewing of the number eleven or a series of the number one are more likely to ascend from the third to the fourth density if they want to. They feel better. Not all are able to.

By the end of the year 2020 or shortly thereafter life on Earth will be very different from what it is now. I am talking about the ascension, life going from the third density to the fourth density. That is a big deal that has been prophesized in many religions. There is such a thing as the ascension and that is going to occur. That will be after the lifetime of those here.

In the forthcoming ascension when the earth moves from the third density to the fourth density, causing some humans to remain on Earth in the fourth density and others to be relocated on third density planets, the same will be true of those spirits now associated with the earth.

Corey Goode is a man who knows much about extraterrestrials and the ascension. You can believe what he says about them. He is correct when he says that only about 300,000 people will move on to the fourth density in the coming ascension. Only a small percentage of humans will remain on Earth in a light body and that most humans will transported elsewhere in the universe.

There is a connection between the predicted solar flash from your sun within the next ten years and the ascension that will occur. Extraterrestrials are using large spheres to delay the solar flash.

Human life in the fourth density, that is; after the forthcoming ascension, will include many aspects of life in the spirit world that you do not currently have. I, in the spirit world, have abilities that humans do not have. After the ascension you will have some of the abilities that I have that you currently don't have. A lot of things that extraterrestrials can do that you cannot do because you have not reached their level of evolution. For example, like spirits, many of the advanced groups can create things by just using their minds. Most humans do not create things by just using their minds. When you want to create something you have to get the idea in your head first, then you have to use your will regarding what to do about it and then you very often have to do physical-type labor very often to create something. You don't just do it directly with your mind. Humans will reach the point where they can do things with just their minds. Some humans are doing it now.

6. After the human state

If you are no longer required to reincarnate, most energy beings remain on the astral plane indefinitely or eventually move to a higher realm or to a lower realm, wherever you wish, wherever you feel comfort and solace. A lower realm is other star systems. The earth is not the only place for us to arrive in. (B)

After they have reached the level of evolution where they are no longer required to remain in the spirit realm, spirits cast off their spirit bodies much the same as you cast off your physical bodies when you enter the spirit world. After the spirits cast off their spirit form, some go to a higher realm. Some are left back and they have to come back and learn. Above my world, we go on and on and angels take over.

Those in the human or spirit kingdom will never evolve into the angelic kingdom. The two kingdoms are always separate. No one from the human kingdom or from the spirit kingdom can ever become an angel. Humans can evolve to a state that they are like angels but they will not be angels. We refer to them as what is commonly called the "masters". Some of us are not able to reach that plateau. Some can and will. Very few can and will reach the "angel state". There is potential for humans to eventually evolve to a level above that of the angels. Don't we call people who are kind an angel? (J)

Humans and spirits will eventually evolve to a higher plane of existence. They will not be dissolved or relegated to a lower plane of existence. The goal of all humans and spirits is to go up to an even higher realm of existence above that of spirits. That is very important for the spiritual aspect.

All souls manifest themselves in various stages in their upward evolution such as the physical human body, the spirit form as well as various cosmic entities such as planets, moons, stars etc. It goes on from where you are and manifests itself in heavenly bodies. It is a natural course of events that I and the rest of you will eventually evolve to the point that we become stars. All the billions of stars out there are souls. A psychic friend whom you knew many years ago and has since passed on told people that after she died she would become a planet. That was possible. She went there. I don't have her in my world.

Sometimes people have to be peasants before they become kings and queens. All the billions and billions of stars are souls but not all have gone through the process of being a human first.

Humans have the potential of eventually evolving to a level much further than you can now conceive more than even cosmic entities. We are all able to reach a higher level. We all can climb up and do well. Helping people, being with people, being of aid is an asset to people. Help others and you will feel better and be better. That is the best way to evolve; to give, to help others. Give and you will receive. When you give, the happiness you receive inside cannot be expressed.

History repeats itself in cycles of a specific numbers of years such as every 539 years or every 720 years etc is a reality. The same souls can reincarnate on those occasions to complete their mission or karma.

7. Miscellaneous

There aren't any planets or moons in your solar system in which there are inhabitants who are less evolved that Earth humans. The Earth inhabitants are the least evolved. There are other planets that are looking in on Earth and their advice is minimal. The Earth humans are the least evolved of any humans in your galaxy because they are the least informed. They are not able to conceive what is given to them. They are limited. At the present time most extraterrestrials are desirous of helping Earth humans evolve to a higher level.

The origin of the different human races on Earth was not related to the activities of various extraterrestrial groups. They absolutely had no influence on the development of the human races. The development of the different races was based more on climate than anything else. The human race was born in Africa and the migrated out from that.

Members of the black race and the aborigines are closer to the original Earth race of humans than the other races. The DNA of those of the other races was affected by the injection or the manipulation of their DNA by extraterrestrials [This appears to contradict the previous entry.]

It is very accurate that according to Hindu scriptures the Aryan race began in Siberia and migrated westward to Europe. (Q)

Natural, cataclysmic events such as comets or meteors played a major role in forming human civilization.

Some people are destined to win the lottery and other people destined to not win the lottery and winning can be solely by chance.

Sometimes people are supposed to win, sometimes they are supposed not to win and sometimes it is by chance. If you are destined to win the lottery it does not matter how many lottery tickets you buy. You can buy one ticket or a hundred. Just one ticket is enough.

Some Earth people originated on Mars and then migrated to Earth. When on Mars all civilizations were more technologically advanced than you are now. The same is not necessarily true of their spiritual advancement. That is individual. It didn't depend on the civilization. It could be humans or elsewhere. It depends on each individual.

Some situations or incidents in a person's life occur because they are destined to occur and other situations or incidents occur because they are simply the result of the roll of the dice. The role of the dice is imminent. Some situations are predestined to occur before you are born, such as meeting a certain person. It is all planned ahead of time while you are in the spirit world. Sometimes you can miss the plane and you cannot judge it. Your judgment is off at times. Sometimes you miscalculate. Your thinking is not good and you make wrong decisions.

When something that you consider extremely bad happens to you and you feel that if only you had not been at that place at that time it would not have happened, the condition would have occurred anyway because it is part of your destiny. You were destined to be there at that moment. If you wish, you could have said that "If only I had not been there." but it wouldn't have made any difference.

The children currently entering physical life on Earth are of a higher vibrational level than most of the adults on Earth. Some are what is referred to as wanderers; that is, entities from other star systems that incarnate on Earth specifically for the purpose of helping to raise the level of consciousness of humans.

The size of the human brain has increased by more than the size of tennis ball within the last two centuries. The IQ level has also increased. There is more to learn. The major social changes now taking place are related to the increase of the brain size. There are different parts of the brain that you will be able to accept. You will use a greater percentage of your brain than you now use.

All of the entities on an advanced planet will eventually evolve to be merged into a single consciousness.

L. HUMAN QUALITIES, ACTIVITIES AND ABILITIES

1. Level of consciousness

All things in the physical world, whether they are animal, vegetable or mineral, have some level or form of consciousness I have said that you humans are stupid; but I would also say that you are more ignorant than stupid. You are not knowledgeable. Both your ignorance and your stupidity are overwhelming. I am being very kind. Humans on Earth are among the least advanced entities in the various star systems. They just cannot see ahead. You just don't know but you do have the potential to learn. Some Earth beings need more incarnations than those on other planets. I had many incarnations because I was a slow learner. I am still a slow learner but I can tell you what to do.

Ignorant means that you just don't know but stupid implies that you don't have the capacity to learn readily. There are some people that are ignorant and you cannot make any sense to them. They are stubborn. They are in their own world and you cannot deal with any person or people that think they are always right. By these questions that I am answering you, I am helping you to become more aware, in other words to become less ignorant. That is what my existence here is for, to be with you, and help you, and serve you and answer your questions. I am helping you to raise your level of awareness or consciousness, some of you. For some we cannot open the door because it is stuck with Crazy Glue. Some people in the physical world have a greater degree of awareness than some of those in the spirit world.

Humans don't have as great a capacity to learn as do those in other star systems. I would also say that you are stupid and make wrong decisions because you let your emotions take control of your thinking. Those in other star systems do not make the right decisions more than humans do but they know the right decisions for them to succeed. In other systems emotions do not influence a person's thinking as they do with humans because there aren't such emotions in other systems. I have explained that the Grays don't have emotions and that they are humans from the future. They are coming into your future now. As humans evolve you will feel less emotion. Emotions will play less of a role in your lives. Emotions get you nowhere except hurt. If a stupid person keeps his mouth shut nobody will know he is stupid.

Evil is a form of spiritual blindness. Humans would be less evil if they were not so ignorant. Evil is an outgrowth of ignorance. It is just an appetite. Another way of saying that might be that if people were truly knowledgeable they wouldn't be evil. Once people overcome ignorance and become knowledgeable, evil will dissipate. Evil will affect only those who are themselves evil.

The ability of an individual to easily feel love for others (not physical love) is an indication of that person's level of evolution. The more you can be sensitive and feel love for people, the more spiritual you are.

In both your world and our world, individuals who have a good sense of humor are usually more highly evolved than those with very little sense of humor. Those who have more humor have more strength. Those with very little sense of humor are not as evolved. (B)

There is a relationship between the kinds of music you enjoy listening to and the functioning of your chakras. You actually raise your level of consciousness by listening to classical music. If the music doesn't get on your nerves and it does not tear you apart, if it brings peace to you, you can control it. You advance more spiritually if you listen to classical music rather than rap type music.

It is not an important means for raising the level of a person's awareness to spend time in nature and vegetation rather than in metropolitan areas. If you want to think like a bug, go where the bugs are. It is ridiculous that you will raise your level of consciousness if you are in pure nature rather than in the city. Although I have said that being in the countryside rather than in urban areas will not help you raise your kevel of consciousness, there are places on Earth where you could help raise your level of consciousness simply by being there. Every individual is an individual. Every stone has a different need. Everyone has a different answer. It depends on the person where it would be best to raise the level of consciousness. Wouldn't it be interesting if all were to gather in one place!

Eating meat is a reflection of lower level consciousness. You can definitely raise your level of consciousness by avoiding red meat. Eating red meat is not beneficial to your health.

Cursing or using foul language does not have any repercussions on the individual's evolution. It is release. I feel better when I don't give a damn what I say.

When a person has a disease such as Alzheimer's, that person's consciousness is neither in the physical world nor in the spirit world. Confusion exists in that person. They are not in any world. They are out of this world.

There is a danger for humans to learn to activate the rising of the kundalini energy. Be careful.

2. Human abilities

Since there is no time or space in the spirit dimension, the closest thing to what humans can experience is that they can instantaneously take their thoughts to any place or any time. Since time does not exist in my dimension, it is correct to assume that no medium or psychic on your plateau can accurately predict the dates when future events will occur. If they are good, yes they can, but accuracy does not exist. The future does exist.

When I see a person's future that means that I can tell how that person will exercise his free will. The results of a person's exercise of his free will are known in advance by the higher powers. We can tell how that person will exercise his free will. It depends upon the individual whether free will is predestined. Remember the word *free will*. You have a choice: to do it or not to do it. You are where you are in life right now because of the series of sequences in exercising your free will. When we see your future we get together and we gamble at what you are going to do and what you are not going to do. That is based on how you have exercised your free will in the past. You can change your mind.

The use of a person's free will can overcome any astrological influences. Look at your wife. Is she not suffering today from the astrological influences? She has a very strong will and the personality to overcome the dreadful pain and illness that she has. She is remarkable in the way that she can help and wants to be there to share with others. She wants only peace and happiness for others. They need not suffer like she does.

Humans are able to create with their minds. They are able to cause fear, apprehension or alarm. They can also cause happiness. Extraterrestrials far more advanced than you can actually create physical objects just using their minds. Humans also are able to do anything they want to do with their minds. Although I have said that humans have the ability to create physical things with just their minds, they do not use that ability. However, there are some people who perform as magicians, even on television, who actually do appear to create with their minds. It is more than just sleight of hand. You can do anything you wish. I am talking about [for example] someone like Uri Geller who could bend spoons with his mind. Humans can do that.

Some humans are more knowledgeable than some spirits in understanding the world and others around them. The same is true regarding foreseeing the future. Some humans can see the future better than some spirits. However, there are very few that can.

The explanation of what happens in fire walking events to enable a person to do so without harm is that they do not actually walk on fire. They walk on dead coals. You can do it any place you wish to if you can do it fast and run right through it. I've seen many a dumb thing done.

Mediums are not the only ones who can see spirits. Many people can see spirits but they do not trust their vision or do not trust their mental abilities. Anything, including an injury to the head, can trigger you to become a medium.

It is possible that as you age you can; even while in the physical, begin to live life on the spirits' level. For some this is true; for others it is a fallacy. Each person or individual has to know the difference. It is imperative to know the difference.

There are civilizations on other planets where the inhabitants do not need mechanical means to travel from one place to another but instead are able to use their minds to teleport themselves wherever they wish to go in the physical. Earth people can learn teleportation. Instant teleportation of a person from one place to another is possible both through the use of technology and also through the use of the human mind. Some humans can instantly appear in a different place from where they were before.

Just like animals such as dogs that can smell or sense certain diseases in humans, some humans are capable of smelling diseases such as Parkinson's as well. That is prominent now.

One thing humans can do to keep secrets from spirits is to keep your mouths shut. Spirits can read the thoughts of humans but not the words in their minds. Humans cannot keep secrets from spirits.

Humans have the potential ability to receive communication from everything in the mineral, vegetable and animal kingdoms. Angels and spirits can project thoughts into the minds of humans. Humans also have the potential for that ability. (D)

The thoughts or prayers of humans can generate storms such as hurricanes. You have control. Extraterrestrials can use an advanced part of their mind to do that. There are humans who can do that also. There are quite a few humans who have that ability. They are the more highly evolved humans.

Praying that another person not die can be of some sort of help in saving that person from dying. [This statement appears to contradict entries elsewhere.]

Humans can send telepathic thoughts to another person. Those thoughts are sometimes intentionally and sometimes they are sent without the awareness of the sender. It does not make any difference if the two people are near each other or if they are at a distance. The best way of intentionally sending telepathic thoughts to another person is to just think it and review it.

3. Time Traveling, astral projection and near death experiences

Time travel exists and there are some people on Earth right now who are from your future. We all can time travel. We can go forward or we can go back. It is easier to go back but you can also go forward. Time travelers can go back in time and change their history. They can go back and change themselves; not the world history, but their own history. A time traveler can go back in time and visit himself. As Sondra saw, it is true that Charles is a time traveler from the future.

When a person is having an astral projection he is able to travel anywhere in the universe much the same as the spirits do. The person is also able to travel in time, both to the past and to the future much the same as do spirits.

Human encounters with extraterrestrials are sometimes not really encounters with extraterrestrials but rather encounters with human time travelers from your future. You thought they were extraterrestrials but they were imposters. They were you from the future. There are also currently humans on Earth who are not from the future but who are time travelers to their future.

147

Everyone has an out-of-body experience at least once in a lifetime. In one form or another that is true but it may be misinterpreted what an out-of-body experience is. We have gone through many, many out-of-body experiences. One is when a person is asleep.

4. Validating information from other sources

The information about the root races as depicted in the Theosophical belief system is indeed accurate. Blavatsky is correct. She is telling me to tell you yes. Homosapiens are gradually evolving into what some call Homonoeticus. You will not have to use your voice in the future. Homonoeticus will be more psychic and telepathic. The forerunners, the indigo children, are here right now, beginning slowly amongst your younger children. There are many people who can foretell and foresee. The fundamental principles presented in Theosophy are correct for the most part. You could learn and grow if you looked into Blavatsky's work, the *Secret Doctrine* and things like that. It is of use to find out where others have failed so you can prevail. You will do so.

There is some accuracy in the letters of those individuals in my realm who channeled the Urantia Book.

Erich Von Daniken is on the right track in his book *Chariots of the Gods.* There is some truth in what he has written.

The information that David Wilcock provides for you is generally worthy of your consideration. It is something to think about. I would suggest that you read about what he has written or listen to what he says. Not all is fallacy. There is some truth that lies within.

Darwin's theory of evolution is somewhat correct. Brilliant man, you know.

5. Homosexuality and the Vanishing Twin Syndrome

I have indicated that homosexuals are so by choice. The choice can be made either before birth or after but mainly after birth. This is not done at the conscious level. Sometimes there are times that people cannot finish their gender and come back to finish even though they are in a different gender body. Sometimes you just like the same people. You find it appealing. That's why so many wish to transfer.

Although it seems that there are a greater percentage of homosexuals today than in the past, it is just the way it has always been. More individuals have been acknowledged and more people have been educated and they are not stupid.

Through psychological therapy homosexuals can become heterosexuals. They can be both if they wish, you know. They can attain any wish they desire. It is not uncommon. 'Tis very common.

The theory of the vanishing twin syndrome is a reality. It occurs frequently but it is not important. Some of it is not digested well. Miscarriages are also part of the vanishing twin. All babies have a twin in the womb with them. The surviving twin will be aware. The gender of the surviving twin will be whatever it wishes to be. If it wishes to be female, it will be female. The twin that disappears has no affect on the surviving twin.

It is very difficult to attract your twin flame. That is your twin self. We all have a twin self and sometimes it is not for the best because the twin is not always the best. It is contrary to you. The twin flame is related to the vanishing twin syndrome. That is the other part of you. Your twin flame is not in the physical. It is still in the spirit world because it did not incarnate. If you are looking for a twin flame in the physical, you will not find your twin flame. Very often when people speak of twin flames they think of the person that they will relate to a hundred percent and it will be a perfect union. That will never happen. You love yourself and you hate yourself. In actuality, you will never find your twin flame. It is nonsense that this is supposed to be the last time that we have lives on this planet and that twin flames are supposed to be coming together.

When I said that Charles has a twin who has not yet been born, it is not in the skin and bones that I am talking about. He did not come to this Earth. He is part of Charles. He has his skeleton and the other half did not form. Half of his twin is in the spirit world and half is in the physical world. His soul is split into two. Half of him is here and half of him is there. It has to do with his being a situs inversus. It is that way with all situs inversus. They are all half developed. That is also related to the vanishing twin syndrome.

6. Miscellaneous

Intuition is like a brain. It is a brain that you had before and is the feeling of the knowledge that you have lived before. Your intuition is another word for being psychic. Everybody has intuition. Everybody, every single soul is psychic.

A personal astrological chart is a good source for life guidance. It can be helpful if you are able to interpret it in a proper way.

Spontaneous combustion of human beings does exist. A person's body temperature can actually reach three thousand degrees. You can do anything; reach a low degree or a high degree. The source of the combustion comes from within.

The desire for humans to become godlike is not implanted in their DNA. It is implanted in their mental abilities that they have lacking of.

Good luck is how you enlighten yourselves and how you grow inside. It is true that the more light that is inside, the more you can illuminate what is outside for yourself. It is to know yourself. That is most difficult, you know.

If a person repeatedly says negative, but untrue, things about himself such as "My eyesight is poor." there an increased possibility that this will eventually become true. We know how to make it prevail. We talk ourselves into being good and to be not.

There is not more dishonesty among people on Earth nowadays than there was several decades ago. It just appears that way. Your society in America is not more decadent today than it was many years ago. It's the same but it is just advertised. It just appears that there is more dishonesty. It is the same but there are more people on Earth now than in the past.

When you dream at night, in some dreams you are only partly in the physical world but in other dreams your consciousness is fully in the spirit world. It depends upon the dream.

In the earth's sphere there are about ten times as many souls in the spirit world than there are in the physical world.

When a person is in a coma state, that person is not able to think. His mind is shut down. He is sleeping and resting peacefully.

It is true that there are more mentally ill people on Earth today that ever before. We have mentally ill people in my world also. This is a trend in society.

Many human hybrids on Earth appear physically the same as other humans to us but are mentally and psychologically different. They are more psychologically and emotionally different than they are physically different. The hybrids that are being integrated into your society are noticed by the way they think and act, not by the way they look.

If we do not forgive, anger and hate become part of us. If we do not forgive, that means we do not understand and if we do not understand that will continue to carry on. That will not necessarily bring negativity to us. That can bring changes to our environment. What we don't understand as we grow we will understand. So growth will help us to understand. The best way to understand is to teach.

The use of the royal crown does not have any connection with extraterrestrial communication or an astronaut helmet. It is related to the halo. By halo I am referring to the aura which surrounds a person and is strongest at the head. Each one of us had a halo around the head. The crown is used a physical depiction of that aura around the head.

The human brain distinguishes what is or was real from what is imagined or visualized. There is a difference in the brain. The human brain knows that what is visualized is not real. That is why honesty is very important.

There are humans on Earth today whose beings were not modified by extraterrestrials. In other words there are some humans who are not hybrids. Their bodies have not been modified at all by extraterrestrials.

Although only about 15% of humans have negative Rh blood types, the Basques in Spain and France have a very high percentage of people with Rh negative blood type. They are smarter. They think better than you do. They are more intelligent. There is a relationship between Rh blood types and intelligence. The Basques are originally from elsewhere.

Everything that happens to you occurs either for a purpose or is simply the result of a cause. Watch what you do. Watch what you say.

When a person has multiple personalities, the different personalities can be from one soul that is reincarnating again and again and it can also be from different souls.

It is not unusual for a birthmark to be inherited. Birthmarks can be similar.

When a cell in a person's body dies and is replaced by a new cell, that is similar to a person dying and leaving the physical remains to decay while the life force that animated that body continues to exist elsewhere. The life force of the cell has no personality of its own but rather returns to a collective life force, if you wish to phrase it that way. There are many different ways of phrasing that. In other words, when it leaves, the life force does not maintain its individuality but returns to its source.

There are human beings that are not the manifestation of souls, or as you tend to say, humans without souls. There are so many humans without souls. They are there without a heart, without a soul. They are heartless.

A person's birth name is very important because it reflects the true character or self to a point. Any appliance will affect. When a person feels the desire to change his name, that desire often comes from the higher self in order to reflect the change of character. Conversely, if a person changes his name, that can have an impact on his character. If you wanted people to call you by a different name your personality would change to reflect that name. It would give you a feeling of being better.

Human life on Earth is an experimental laboratory for extraterrestrials. Right now, extraterrestrials are continuing to have an influence on the consciousness and physical form of humans.

There are humans on Earth who are immortal in the physical world. There are some people in the physical world that will never die if they choose not to. There are humans in the world today that will not go away.

The pineal gland is in the center of the forehead and its interior is like the retina of the eye. There is a connection between the function of the pineal gland and what we call the third eye. It is also your psychic ability if you don't wipe it away. It will help you. Your first thought will help you, which you often decline.

World changes, such as a reduction in terrorism, do not necessarily occur if a large number of people simultaneously meditate on or pray for such but you can change your condition. You can only change your own conditions, not world conditions. [This appears to contradict other entries.]

It is true regarding John of God in Brazil, that more than 600 women came forward and accused him of raping them. A person can actually do what you call miracles such as healing a person from disease and yet perform evil acts. That goes on all the time, right before your nose. Let's see you pick the next president. A person can be evil and yet do good things at the same time.

When people enjoy hugging trees, that can have a greater consequence other than just making the people happy. The sharing of energies has an effect on the trees. The trees can sense the hugging.

M. GOD, CREATION AND THE UNIVERSE

1. God

You humans do not know God. No one knows God. My vision of God is tremendous and not explainable and it lies within each of us. We do not have any worship on this plateau. We do not worship other than ourselves. Each individual is an extension of God. We use the word God so loosely. I do not know what is meant or what is referred to as God. I am God within myself. Within me is a god. Within each one of you there is a god. We call that god intuition. Within every soul there is intuition and there is a god. Within ourselves we are strong. Do not allow someone else to appoint what should be done or what will be done or could be. God could be defined as a conglomerate of all that exists. God is everything. Everything is a word that cannot be explained or expressed. God is so unexplainable and so far above comprehension that God can't even be described as an entity or as a being. God is more a force or energy. It is more a will. We leave things in God's hands. Who is God? It is us. God doesn't do anything. We do everything. Humans will never be able to comprehend God.

There is no single entity watching over all of creation. We have no god. There are many entities. God is within each individual. Like on your earth, everyone has their own soul. There are different gods, different beliefs, and different standards. There is no one specific entity in charge. We have groups of intelligent entities that get together and aid us to aid you. The work is done by committee. Although there is no single entity that we might think of as God overseeing everything in our universe, there is a hierarchy or committee of what we might think of as gods that oversee it. I must admit a smile on my face and show you there is such and it is not a single entity but "committees".

God as you understand it is all powerful and all knowledgeable and is the oneness of all and that somehow you became separated from that. Although you are told in your scriptures that the devil or someone made the wrong decision, that is not correct. It was not the wrong decision that was made. It was a different decision.

Each star system has some form of a conscious entity that oversees the development of that star system. We have different rules and organizations on our different star systems. We are the overseer of all creation. We have someone to put our efforts on, so why not blame God. We will not blame ourselves and sometimes we blame God. All of us together make up God.

Since God is everything and nothing exists without God, then evil is part of God. The good and the bad. Sometimes the same thing is good for one person but evil for another.

There is actually a center of our universe from which the God force emanates. There are places in your universe in which the God force is stronger, such as black holes.

2. Places in the universe

There is another planet in your solar system that your scientists refer to as planet nine which is twenty times further away from the sun than the planet Neptune. Such a planet exists. That planet was always in your solar system. This is the planet that the ancient Sumerian stone tablets refer to as Niburu.

There are additional undiscovered planets in your solar system. There are planets in your solar system that you don't know about. There are seven or nine undiscovered planets as large as the earth. They are as far out as the planet Niburu. The planet Pluto was originally a moon of Saturn that was hit by the planet Niburu. Pluto was originally revolving around the planet Saturn. Then the planet Niburu influenced it and threw it out of the orbit of Saturn. There are many planets similar to your Earth. The planet Niburu is one that can cause harm when it comes near Earth but that will not be in your lifetime.

Zachariah Sitchin was correct when he interpreted an ancient Sumerian tablet that said that there was once a planet between Jupiter and Mars that they called Tiamat. That is why your horoscopes are changing. The planet that broke up created both the asteroid belt and the planet Earth. Indeed it was hit by Niburu and splintered off, having children. I am not quite sure but I will tell you that it is partially true that the earth was once part of that planet. Zachariah Sitchin is with me on this plane. He is here now and is telling Sondra he loves her and wanted so much to meet her and he is holding her and he is charming. He loves the work that she is doing to assist and aid people and let average people know what it is to feel good about themselves.

The destruction of the planet Tiamat that was once between Mars and Jupiter was not the result of warring extraterrestrial groups. Some of the survivors of that planet went to the dwarf planet Ceres and some went to Earth. They went to where you came from. You will not like the inhabitants of Ceres but you will come in contact with them on a widespread basis. You have concerns. There is much to learn. There are more rules and regulations on Earth than there are on other planets. The people, or entities, on other planets are nicer to each other than Earth people are to each other. We don't use the word "don't ". What makes the earth the most difficult planet to live on is not nature. It is people.

Many other universes in addition to your universe exist. When a soul experiences parallel lives, those lives are sometimes in different universes. There is a center of your universe as some scientists feel. It is from that location that the life force emanates. There are no stars at the very center of your constellation, the Milky Way, because there is something very powerful there. There is energy at the center. It is because of that energy that there are no stars present.

There other planets outside of your solar system which could support Earth humans in the physical as you now are.

Places exist in the physical world that you call wormholes, black holes or star gates where you can go through some kind of portal and emerge in faraway places in the universe. Not only through one's mind but in the future. You can go into the future and into the past. They are what you may call black spaces. It is available to you. There is a network of underwater portals used by extraterrestrials. There are many star gates within the borders of your country but they are mostly in the water. The earth is made of water. Those that are on land are not mostly on mountain tops as some people believe. We look above but we do not look below. We must look below. Some are in your lakes and oceans and they are near here.

As according to your scientists there is a black hole in your galaxy that has a white hole at the other end of it, thus causing a tunnel that aliens could travel through.

From my own experience, I would say that physical life on Earth is more difficult than that physical life in other star systems. Here on Earth you have promises. You have laws. They are all shaking their heads. They do not want to come back. So I would assume that from this experience, no one wants to come back.

It was because of Lucifer's actions that the earth became a most difficult place for physical life. Lucifer has definite intentions and they are not misguided. Lucifer's intentions in regard to the involvement with Earth are usually good but perhaps not to you. The people made it difficult. The people disagree no matter what you do, no matter what you say. They don't know what they mean.

There are pyramids on the moon and on Mars. There are pyramids on other planets in addition to Earth and Mars. Why should they be special? There are absolutely pyramids beneath the water in the earth. The earth has fallen. That is why there are pyramids beneath the level of the water.

Mars at one time resembled Earth in regard to land features, vegetation and animal life. It was once like Earth with water, land features, vegetation and atmosphere. Humans originated on Mars and gradually came to Earth. Earth human life actually began on Mars and then migrated to Earth. So you are all ancestrally Martians. You are all black. Earth human life began in Africa.

Your moon was originally a natural creation but extraterrestrials modified it to the point that it was no longer a natural creation. The moon was originally somewhere else, but through their technology, extraterrestrials moved it to a specific place so that life on Earth could take place. The moon is hollow. When the astronauts crashed something on the moon, it rang like a bell for about an hour.

The moon is a space station of some kind and there are extraterrestrials inside of it. Your moon was not originally a satellite of the planet Tiamat. It was intentionally parked in its current orbit around the earth by extraterrestrials. There is physical evidence on the dark side of the moon of long ago warring between extraterrestrial groups. China recently sent an expedition to the dark side of the moon. They will discover surprising things on the dark side that you don't know about now.

I am aware of nowhere in the universe where there such a thing as complete silence or no kind of activity whatsoever.

There are entire cities beneath the ice in Antarctica today that are inhabited by extraterrestrials. Air and water are necessary for the entities beneath the surface of Antarctica. It is necessary for flowers and anything that needs air. There is also vegetable and animal life beneath the surface. At one time there was an Earth shift and what was Atlantis became Antarctica. That is why it is a highly evolved civilization. Millions of people live beneath the ice in Antarctica. The Nazis were involved with the civilization in Antarctica. They are still there but not actively involved.

There is more than one star in your solar system. There are many stars. The earth revolves around more than just what you think of as your sun.

Earth one of the most recent planets to be inhabited by human-like entities. There are more than Earth. There is another planet that is exactly like Earth. I have told you that human life on Earth is the least advanced of all planets. The beings on the other planet that is just like Earth are at the same level as humans. You will have contact with those beings if you live long enough. That planet is in your solar system. It will be difficult to communicate with them. I'm not talking about Ceres but something further away.

Spirit worlds exist on planets and other celestial bodies where no physical humanoid life exists. There can be spirits on the moon but no humanoid life on the moon. There is energy everywhere. Spirits are energy. When I say there is energy everywhere, I am saying that there are spirits everywhere even though physical beings are not everywhere. Just as there are many different physical worlds, there are also many different spirit worlds. Each planet that has humanoid life has a spirit world. All spirit worlds are not alike. The character of a spirit world depends on the planet it is part of. Earth was inhabited by spirits before it was inhabited by humans.

There are multiple spirit worlds just as there are multiple physical worlds. Spirits such as I can instantaneously travel from one spirit world to another. My origin is not on this earth. Thank goodness for that. That is why it takes me a lot of energy to travel to you, from one spirit world to another. (E)

Just as the outward universe with all the celestial bodies is infinite, forever expanding, the inward universe inside the atom is also infinite. There is a whole universe inside the atom also. It is coming to light. There are certain people who can actually see inside the atom. Your wife has gone inside the atom and described it. There are many others who can see inside the atom. Your wife is not the only one. She does not profess to be the only one. She is not alone.

There is just as much animal life in the sea as there is on land on your planet. There is just as much vegetation in the sea as there is on land. Vegetables on the land walk among you, too.

As some scientists say, it is more likely that life exists on the moons of planets that are very far away from their star rather than on the planet itself.

There are technological ruins from ancient civilizations, such as things comparable to your computers, in the rings of the planet Saturn. You can assume that at one time that was a flourishing highly advanced civilization, more than that. There are civilizations that have been long gone. The rings around Saturn were originally a band around the planet built by humans or humanoid beings to be a super weapon that could destroy other planets. It was a very powerful weapon for protection. That band was destroyed by warring extraterrestrials. That is what broke it up to become the rings.

There are hundreds of millions of planets within our galaxy, the Milky Way, which could support human life. Definitely hundreds of millions could support life just like you have on Earth. Earth is not alone.

Your solar system was originally inhabited by humanoids that were brought here from other star systems. They were brought here because they were removed from elsewhere because they were too warlike to coexist with them. The original inhabitants of your solar system were the cast outs, the lowlife of the universe. The extraterrestrials are coming back to reverse it.

The planet Mars was once a moon of the giant planet that we call Tiamat which exploded and became the asteroid belt about 800,000 years ago.

Just as there are wormholes that you can go into and end up somewhere else in the universe, there is also something comparable regarding time rather than space, some kind of portal to go somewhere else in time. You can go back and forth in time. You can do that in your mind.

Your sun has a companion star which has been referred to as the black star in ancient writings.

3. Evolution of cosmic entities

Highly advanced entities that were once on your plateau can eventually evolve to the state in which they can become a planet or a star. That is at a higher level. Souls can evolve into the sun or things like that. These are highly advanced souls. There are many stars. You can always be a star. So we can say that all the billions of stars out there are souls. It's hard to believe. That's why we wish upon a star. Do we not? Planets and stars have a level of consciousness that is above the level of that of humans. I will not start up with a star. To become a star you must be knowledgeable. Humans have the potential of someday becoming a star. Indeed if you are good in school, you will become a star. I will not tangle with a star because they are more knowledgeable. (G)

Planets and stars are highly evolved souls and those souls sometimes withdraw from the planets and stars just as your souls withdraw from your physical bodies. A burnt out star is a body that has been left after the soul has departed just like your bodies after the soul has departed. After the soul withdraws, it goes on to another. It goes on and on. It's like playing hopscotch. The planet or stars continue to exist without a soul. They are mightier than we are. Your sun has a soul, many bright lights, and many peaks of energy. When they refer to your sun as the logos of your solar system that implies that the sun has a soul.

Your souls are manifested as physical humans but eventually as you continue to evolve in the physical, your soul can manifest itself as a planet. In addition to planets and stars, celestial beings, such as comets and meteors, are also the manifestations of souls. Many souls are resting on different stars. The same is true of comets and meteors. They are different energies.

There are celestial bodies in the spirit world as well as in the physical. Celestial bodies have a spirit component just as humans have both physical and spirit components.

All life in the universe began at one specific location and then spread throughout the universe. It was like an ant. It keeps spreading and spreading. The process of spreading out is continuing even today. Your solar system is one of the youngest in the universe. New solar systems are continuously being created.

Life on Earth began because organic material was brought here from elsewhere. Extraterrestrials were able to bring organic materials to start off physical life. They had manipulated and they are still doing so. They are here where we need the most help. Earth human beings are the least advanced in the universe but I see them evolving to the status of extraterrestrials. They have a long ways to go, a very long ways.

Your entire solar system is changing from the third density to the fourth density, not just the earth but the entire solar system. It has been changing so slowly and will continue to change. Your global warming is related to what the entire solar system is going through. This is part of what is referred to as the ascension, very slow and not able to be recognized. There will be major changes in the orbits of some of your planets. It has been and will continue to change.

4. Other Kingdoms

Nature spirits or elementals watch over nature and the vegetable kingdoms as do angels over the animal and human kingdoms. There is a force watching over the mineral kingdom. It's something comparable to angels watching over the human kingdom. Elementals such as gnomes, fairies, leprechauns etc. really exist. I can perceive them. I do not like the elementals, leprechauns, gnomes and things like that. They cause turbulence in any kingdom. They can get in your way and help you to fall or trip. They can move up to a higher level when they come back. It may take time to become humans but they can do that. It does take time

Vegetables have consciousness of some kind for a moment. They communicate with other vegetables. It is possible that they communicate with people for a very short period while they are alive. The purpose of vegetables is to provide nutrition for insects, animals and humans.

I am told that there is a blending of the vegetable world and the animal world. There are creatures that are part vegetable and part animal. This is true on other planets as well. That is true everywhere you go.

I have said in the past to you that animals can evolve into humans and that birds can evolve into angels. Fish are just as a vegetable. A fish does not have a brain, depending upon the fish, if you are talking about a goldfish or an octopus. What category do you put fish in? They do evolve further, just as a rock does. Even a rock progresses.

There is no distinction between male and female in the spirit world. When we speak of both gods and goddesses, in that realm the gender distinction does not exist either. Society is progressing so that there is increasingly less distinction between male and female. The future shows that there will be less distinction. Notice the clothing. Notice the hairdos. Notice the people. Notice how everything is going away from gender to gender. This is a natural or normal type of progression or evolution.

I have said that the greatest of goals for humans and spirits is to be of service to others but the same can be said for entities in the mineral, vegetable and the animal kingdoms. In all kingdoms, the best goal is to be of service to others.

Leprechauns have a humanoid form: two legs, two arms, a head and a torso. You will see whatever you wish. They are in both the physical world as well as in the spirit world. They are not more abundant in Ireland than in other places in the world. There are nature spirits all over, in Africa and in your own garden.

Nature spirits such as leprechauns, fairies, gnomes and trolls, go through the same evolutionary path as humans and angels; that is, their awareness begins in the mineral kingdom and then proceeds to the vegetable and animal kingdoms before transitioning as an elemental.

5. Miscellaneous

The information about the root races as depicted in the Theosophical belief system is indeed accurate. Blavatsky is correct. She is telling me to tell you yes. Homosapiens are gradually evolving into Homonoeticus. You will not have to use your voice in the future. Homonoeticus will be more psychic and telepathic. The forerunners, the indigo children, are here right now, beginning slowly amongst your younger children. There are many people who can foretell and foresee. The fundamental principles presented in Theosophy are correct for the most part. You could learn and grow if you looked into Blavatsky's work, the Secret Doctrine and things like that. It is of use to find out where others have failed so you can prevail. You will do so. (L)

There is some accuracy in the letters of those individuals in my realm who channeled the Urantia Book. (L)

The information in the book called the Kolbrin Bible is worthy of your consideration to be knowledgeable.

There are about ten times as many entities in the earth's spirit world as there are in its physical world. Of those in the spirit world, there is a large number who no longer have the need to come back into the physical

A soul must follow the same line of evolution in all star systems when in the physical; that is, a progression from the mineral, to the vegetable, to the animal before evolving as a human-type being.

Some form of individual entities existed before the creation of your universe.

If a large meteorite should totally destroy the earth, the spirits of all those in the earth's spirit world would have to find somewhere else to go. In other words the earth's spirit world would no longer exist and those spirits would have to go to the spirit world of a different planet.

There is such a thing as what scientists call the God particle. It is held by people that are together as they are here before me. I am saying that the God particle is like a conglomeration of souls or something like that.

The soul does not manifest itself only in the physical realm and in the astral realm. There are other realms. I have visited those realms if you wish to refer to them as higher realms.

A thirteenth constellation should be added to astrological charts. That change was in consideration sometime ago. Readings would be more accurate if there were that thirteenth constellation, more accurate and a little more disturbing.

Major solar storms eject a great deal of energy that disturbs the Earth's electromagnetic fields. This also affects the nervous systems of people on Earth causing increased flow of adrenaline and both physical and emotional agitation and sexual agitation. It has also affected the level of consciousness or psychic abilities of some. It has made them more aware, like waking up a doorbell that hasn't been rung. You can say that in general, solar storms have not only an effect on the planet earth but also on the inhabitants of the planet.

Micro-organisms such as bacteria, viruses and fungi have some form of consciousness. You could expand on that and say that anything that exists in the physical has some form of consciousness, although quite different from human consciousness.

Intelligent life exists within the atom. There are whole universes of worlds within the structure of the atom.

I am not aware of any planets whose inhabitants are that are less evolved than those of Earth.

There are 72 dimensions.

Amphibious humanoid beings existed on Earth and they still are.

What you call global warming is now occurring on all the planets in your solar system. Your solar system is changing. This is causing a change in human DNA that will raise your level of consciousness. This is related to the approaching of the tenth planet, the one referred to by the Sumerians as Niburu.

There are indeed physical entities on Earth who have a higher level of consciousness than humans. There are also people among you who can see. They see much more than they wish. There are different levels of consciousness among various humans. Some are practically at the level of animals at the lower end. The same is true on other planets. We do travel from planet to planet. We will end up doing that more as time goes on. We will not all be on Earth. Some of us are going to Mars and some will be leaving Earth. Some have already left.

There is such a thing as sacred geometry. That is, the universe has been created according to a geometric plan in which certain physical shapes and designs have significance. They are not hidden but they are significant. They have meaning. Geometry used in the design and construction of religious structures is often based on what is believed to be sacred geometry. It is based on numbers. Numbers are part of sacred geometry.

There is no limit to how many humans the Earth can support. You do not have too many humans on Earth now. The earth will be able to supply even more humans with nutrition, air etc.

There is a mystical significance to the Jewish Star of David. The star is a two dimensional representation of a three dimensional geometric figure which is the building block for all of creation.

N. EXTRATERRESTRIAL INVOLVEMENT WITH EARTH

1. Extraterrestrials and the U.S. government

NASA is withholding some very significant information from you regarding the universe and extraterrestrial life. There is secret cooperation between your government and aliens. Your government has been spending much money each year for secret facilities and searching for extraterrestrial life. The amount is not for public airing. NASA has a secret space program in addition to their publicized program. You know that in America everything is a secret. They have secrets regarding the planet Mars. NASA is doing things on Mars that they are not telling anybody about. Your government is not without an odor.

The United States has military installations that house extraterrestrial beings. They are around you everywhere and they change their form and position so often. There is a hidden city beneath the earth near Dulce, New Mexico in which thousands of extraterrestrials live under the cooperation and observation of the United States government. There has been a pact between you and the aliens. These extraterrestrials experiment on humans there. They share their technology with you. They keep up to their part of the agreement, sort of. In addition to the installation in Dulce New Mexico, there are others that house extraterrestrials. There are more secret underground military installations in the United States. The government installation in Roswell, New Mexico is still the home of aliens. (Laughing) I must see my family there. I am not able to share the information regarding a secret government installation beneath the Denver airport.

The reason for the intense secrecy surrounding Area 51 in the air force base in Nevada is that security is needed. Your government chooses that. They wish that it is a secret. They are hiding information about aliens, UFOs, equipment and things like that. They're hiding it without too much success, you know.

The HAARP facility in Alaska to control weather is a potentially dangerous experiment to the earth and mankind. You cannot control anything that's going to happen regarding the weather. The danger will be when the people doing the experiment drown. There is no extraterrestrial involvement at this time. There will be a time that others will need help but at this time, no. Your government is using the HAARP facility in Alaska for nefarious purposes, such as mind control. There is secrecy about the HAARP facility that the government is not publicizing.

Some of your technologies have been achieved through analyzing equipment found on crashed UFO's. They have been there for years. What is so different? There is nothing different you know. The United States government is involved in programs of reverse engineering of alien spacecraft or other alien technology. They are examining things they found and then cover it.

There are members of your government who are aliens disguised as Earth human beings. Some mean to do you good and others mean to do you harm. They do not know that they are aliens.

Extraterrestrials are monitoring your nuclear facilities because they are concerned about the direction your civilization is taking. They are very concerned about these directions. They are very curious and they wish to be in control. They are not fearful of what you might do. There may be a potential for nuclear warfare but it will not come to that end. You will wipe ISIS out and you will come to the aid of Israel. Israel has forces as such that no man has created. The Jews have secrets. Indeed, Israel is being guided by a powerful extraterrestrial force. They want so much to be existing.

The information in the U.S. government *Project Blue Book* about human encounters with extraterrestrials is mostly accurate. It was declassified to make it seem as though it was not true, even though it was true. They do not wish you to be anxious or cause raucous or cause another war. Sometimes when the government declassifies information it is to make you believe it was false.

Other countries are covertly influencing American politics at this time. Everybody is busy. One of those countries is Russia. Americans are very confused and not together. They are split. They should join each other. Extraterrestrials are influencing American politics. Different extraterrestrials are influencing one party and other groups are influencing the other party. Your politics are a contest between different extraterrestrials groups.

There are absolutely people in your government, in Congress, senators or those in the House of Representatives, who are actually extraterrestrials that look like Earth humans.

All of the U.S. presidents in the 20th and 21st centuries have knowingly had face-to-face contact with extraterrestrials, but they are fearful that they will be humiliated if they publicize that. Some of those extraterrestrials looked just like humans. Others did not.

2. Extraterrestrials and the evolution of mankind

Note: Information about the Anunnaki regarding the evolution of mankind appeared in Section K: *The Evolution of Humans.*

Everyone who serves a purpose whether you wish to call it significant or useful or non-sense is up to you. They come from another star system. There are star systems other than the earth. They raised human consciousness. Now the humans have a greater sense of responsibility which not every race has.

Adam and Eve were super humans who came here from somewhere else to infuse their DNA with that of the humans on Earth at that time. It was a long time ago, even before my time. They were here before any of us were here.

Some of the royal lines of kings and queens originated with extraterrestrial involvement. Some are from alien beings and some are a mixture. You can call them blue bloods because their blood is blue indeed. When it hits oxygen it turns red and sometimes yellow which is ill. It started from nonsense to begin with. They had the same blood as everyone else. There is nothing special about the royal bloodline. We make people into royals by idolizing them and putting them on pedestals.

Epidemics or plagues that have affected humans have been caused by microbes on meteorites and asteroids that have hit the earth. Some were deliberately sent by extraterrestrial entities to reduce the population. Some diseases afflicting humans in today's world were caused by extraterrestrials. They meant no harm. It was not intentional. It was experimental. Those diseases are neurological in nature.

The Atlanteans were hybrids of humans and extraterrestrials as you are. The origin of the system of priests in various religions was actually humans who were able to communicate with extraterrestrials and act as intermediaries between them and Earth people Aaron, the brother of Moses, was one such person; not well liked but Moses was well liked. I was on Earth at the time of Moses.

There is interbreeding between extraterrestrials and humans. If an extraterrestrial should interbreed with a human, that child will not look completely different from a human. He would not be likely to have any noticeable physical extraterrestrial features. It would skip a generation. It is recessive and occurs in alternate generations. (K)

Babies with reptilian features are sometimes born of human mothers who have had sexual contact with extraterrestrials. They are being raised by Earth mothers rather than by the extraterrestrials.

The early forms of writing such as the Egyptian hieroglyphs, runes, and the Sumerian alphabet were invented by humans at that time, some with input from extraterrestrials. After the extraterrestrials left, the humans came up with different ways of putting the events into writing in order to record them.

Throughout the history of the earth, including the present time, there have been both good and evil extraterrestrials attempting to direct the evolution of mankind on Earth. Right now you have good intended and bad intended extraterrestrials involved with you as always.

Various extraterrestrial groups colonized different areas of the planet Earth such as a group in China, India, Mesopotamia, South America and Africa. Just as you have humans colonizing different areas on Earth, there were several different extraterrestrial groups, not just one.

In the past there were a number of ancient civilizations that disappeared without a trace. Large groups of people, even entire civilizations, can be moved off the earth to somewhere else in the universe through some kind of portal. The extraterrestrials took them away. People have disappeared in the Bermuda Triangle. When a physical being goes through a star gate, a wormhole, a portal or whatever you want to call it, that person can survive physically. They don't die when they go through places like the Bermuda Triangle.

Extraterrestrials that are in the physical can telepathically send thoughts to a person in order to influence the person's thinking if you allow it. It doesn't mean that you have to listen or have to do what they say. It is the exercise of your will that determines whether or not you obey. Extraterrestrials do not have to be within a few feet of you to influence your thinking. The thoughts that they put into your head are generally helpful thoughts but it doesn't mean that they are always correct. They might be sincere but wrong. (D)

The origin of the enmity between the Arabs and the Jews was not related to opposing extraterrestrials. It was created from sibling rivalry, similar to what any sibling rivalry would be. The cause of anti-Semitism is often the result of extraterrestrials having spliced some of their own DNA into the DNA of humans. You have mixes like you have races. The [most] mixed race of all is the Eurasians. (I)

On Earth today, there are some purebred Earth people who are not extraterrestrial hybrids, in other words people whose DNA was not changed by extraterrestrials. They absolutely cannot be distinguished from the rest of you. They know exactly what to do. Most humans are hybrids Extraterrestrials can imbue some of their own attitudes and desires into the DNA of humans to make humans more like them. Extraterrestrials mess around with your DNA. Opposing groups of extraterrestrials have spliced some of their own DNA into different groups of humans in the past. The imbued DNA passed on from generation to generation. That is a major cause of the wide political division in our politics today. The division between the Democrats and the Republicans goes way back in history and it started with opposing extraterrestrial groups. (K)

Members of the black race and the aborigines are closer to the original Earth race of humans than the other races. The DNA of those of the other races was affected by the injection or the manipulation of their DNA by extraterrestrials. (K)

There are many different species of extraterrestrials, some positive and some a little negative, involved with Earth humans at the present time. In regard to the evolution of humans more of them are positive rather that negative.

Extraterrestrials are far more advanced than humans and Earth humans are the least advanced among the various galaxies. Extraterrestrials with their advanced abilities had a role in making the human body look like it does today. You are not the same as the original humans on Earth. Extraterrestrials injected some of their own DNA into them to make them like they are today.

Extraterrestrials have intentionally spread viruses and plagues on Earth for the purpose of reducing the population.

A sizable percentage of Americans express extreme hatred of Donald Trump and another sizable portion of Americans express intense support for Donald Trump. These extremely intense attitudes are the result of manipulation of our DNA by highly advanced extraterrestrials. In other words the attitudes that people have is built into their DNA. They cannot change their attitudes but can change their knowledge. There is also a sizeable percentage of Americans whose attitudes are not affected by their DNA.

3. Extraterrestrials and the development of the planet Earth

The cause of the Great Flood that is mentioned in your Bible and in the lore of other ancient civilizations throughout the world was the accumulation of weather that had formed. It was not an accident. It was precisely planned by alien intelligence to be helpful. The Flood was caused by the Anunnaki to purge the earth. It was not to rid of any specific species. It was a great cleansing. It was engineered by the Anunnaki. At the time of the Flood were there cultures throughout the world that survived by going underground. It was safer to be underground than above ground, as it will be in the future. Underground will be more positive for you. (I)

The Gulf Stream was engineered by intelligent entities, not a natural phenomenon, not the Atlanteans but by many extraterrestrials. The purpose was to keep the lands to the north warmer.

Ages ago extraterrestrials who visited the earth encouraged animal sacrifices. They believed the animals were beneath them and they were not all animals. They were creatures.

Your moon was originally a natural creation but extraterrestrials modified it to the point that it was no longer a natural creation. The moon was originally somewhere else, but through their technology, extraterrestrials moved it to a specific place so that life on Earth could take place. The moon is hollow. When the astronauts crashed something on the moon, it rang like a bell for about an hour. (M)

Entities from other star systems have had an effect on your weather. In the past, extraterrestrials have been able to affect your weather. The manipulation of the weather was used as a weapon in warfare in the past. It was done by extraterrestrials on the planet Earth. They are still sometimes involved in affecting the weather of Earth. They can have influence. You also affect your weather by seeding clouds so it will rain. They can do that and far more to affect your weather.

In 1990 and 1991 extraterrestrials caused worldwide nuclear weapon programs to cease to function for a period of time. That was because they were trying to help you. You will never have a nuclear war because extraterrestrials that watch over the earth will not permit it.

Your planet has a defense grid around it that was erected by extraterrestrials to protect you and not allow entry of negative extraterrestrials into your atmosphere. There is something built around your planet.

4. Physical evidence of ancient extraterrestrials

Most of the mysterious ancient structures found on Earth today were built by extraterrestrials for their own activities rather than for the use by or the good of humans.

The ancient elongated skulls found in Egypt and in the Americas were of alien origin and some were a mixture of humans. The humans didn't try to imitate the aliens by forcing the skulls to become longer. They did it by having relationships. They had fun with each other.

The drawings of the caves of Lascaux in France are ways of communication, what we would say to you is writings by both Earth people and extraterrestrials. They are on this planet and they have not left. They have been here many a century.

Aliens were involved in the construction of the Coral Castle in Homestead, Florida to help Edward Leedskalnin. He was too little to do this himself. His ability to communicate was remarkable.

The architects and builders of the pyramids in the Yucatan and Guatemala were people that are striving from your past. They are reaching out and wish to serve in your future. They were actually built by those of another star system, the Pleiades. They also built the pyramids in Egypt and that is how they got to the top. The Pleiades are one of the most advanced groups. Our secret people were building your pyramids that they could reach from the top down. Humans provided a lot of the labor but extraterrestrials provided the technology.

The purpose of the numerous very long lines, drawings of animals, geometrical shapes and mathematical diagrams in South America that can only be seen from the air was for those that were up high in the sky so they could read it easier when above the land it is written on. I am talking about extraterrestrial UFO's. They were constructed by extraterrestrials for the purpose of providing instructions or information to the people of Earth.

The same could be said about the various crop circles that have been appearing throughout the world. They are messages or instructions to Earth people from extraterrestrials. They are in your face. They are right there. They are trying to assist you and aid you. They are trying to be heard.

A form of geometry is being used in the creation of crop circles throughout the world. Geometry can be used as a key to communications between humans and higher dimensions. Life is all numbers. The extraterrestrials that create the crop circles are trying to communicate to you. There is meaning in the designs of the crop circles. You should be trying to interpret those meanings and you can use them for your own pleasure. (D)

Extraterrestrials have imbued thirteen crystal sculls with special powers. They have been cleansed and are very clever and very intelligent. If they gather together that will be a tremendous powerful force, a controlling force. When those glass skulls are brought together, power will occur; power to the extraterrestrial groups that made them. They are extremely powerful. There are other objects located on Earth that are endowed with powers, such as you humans have power that was endowed by extraterrestrials. Humans will be using the crystal skulls relatively soon to communicate with extraterrestrials.

Extraterrestrials were involved in the formation of the Devil's Tower in Wyoming. We have been there and we created it. Extraterrestrials are still involved in the Devil's Tower. We are everywhere. We have been here for centuries.

The dress of Betty Hill, who claims she and her husband were abducted by aliens in 1961, actually contains DNA evidence from an extraterrestrial.

The ancient astronauts that are depicted in stone carvings throughout the world are both extraterrestrials and human time travelers from your future. There are ruins of whole cities on Earth both on the land and in the waters that were built by extraterrestrials.

The Dogu (Dogoo) statues found in Japan represent aliens in space suits.

5. Extraterrestrials currently on our planet

There are extraterrestrials on Earth not only from other star systems in your galaxy but from other star systems in other galaxies as well. Extraterrestrials are now as active on your planet as they were a thousand or so years ago. They are not easily accepted depending on time. Messages are left and found. Not only have you been watched over for many thousands of years but you have been joined by them. It is important to note that many are noble but some are not so noble. Aliens are showing themselves but they are not taken seriously. The time is coming that they will show themselves. They are not in a robot form.

Extraterrestrials that looked different from humans openly existed with humans on Earth in ages past. Nowadays there are extraterrestrials living on Earth who look different from humans and others who take on the form of humans. They are underground, in the ocean and in caves. There are also extraterrestrials that you call ant people that look like you but have heads that look like the heads of ants in the caves of America. They have humanoid form with two legs, two arms, a torso and one nose. Those that look like humans are amongst you also. There are many aliens among you who look exactly like humans and there are also extraterrestrial beings on Earth who look different from humans. It is not what I would suggest you call communities of those who look different. It is fragments: lightning, the clouds, and the rain. There are many differences that are shown here.

Extraterrestrials that look like humans are not in this room right now but they do attend your meetings. They sit among you here in this room. They are very welcome here. The extraterrestrials are bringing protection to this house and to you.

There are many different alien races currently residing on Earth. Extraterrestrials can show themselves in the physical to people on Earth as something different from what they actually are, much the same as angels do. They can make themselves look like a human if they so choose. They can make themselves look like an animal. Some are.

What you refer to as shape shifters are actually alien creations disguised as humans. There are not certain features that you can look for to identify them. There is nothing that you can see. They are made to be identified yet you cannot identify them. They are not dangerous to humanity. They are there to help you and comfort you. You have shape shifters in your government.

There are aliens on Earth who are more intelligent than you who are among you whose agenda is to be wise and kind and helpful. They will continue to do so and will help and guide and aid you.

There are what is often referred to as "little people" from other systems living in isolated places on Earth and there are tall giant people too.

What you call "Black Eyed Children are knowledgeable children who seek deep within. There is something evil about them and they cause damage and distress that comes from within. They are selected children that come back again with anger. They are extraterrestrials.

There is a connection between the Grand Canyon and star beings as thought by Native American Indians in that area. Star beings are from the Grand Canyon and are imbedded in the Grand Canyon and remain so for protection.

There are undersea UFO bases on the earth. There are activities under the sea. If you wish to give them a name, I would call them extraterrestrials that know how to swim. Air is not needed.

Aliens are here with you now and they are here to help you. They show themselves to you but they are not acknowledged. Sondra can tell you where they have helped her and they have disappeared into the earth or into their dwellings.

Hitler played a predestined role and was guided by extraterrestrials. It was not the goal of that group of extraterrestrials to take over the world. They were following his orders, not their own orders. This is the same group of extraterrestrials that is assisting ISIS today. We must get rid of them. You are on the same path with ISIS as you were with Hitler. They are a fungus.

Long ago some ancient extraterrestrials sought to have humans worship them as gods if you wish to term them gods. What are gods? Extraterrestrials on Earth today are just like most humans. Some are of a positive nature and some are of a negative nature. There are extraterrestrials who try to influence humans by tricking them into believing they are something they are not. Some people call them trixter gods. They are evil.

There is a large system of caves in the state of Washington in which a lot of people from other planets live. The caves were put here many years ago.

A lot of your current political situation originated with battling extraterrestrials. It is like struggling for power. That can be funneled or translated into the point of democrats versus republicans now. It originated millennia ago with opposing extraterrestrials. It is completely ridiculous.

Many, many more UFO's have been congregating around the areas that are prone to earthquakes. The UFO's are not trying to get energy from the openings in your Earth. They are trying to develop more information so they can help you more. They want to help you survive.

Humans with bird-like faces exist on the earth today. They are mainly an underground civilization although some are actually on the surface of the earth also and above the earth. Area 51 is involved in that.

6. Current extraterrestrial activities on Earth

At the present time, there is no one star system that has more influence on the activities on Earth than other star systems. They are working as a unified group. They are not in conflict with each other at this time. Different species or visitors from other planets are not at war with each other. There are not physical battles but disagreements. Opposing forces among the extraterrestrials do not pose a serious potential threat to mankind.

There are extraterrestrial groups that want to destroy Earth humanity. If they were to be successful they could destroy your bodies but not your souls. You destroy your own souls yourselves. No one can do any harm to your soul. You harm yourselves. You are dangerous to your own self. You make your own decisions and non-decisions. No one can destroy your soul but they can destroy your body. There are extraterrestrials helping on both sides with ISIS. There multiple alien races fighting each other on Earth. You have both good and bad. You can get hurt sometimes because of that. There is no way to tell the difference. [This appears to contradict the previous comment.]

Some extraterrestrials do cause wars and some try to cause peace. So we have man who causes wars and man who causes peace. We are waiting for the extraterrestrials to appear and we don't know whether they will be good or bad. So let's pray for good.

Some of the extraterrestrials that are influencing Earth people are from your future controlling your present time.

Israel receives help with their technology, such as the Iron Dome, from extraterrestrial intelligence. Israel knows much more than you know. They are more capable. You know those Jews keep secrets. Jehovah is an extraterrestrial who still involved with guiding the Jews.

Extraterrestrials communicate with you through dreams at times but how many of you remember our dreams?

Extraterrestrials were the cause of the numerous mutilizations of animals across America in recent years in which certain organs had been surgically removed. It happened for experimental reasons for research.

People are currently being abducted by extraterrestrials for sexual experimentation and breeding. They come here on UFO's and actually have sexual contact. They are having fun, you know. They won't harm anyone, just blood sharing blood as you well know.

In your times extraterrestrials have abducted humans and implanted devises beneath their skin for sending information back to them. That is also for manipulating and controlling them. There are people in this room who have been abducted without their knowledge. There has also been a pregnancy by an extraterrestrial by someone in this room but not your wife. Someone has been impregnated by an extraterrestrial in the past, not recently. The child is an adult now.

Extraterrestrials are still interested in getting gold from your planet. They still are in more groups than just the Anunnaki. Gold has tremendous healing. Gold heals.

The St. Louis Arch has an effect on the weather in that region. Extraterrestrials were instrumental in providing information for its design. They want to know if they were good designers. Part of the purpose was to affect the weather.

The research and information presented by Barbara Lamb regarding extraterrestrials and their interaction with humans is very credible.

There is such a thing as an intergalactic federation composed of various extraterrestrial groups. There are many. Human hybrids are placed on Earth to help humans to connect with extraterrestrials to the point that Earth may become part of the federation. Indeed just as the young lady that I have just spoken to, there are a number of you in this room who are hybrids.

There is an intergalactic council of nine gods that oversees or dictates the course of humanity on Earth. They are advising me now on how to answer your questions. They are working in conjunction with the Illuminati. Everyone in the group works together. They do not work against each other. They all agree. This group of nine extraterrestrials are overseeing or protecting the development of humanity. (D)

Extraterrestrials have placed artificial satellites that orbit around the earth. Those satellites are for your protection. They are also giving them information about what is happening on Earth. They are not afraid of the miserable man who has no brain. The Van Allen radiation belt that surrounds the earth was placed there by extraterrestrials.

In the ancient past extraterrestrials were more warlike in the skies above the earth than they are now. Now they have mental warfare in your skies.

The islands that the Chinese are building in the sea do not have anything to do with star gates but there are UFO bases in the China Sea. The Chinese are doing much more than your government in regard to the exploration of space. They are way ahead of the United States. Their involvement with space exploration will help the Chinese inherit the earth. Extraterrestrials will help the Chinese. They are at this moment.

Alien marine life forms exist in the deepest part of the oceans under hundreds of pounds of pressure. They are alien life forms, not originated on Earth.

The widening passionate disparity and enmity between the two political parties in our country is somewhat directed, influenced or exacerbated by opposing extraterrestrial groups. There is far more influence from extraterrestrials than you think there is. But it will be calmness. They are here to protect you but some are not friends. Some are enemies. Not all extraterrestrials work for the good. Some don't. The good side will survive and he will be elected again next year.

Extraterrestrials sometimes abduct the consciousness or minds of people without abducting their bodies. Some people are worth getting some of their consciousness. Some are not worth it. It is the matter of their brain we are looking at. That is very complicated.

There are extraterrestrials or other beings on Earth that feed off of our negative emotions and need negativity for their survival. When you are negative, that makes them stronger.

There is much hidden information about the town Paradise, California which was recently completely destroyed by fire. Extraterrestrials from

Alpha Centauri had some kind of treaty with humans there that permitted them to have a safe haven and live there peacefully because they were kind people and were nearly identical to humans. The fire was created and enhanced by laser beams by the Cabal to destroy the Centaurians because they were on the verge of disclosing their existence to the public and the public was fearful. There was a connection between the fire and the shooting incident in which several people were killed when a gunman opened fire at a restaurant in Thousand Oaks, California.

Iran is being directed or assisted by the lizard headed extraterrestrials called the Draco. Iran has a problem. Iran opens its mouth and its mouth will be closed by Israel. No matter what, Israel will not give in. The extraterrestrials called the Draco are for you dangerous but they are influencing Iran. (S)

Warfare among some extraterrestrial groups continues today as it did thousands of years ago. They are of different opinions. In a way, opposing extraterrestrials are using Earth people to fight a proxy war for them. It is a ridiculous war. It has no pleasure and no meaning. One of the dangerous groups is the Draco. You are having warfare with the Draco extraterrestrials. The physical warfare is now showing.

7. The Grays and other extraterrestrial entities

Note: Information about the Anunnaki was included in Section I: Religion.

The intent of the alien beings that we call the Grays is that they wish to dominate, and they may. They are a mixture of Earthlings in a star system at this time and there is another system that has been recently discovered by your people on Earth. The Grays are mostly short but there are some tall. Some Grays are actually robots.

The Aztec Indians worshipped Quetzalcoatl. It was their god, what they called god. There was such a person. He is of extraterrestrial nature. He is with me now. He says hello. He can communicate with me. He is not on Earth. He thanks you for the recognition.

Many of the ancient Sumerian gods were actually extraterrestrial beings. Many of the world's great religions today came about as the result of encounters with extraterrestrials, causing many of the confusions. It could be said that Jehovah was an extraterrestrial. Jehovah gave the

Ten Commandments directly to Moses. Jehovah still guides the Jews in modern times. He is here now. I am telling some of your questions for him to aid me in guiding you. In answering your questions now, I have assistance from Jehovah. (I)

In regard to the ultimate agenda of the Anunnaki concerning the current human race, it doesn't matter what they feel. It is their opinion against your opinion. There is no feeling of control. They are about to leave.

There are inscriptions written in the ancient Sumerian language in Tiahuanaco Bolivia as well as in ancient Sumer because the Anunnaki visited both places. It is like Americans. They are everywhere.

The majority of extraterrestrials are of a benevolent nature to humans rather than malevolent. The lizard-like extraterrestrials are usually malevolent.

Lucifer who was with the fallen angels was actually a physical extraterrestrial who lead a group of very tall humanoid beings to Earth. I see him leading along with Jesus. He means well. I would like to say he is misunderstood. The Luciferians are part of the Cabal, of which the Illuminati and other groups are part.

The extraterrestrials known as the Draco reptilians are the major negative group of extraterrestrials involved with our world now. They were involved with assisting the Nazis in World War Two. The Nazis are still alive in the United States Government. George Bush is involved with them. The Nordic extraterrestrials oppose the Draco. The Draco extraterrestrials are somewhat the same as the Anunnaki. They and the Nazis are working toward the same goal: world domination. They are the force behind the Illuminati.

8. Extraterrestrials in recorded history and mythology

Many of the gods portrayed in the various mythologies throughout the world were actually extraterrestrial entities. There is some truth in the foundation of mythology even though it is distorted. You have people here that are aware of the truth. You go back to your India and your mythology which is correct. In some ways it true that much of the ancient mythologies regarding the various gods and goddesses are actually references to aliens who visited the earth. Some facts come through. In a way, there is no doubt. Gods like Zeus or Jupiter actually were extraterrestrials. Long ago, as people believed, gods lived on the top of Mount Olympus. They were actually extraterrestrials that made their home there.

In ancient times there were wars on the earth or in the skies above the earth between opposing groups of extraterrestrials which were often portrayed in various mythologies. There was not a physical war that we call the Clash of the Titans between Zeus and his siblings. The Clash of the Titans did exist but was not important. It was a battle of tongues, all extraterrestrials.

There is factual historical significance to the American Indian mythologies which often portray beings that are part ants and part humans. Such beings did exist and they still exist on Earth.

The early Egyptian pharaohs were either extraterrestrials or descendants of extraterrestrials. Queen Nefertiti in ancient Egypt was an extraterrestrial but she showed herself as an Earth human. The same is true of the Egyptian King Akhenaton. They are buried near King Tut's tomb but not in the same place. The ancient Egyptians tried to erase evidence to references that Queen Nefertiti and King Akhenaton ever existed because they felt that they had too much power and they wanted the dead to be deceased. They were full-fledged extraterrestrials, not hybrids.

The Incan empire was created and significantly influenced by extraterrestrials.

George Washington had encounters with non-human intelligences during the Revolutionary War. He thought people were being misled. He appeared to think that people were going not well mentally. Extraterrestrials helped him with the war.

In ancient times there were warring groups of extraterrestrials in the earth's sky whose battles were witnessed by Earth people. Those scenes were often portrayed in drawings. A lot of your mythologies, whether they be the Norse mythologies, the Greek mythologies or the oriental mythologies were based on extraterrestrials that they observed.

The rulers of the Mayas, the Egyptians, the Sumerians and many of the ancient civilizations with elongated skulls that protruded in the back of their heads, such as Queen Nefertiti or King Akhenaton had bigger brains and were a mixture, part extraterrestrial and part human.

9. Extraterrestrial travel

Places exist in the physical world where you can go through some kind of portal and emerge in faraway places in the universe. Not only through one's mind but in the future. You can go into the future and into the past. They are what you may call black spaces. It is available to you. There is a network of underwater portals used by extraterrestrials. We look above but we do not look below. We must look below. Some are in your lakes and oceans and they are near here. As according to your scientists there is a black hole in your galaxy that has a white hole at the other end of it, thus causing a tunnel that aliens could travel through. (L)

Humans will be able to travel to the home planet of the extraterrestrials that helped build the pyramids. It is coming shortly. They will travel the same way they arrived. I am not able to give the information about how humans will travel but with your mind you can do so much. So many of you have bright minds and you don't use your minds. We have so much to offer and so much to give. So we come therefore to give more help. Open up your minds and you will get there.

The Anunnaki used spaceships to travel from their home planet to Earth. They did not use any type of vortex or wormhole to travel here. They are here.

Some entities that we call extraterrestrials are actually time travelers from your own future. The Grays are such.

There are not more UFO sightings in America than in other parts of the world. They are all over. They are everywhere. It is not that you are more observant but you are more forceful. You are more talkative. You have more freedom. There are just as many UFO's in Africa, Australia and other places. Alien life forms enter your world through underwater star gates as well as in unidentified flying objects. At this time there are not UFO's from other star systems large enough to transport hundreds of people.

10. Miscellaneous

Note: Information about extraterrestrials in the bible was included in Section I: <u>Religion.</u>

You know that when I speak to you, you are communicating with an extraterrestrial through a channeler but a time will come within the near future that there will be overt face-to-face physical communication with extraterrestrials whose appearance is noticeably different from yours. That will be in the lifetime of people already here. Some people in this room will meet face-to-face with humanoid beings in the physical from a different planet that appear totally unhuman. They will see people that look like me, but not me. There are extraterrestrials that look like humans and there are extraterrestrials that look very different from humans.

There are people in your world who have already seen these extraterrestrials. A lot of those beings are housed in Area 51 in Nevada beneath the ground now and in other places in the United States. They look totally different from humans and live mostly underground. They can change. Your government is aware of that. The government has shown it. They have presented it.

I have contact with human-like beings in other star systems. They are all the same or similar, just different systems. (E)

Erich Von Daniken is on the right track in his book *Chariots of the Gods.* There is some truth in what he has written.

Mathematics would provide a universal means of communication between those on Earth and physical entities in every civilization in other worlds. Mathematics is an answer to all your questions. Some of it you have yet to learn.

The activities of L. Ron Hubbard, the founder of Scientology, and Jack Parsons did not have any involvement with increased UFO activities as some people believe.

There is a high degree of accuracy in the television program called *Ancient Aliens* on the History Channel. Your government is not promoting the program. The government is withholding. They are trying to condition the American people to accept extraterrestrials. They are walking among you. They are right next to you. You are holding their hand. You are them. They do look like the typical human beings. Some, such as the Grays, don't look like human beings. The next will be the robots. There are many people without a brain.

The Vatican secretly accepts the fact that they believe in the possibility that extraterrestrials may exist on Earth. There are secret files in the Vatican that support the existence of UFO's and extraterrestrials, files and rows of books. That is why we are here. I am saying that the Catholic Church does know it but they're keeping it secret. They do not want to make you aware you and scare you. Aware and scare! That is not the main reason they are keeping it a secret. The main reason is control. (I)

The reason that you sometimes cannot see extraterrestrials is because they are of a higher dimension. Extraterrestrials do not have disease because they are in a higher dimension and the reason that you have disease is because we are in a lower division.

Highly advanced extraterrestrial civilizations have absolutely been able to imbue robots with sentience or some level of consciousness.

There are underground facilities at Rudloe Manor in England that are used for extraterrestrial research. Not only at that particular area but there are other areas also. Many countries are doing research on extra terrestrials.

The majority of the world's great scientists of both the past and the present received information from extraterrestrials. The extraterrestrials are having a great deal more influence than you might think on the thinking of humans because they can project their thoughts. They were not recognizable but they have always existed.

Certain alien factions do not consider Earth humans a threat to them but they are a threat. Most of the time your first thought is even better than theirs. They are not afraid of humans hurting the aliens but they are afraid of humans hurting each other.

Some extraterrestrials are capable of creating physical objects by simply using their minds. Humans are able to do that. With humans, they are able to cause fear. They can cause apprehension. They can cause alarm. They can cause happiness. They are able to do anything they want to do with their minds. Extraterrestrials who are far more advanced than you can actually create physical objects just using their minds. Some humans can do that now. You can move your glass by holding it. You can do anything you wish. I am talking about [for example] someone like Uri Geller who could bend spoons with his mind. Humans can do that.

Interstellar slave trade exists. That is, people are abducted from various planets and used as slaves. It depends upon the forcefulness of the individual. If they are strong [willed] they are not able to be abducted. If they are not strong they can be abducted and used as slaves. People from Earth are abducted and taken on UFO's and used as slaves elsewhere.

The information that a man named Corey Goode presents on You Tube is worth your interest. Obviously it is worth your interest so there must be some message that is given to you. I am saying that his message is credible not just to you but to others. He is not the only one. It is given to several people. I would say the same about David Wilcock. He is a darling soul.

Extraterrestrials can erase specific memories from our minds. That is not an ability that they have but they can express it.

Artificial spheres, some as large as our moon, come into your solar system to investigate. They are not natural creations, but creations by more intelligent entities to investigate your solar system

Ancient extraterrestrials built moons using their technology around their planets for protection against other invading extraterrestrials. It seems that it would appear that your moon was created by extraterrestrials but it wasn't exactly so. It was both natural and technological.

Extraterrestrials have the ability to render your atomic weapons inoperable and have done so.

O. OTHER PLANETS AND THEIR INHABITANTS

Because of the wide diversity of the features of other planets and of the humanoid beings that inhabit them, they cannot be described with a single stroke of the brush. Therefore the information in this section does not always refer to all of the planets but sometimes only to the majority of the planets and the inhabitants, but not necessarily to all.

1. Other planets in the universe

There is another planet in your solar system, often referred to as Niburu, that revolves around your sun in a huge elliptical orbit. What you refer to as the planet Niburu is actually a dwarf brown star with planets circling it, as some scientists claim. The Anunnaki are still on that planet. Scientists are men who do not know all that is given. There are more than that, many more stars and planets. There are many planets revolving around your sun.

Some planets have both days and nights and others have no distinction between day and night. Most inhabited planets have one or more moons. Some planets do not have skies like yours. There is always atmosphere. All planets in other star systems which support human life have both climate and weather as does your earth. There are planets which have a very different kind of air from that on Earth.

Many other planets, like Earth, have several land masses surrounded by water. All inhabited planets have water. There are planets that have only surface water and no dry land. Surface water sometimes freezes and turns to ice on other planets. The water on all other planets is not the same as on Earth; that is, chemically not H_2O. There are other kinds of water on other planets.

There are more elements that are not on Earth that are on other planets. Earth does not contain more gold than other planets. Extraterrestrials wish they had the ability to change other elements into gold but they are still trying. Just like salt at one time was more worthy than gold.

There are planets which once supported physical life but no longer do so. A planet which does not have physical life on it can have spirit life on it. Most all of them do so even though they may not have physical life. There are other planets or moons in your solar system that were once inhabited by physical beings that you would not call them human. Physical, yes but they did not look like you.

Other worlds are more advanced than Earth. They've been here before. Go back in the centuries and the earth is the last to be involved.

There are planets or moons in other star systems that could support human life exactly as the earth does (light, air, temperature, nutrition, etc.). You will be amazed to find out how Mars has many features that are on your earth. There are human-like entities on Mars right now in the physical.

The asteroid belt between Mars and Jupiter was once a planet but not in the traditional sense that you call planets. It is broken up into many pieces. It was a once single piece. It was broken up by the atmosphere of the planet. There is a civilization on planets other than Earth. There is a civilization on the dwarf planet called Ceres. You will not like them. The appearance of their planet will not entice you. Humanoids on the dwarf planet Ceres in the asteroid belt resemble Earth humans. Human life on the asteroid Ceres is similar to life on Earth. You won't like them because they are not like you. You have differences of opinions. On the bright side, they do look similar to you.

At one time you were all on the same planet. You were fighting. You were of different beliefs, different bearings. It wasn't physical warfare but mental disagreement. You are now in contact with them physically. The planet that was once between Jupiter and Mars was destroyed because of being close to Earth. There were warring extraterrestrials. Some Earth people are the descendants of the winners. Extraterrestrials do not war against each other in your times like you have war. They are not one of extinguishing each another. They are at war with words not with extinguishing like you have. We do not diminish each other.

There is such a thing as an intergalactic federation composed of various extraterrestrial groups. There are many. Human hybrids are placed on Earth to help humans to connect with extraterrestrials to the point that Earth may become part of the federation. Indeed just as the young lady that I have just spoken to, there are a number of you in this room who are hybrids. (N)

There are political land divisions on some other planets, such as the various countries of Earth. There are divisions on all planets. The mere fact that there are people on planets makes it so that there are political divisions.

A large percentage of the forty billion Earth-like planets in the Milky Way have human-type inhabitants.

2. Nature, climate, and land features

The land features of some other planets are similar to those on Earth; that is, there are mountains, valleys, deserts, jungles, rivers, oceans etc. There are other planets that are inhabited by human-type beings where the land features are noticeably different from those on Earth. There are some other planets where the vegetation is similar to that on Earth, but on those planets the basic color is not always green. There can be other colors other than green grass and green trees. There are some planets where the vegetation is totally different from the vegetation on Earth. That is why there will be people that will be blue. What they eat will have an effect on their skin color. Most other planets have what you might call vegetables and flowers if you wish to give it a name.

The vegetation on Earth is comparable to that on other planets. Leaves on trees on Earth are usually green but the same is not true on other planets. Trees can be different colors. Other planets have fruits and vegetables very similar to those on Earth but they can vary. There are many different kinds of fruits and vegetables on different planets. Some of your fruits and vegetables have been brought to Earth by extraterrestrials by mistake. It is on its way to be discovered that there are other planets that have just as much vitality. If you want to compare animal life to Earth, it is difficult to say because there are different animals.

Other planets have periodic cataclysms such as earthquakes, floods, tornados, hurricanes etc. as on Earth. It is somewhat the same as Earth as far as weather conditions. It rains and snows on other inhabited planets. There is a wide range of atmospheric temperatures on most of the other planets as there is on Earth. Some planets have a very limited range of temperatures.

Other planets have mineral, vegetable and animal kingdoms. There are planets that do not have human-like beings. There many varieties of insects, birds, land animals and sea creatures on other planets. Some of those are the same as those on Earth. Actually, every planet has life; different forms of life, insect life and animal life. Every inhabited planet has something similar to human life.

Visible fire that the inhabitants can make use of exists on all other inhabited planets. That is a strong thing. That is your weapon on Earth, fire. Your only natural weapon on Earth is fire. Guns are manmade. Since fire exists on all inhabited planets you can assume that hydrogen and oxygen exist on all planets. There is water but on some planets it is a different kind of water than what you have, a different formula. Too much oxygen can be poisonous to the humanoid beings on some planets.

3. Physical appearance of inhabitants

There are entities on other planets that are very similar to Earth people in appearance and there are still others who do not have a humanoid form. They are not human beings. They are on other planets and they do not look like you. There is no other place in the universe that looks exactly like you. They can be very similar to you. We have many other plateaus, not only on Earth. There are others who are very different but have a humanoid form; a head, torso, arms, legs etc. Whether they have a humanoid form depends on what planet they are; what planet that will elevate their souls. Some planets have entities with a form like yours, although they may be different. They are all different. There are some that are not human-like that are living among you now. They do not look like people. You can recognize those conscious entities. It is not the cockroaches. It is animals, some animals like cats and dogs, closer to humans that understand the human language.

There are humanoid beings on other planets whose physical bodies are not as dense as those of Earth people. They are more like the Lemurians in your history. Some have larger heads and more brains. There are planets whose humanoid beings are of greater density than those of Earth. In addition to having arms, legs, a head and a torso, there are extraterrestrial humanoids that have other visible human-like features such as skin, fingers, fingernails, toes and hair. Not all extraterrestrials have fingers. They do not all have skin.

Humanoid beings on other planets have different kinds of external coverings rather than human-type skin. For example some extraterrestrials have scales like reptiles. Some are covered in feathers or scales or things like that. They do not all have hair. Quetzalcoatl was covered with feathers rather than with skin. Some extraterrestrials have skin colors different from those of humans

There are alien races which are not as human-like in appearance

187

but rather more like insects, such as ants and praying mantises. Some extraterrestrial groups on other planets have wings and are able to fly. They have a humanoid form and wings.

The physical characteristics of the inhabitants of other planets do not provide any indication of their age, as they do for Earth people. You can look at those from other planets and those who have been in the physical longer don't look any different from those who have recently incarnated. You are what you want to be.

There are physical differences among the people of other planets in regard to their height, weight, skin color, and facial features as there are among Earth people. There is as much variety in the people of other planets as there is among Earth people.

Other humanoid beings that don't look like humans have facial expressions that tell something about their emotions. A prune will always look like a prune. A prune will not look like an apple. [Other comments by the guide state that at least some other extraterrestrials do not have emotions.]

Each star system or planet has a unique form of humanoid being that does not exist elsewhere in the universe and there are some forms of humanoid beings on several different planets. There are planets in the universe which have the same humanoid being. In other words, you can confer with different planets.

There any more races like humans on other planets. They will be visualized and recognized in the future. They have been there for years but not been recognized.

4. Gender and reproduction features of inhabitants

Considering that there are various means of the reproductive process in other star systems, the reproductive process is designed to begin with a pleasurable experience as it is with Earth humans. Although there are many individual exceptions, the need or desire to reproduce is implanted into the minds of individuals in all star systems. To reproduce is very important. It keeps the whole ball rolling. There are planets where the reproductive process is totally different from on Earth. Shaking hands is sometimes a reproduction. Some are hermaphroditic and some are like starfish where you cut off a piece that grows into another being. There is cloning and other means of reproducing. Sometimes it takes just one person, sometimes two or even three in some systems to reproduce but it is always a pleasurable experience. Ask any animal.

On other planets there and genders like male and female and also bisexuals. On some planets there are three genders but in the realm of the spirits there is no such thing as gender. There are many more genders than just two. At times it takes two beings to reproduce. At times a single being can reproduce itself. At times more than two beings get together to reproduce.

There are physical extraterrestrial entities who visit the earth who are neither male nor female. Likewise there are some who are either male or female. I have said that in the spirit world there is no distinction between male or female. I am neither male nor female. The division into sexes is only in the physical world.

The majority of other planets that have human-like beings have both male and female genders, as do Earth people. Homosexuality exists on those planets. There are also planets that do not have the division into sexes, only one sex. Most of those planets are bisexual and all of you human cultures are bisexual. There are planets that have more than two genders, a third gender. There is male, female and something else. They do not need all three genders for reproduction purposes. All you need is one.

5. Internal physical aspects of the inhabitants

The internal organs of the people on some planets are basically similar to those of Earth humans and on other planets they are very different. They all don't have what you call blood or something similar to blood. Some don't need blood to function.

Human-like inhabitants of other planets have the same five senses as do Earth humans. They sometimes have additional senses that Earth people do not have. They have senses that are not physical; and that is intuition. They have senses that are more acute than those of Earth people. They hear sounds that are beyond the frequency range of humans. The same is true of sight and colors. There are colors that they can see that you can't see.

On other planets there are physical beings above the level of animals that can breathe under water and fly as well as walk. They have forms different from that of Earth humans.

6. Non-physical aspects of inhabitants

The overall level of consciousness of Earthlings is mostly lower than that of physical beings on other planets. Conversely, physical beings on other planets are at a higher level of consciousness.

Humanoids in other star systems have attitudes and desires as part of their being. Inhabitants of other planets do not have the depth of emotions as Earth people. There is always unhappiness when we don't get what we want to receive. The Grays do not have emotions. They have facts. They work on facts. That is not emotional. They do not cry like the humans cry or have the fear that the humans fear. At least some of the Grays are human time travelers from the future. They have a sense of humor. All life is a sense of humor, I show you that I have a sense of humor and I am from a different world. People on other planets have a sense of humor. There is variation among the intellectual abilities of the inhabitants of all other planets.

Although they do not have the degree of emotions that Earth humans have, at times parents on most other planets have feelings of attachment to their offspring similar to that of humans. Everything is individual, but in some places they don't have the same feelings of attachments to their children. It is like you being attached to somebody's child.

The Grays do not reproduce exactly the same way as humans but they enjoy it. They have done a lot of cloning over the years and sometimes that does damage to their DNA.

Humanoids on planets in other star systems do not have the propensity for creating warfare as do Earth humans. Warfare is when there is one of the human race that wishes to win when you don't agree with them. They do not kill each other like you do if you don't agree. I would say they are more advanced in their evolution because they do not dissolve the person who does not agree with them. In other systems they are more technologically advanced. Earth people are physically warlike but those on other planets are not physically warlike but still have the same arguing and disagreements. You kill yourselves. You injure yourselves. Extraterrestrials don't dissolve each other.

I could say that life is more peaceful in other systems than it is on Earth. That is one of the reasons I don't like life on Earth. Too many rules here sir and your religion is a rule. Other star systems do not have religions. Religion is manmade.

Those who inhabit other planets appreciate the beauty of plant life and create beautiful gardens such as some of us do on Earth.

Inhabitants of some other planets often keep animals in their homes but not as pets. People on other planets are sensitive to those around them. They get close to certain animals as you do to dogs and cats.

There are other star systems in which physical entities can create physical objects with just their minds, similar to the manner in which spirits create in the astral world. It is going on at this moment. Physical beings can absolutely create physical things with just their minds. We can make things happen and it wasn't until I left your dear Earth that I could make things happen. That is why I do not want to come back. In those systems where the physical entities can create physical things with just their minds, they are not on more highly evolved planets than Earth. It is just an ability that they have developed that you have not. You haven't desired to develop that but if you tried, you could create with just your minds to a great extent.

The mineral, vegetable and animal kingdoms exist on all inhabited planets. Humanoid beings evolve through the mineral, vegetable and animal kingdoms as they do on Earth, somewhat. In other words, some don't start off in the mineral kingdom and some bypass the vegetable kingdom. All humans go through the animal stage before evolving into a human. The animal kingdom is very aggressive and that will be human after the animal.

The lifespan of individuals on other planets is much longer than that of Earth humans. More than five generations of a family can exist together if they want to.

In my opinion there is as much dishonesty among extraterrestrials as there is among humans. Earth humans are not more dishonest than others if you want to call it dishonesty.

Just as there are differences among the physical inhabitants of the various planets, there are also differences in the spirit worlds among the various planets. Each of the spirit worlds of the different planets is unique. Their thinking is different, just as in the physical worlds.

Extraterrestrials have many of the abilities that spirits have but which most humans do not have.

Many extraterrestrial groups have a strong physical resemblance to Earth humans. Many are very much like you. My form is different from yours. That is why I find you all ugly. Except for their physical appearance, all humanoid beings are basically similar. They have thoughts, physical senses, attitudes, emotions, desires etc. The inner core of all these beings is basic similar even though their physical appearance is different. I may come across to you as much like you but I am not an Earth being.

When I say that extraterrestrials are sometimes of different opinions, I meant they argue in their communications with each other but do not have physical warfare with each other as they did in the ancient past. They don't argue but they disagree.

7. Extraterrestrial species

Note: Information about the Anunnaki appeared in Section K: *The Evolution of Humans*

The intent of the alien beings that we call the Grays is that they wish to dominate, and they may. They are a mixture of Earthlings in a star system at this time and there is another system that has been recently discovered by your people on Earth. There is another system with more people as you wish to call people or those or things or it. (N)

At the present time there are human-like physical entities on other planets and moons in your solar system. Some are walking among you on your planet. On other planets, they are above ground and underground. It depends on what area you are. The civilization on Ceres is half and half, the same as Earth. There are physical entities on Mars below the ground. They are above the ground also. They are like lightning. You see them and yet you don't. Like a flash of lightning. You see them for the moment and then you don't but they are human-like entities.

There are human-like beings living beneath the surface of the Earth but they do not look like humans. There are some that have a human-like form but with the head of a bird or a reptile if you wish to refer that way.

The density of population on other planets compared with the density of that on Earth is not greater. It is not lesser. It is the same.

Society has existed on other planets for what you might say hundreds of thousands of years more than Earth society.

For me other planets are more pleasant places to incarnate than is the earth. I do not wish to come back to Earth. For me the earth is not the most comfortable place. There is always war, fighting and destruction. I have had experiences in other places in order to make the comparison.

When you live as long as I have, and I have, you can compare. It can be said that the earth is considered among the least pleasant planets on which to incarnate. The earth is made up of people who only want to profit, as far as what you would call money. Money seems to play an important role on Earth.

Humanoid beings in other star systems also have spirit guides as you have on Earth. You are not alone. I myself assist other physical beings in star systems other than Earth when it is needed. When I am called for, I am there to serve as Charles' mother is and she has learned to deal.

There are physical monuments or structures on other planets or moons in your solar system that are not natural creations but rather created by other physical humanoid beings. When you go to the star systems, you will see these wonderful awarenesses. There are structures on Mars that were created by human-type beings. There are objects created by intelligent beings within the rings around planets.

As the ancient Sanskrit writings state, there are some 400,000 human-like species of extraterrestrials, even more than that.

Earth humans are not the only species in the universe whose physical bodies were created or modified by extraterrestrials. There are humanoid beings and animals on other planets whose physical bodies were modified. There are animals that are more human that are so much not to be taken for granted, like your dogs who know the weather. They know the future.

8. Miscellaneous

Life on other planets is easier than life on Earth. One of the first words you were taught is "no" and they learned "yes". As far as I know, there is nowhere that physical life is more difficult than on Earth.

P. LIFE ON OTHER PLANETS

Just as in the previous section, because of the wide diversity of the features of other planets and of the humanoid beings that inhabit them, they cannot be described with a single stroke of the brush. Therefore the information in this section does not always refer to all of the planets but sometimes only to the majority of the planets and the inhabitants, but not necessarily to all.

1. Institutions and society

The concept of marriage does not exist on other planets. It is not a natural social institution but rather the result of religious doctrine invented by man. Marriage is something that is an Earth feature rather than in other star systems. Your cats and dogs do not get married either. There are some swans that keep one mate but is that marriage? There are some monogamous animals. You can be monogamous without being married. In other star systems, monogamous relationships are not necessary. Monogamy is absolutely not practiced in all other star systems. We are having fun. We do not have rules and restrictions as you do.

The concept of family on other planets is attachment. It doesn't mean that you have to be born into because we are born into the same race. We are all the same. Parents take part in the raising of their young. It is turning toward a communal thing that you are going into. It is like in Israel. Your planet is gradually becoming so that the family unit will not be as important in the raising of the young as a communal. On other planets it is not more communal. On some other planets the family concept does not exist and parents don't oversee the upbringing of their children. There is a different way of raising children. It is more of a community way.

Individuals on other planets have professions or special areas of work. They have activities ahead for them and they are here. Some of them wish to bring rewards to the people here. They are waiting anxiously and happy to be called upon and wish to assist and aid those in pain.

Those on other planets are not more attentive to the needs and care of their planet than are Earth people. Earth people are at this moment more concerned. Earth people should be more concerned about climate warming if they wish to but a lot of what is occurring is natural.

There are other planets where individuals do not need clothing or some kind of covering of the body. Their skin is enough to cover their bodies if they have that. That is not necessary. Some have feathers. They don't have something comparable to your clothing but it is always nice to adorn with clothing.

On some other planets bodies of the dead are not buried in the ground, cremated, or cast in the sea. They evaporate, turn to dust. They just dissolve. They just disintegrate. They make themselves disappear. They make their bodies disintegrate just like the wind. In your language some individuals live a couple of hundred years and some less.

It is not necessarily of interest or a habit for people on other planets to record or preserve their history. They do not have things comparable to your museums. They have no interest in such rubbish.

There are planets which have some form of government, such as you have on Earth, with leaders, laws, or politics etc. if you want to call it that. There are questionable people always who take charge.

Those on other planets treat each other more kindly and cooperate more with each other than do Earth people. They listen more. They are not ones that think while you are talking. Earth people, who, as you are speaking to them, are thinking their own mind and usually their own problems.

There is more of a similarity in the lifestyles among the various extraterrestrial groups than there is between them and Earth people. Extraterrestrials are more homogeneous. Earth people are different from them.

Religions do not exist in any star systems in addition to yours. Religion is manmade. (I)

2. Dwellings and buildings

The residential architecture on other planets is somewhat sometimes similar to yours. It varies a great deal among the different planets. Stone is very common in the materials used in their residences. Wood decays. It is mostly stone, like caves.

Entities that inhabit planets in other star systems live both in what you might call metropolitan areas and in rural areas much the same as those on Earth. There are different areas where people choose to be at rest and that depends. There are people that like to be in rural areas and they lead lives that way much the same as you do.

On other planets dwellings are used as they are on Earth; that is, for individuals or families for both protection and privacy. Those shelters are usually manmade rather than natural. They are often beneath the surface of the planet, sometimes several stories deep.

Some planets have buildings above ground that are many stories in height. Some of those buildings are higher than those on Earth. On many other planets the civilizations are beneath the ground much more than one is aware of at this moment. There is civilization beneath the ground on your Earth, mainly of extraterrestrial nature.

The interiors of the dwellings on other planets do not necessarily have divisions used for specific purposes comparable to your rooms such as kitchens, bedrooms, recreation areas etc. Some extraterrestrials do have furnishings similar yours in their abodes if they are needed or if they wish that. However, they are not needed on all planets. On some planets the inhabitants use nature more for their furnishings. For beds they lie on the ground. They don't have bathrooms. Some humanoid beings on other planets can just live in nature without anything of comfort. Nature is the most comfort.

Both public and private plumbing systems for obtaining water and disposal of sewerage on other planets are nothing compared to yours. Yours is more elaborate if you wish to say it that way.

3. Communication and education

Those on some other planets do not need to communicate to each other through spoken language. They need not speak in words. They can mind read. They do not have spoken language unless you mean hand language. The Earth is the only planet where you have to communicate with voice.

Most extraterrestrial groups communicate with other extraterrestrials from other planets. They use mostly spoken language like you do. In other words, they don't communicate as those in the spirit world. They don't read thoughts but they will be able to read thoughts as most of you think you do. You will eventually evolve as humans where you can read thoughts. [This answer appears to contradict the previous paragraph.]

Those on most other planets have learning centers where they can obtain knowledge but not as you have them. The young are not provided with what might be considered a formal school type of education as they are on Earth. They are educated in some other manner, if you wish to call it educated. They grow up without it. You can grow up without a wisdom tooth.

Those on other planets communicate with the angels, spirits and entities on other worlds if they are friendly. They do communicate with angels the same as you do.

4. Nutrition and health

The consumption of vegetables is a source of nourishment for human or human-like beings on all inhabited planets in the universe. Vegetables are necessary for all human life.

Bodily diseases do not occur among the population of those on other planets. Disease does not exist except on Earth. Disease is manmade. Individuals on other planets can be injured and need help to repair strength. They need strength. The help comes from external but not necessarily just from within. They do not have places where these people can go to have their bodies repaired. We do not have physicians. We do not have medications. We have our own resources which is our own mental ability. There is no equivalent of medical doctors. We need mental people.

Agriculture is practiced on most other worlds to provide nutrition for their inhabitants. Inhabitants on other planets have farms that they create in order to feed the inhabitants and they take things from nature without planning.

For people on most other planets, the intake of nutrition does not occur on a regularly scheduled basis as it does with Earth humans. On some other planets water is all that is mainly needed for nutrition.

Food is not food as you think of as food. They do not eat the way Earth people eat. Earth people eat for taste. Nutrition on other planets is comparable to your putting gas in a car. Different kinds of gasoline are needed. So you purchase the gas your car needs. You don't fill it with sugar. The sense of taste is not as important for extraterrestrials as it is for Earth people. Nutrition comes somewhat from the vegetable kingdom, somewhat from the sea kingdom, not all from the animal kingdom. They consume animals that live in the sea, vegetables that live in the sea and vegetables that live in the earth like worms. I don't want to make a complete vegetarian out of you but I could tell you stories you wouldn't believe. On other planets some of the humanoid beings eat animal flesh also.

Those on other planets do not consume mind altering substances comparable to your alcohol and drugs. They just have their own mind to deal with. That is enough.

The bodies of those on other planets need rest and sleep. Everyone needs rest, but not sleep. Do not worry about sleep. Not everyone in the universe sleeps. You can rejuvenate yourself just by resting. Dreaming when you are asleep belongs more to humans. Sometimes humans dream when they are awake. By dream they hope and they wish. The same is true of extraterrestrials when they are awake. They are no different than the wonderful humans except that they don't sleep and they don't go to the bathroom as you call it.

5. Transportation and technology

When humanoid beings on other planets want to travel from one place to another, they do not need to use land vehicles on roadways comparable to your streets and highways. If they want to travel from one place to another in the physical they can fly instead if you want to use that term. They do have vehicles like your ships that travel on the surface of the earth as well as vehicles that travel beneath the surface. We do not have airplanes. Teleportation is probably the most common means of transportation. People on Earth are now teleporting by their daydreams, their visual dreams. The mind can do it but the body won't.

There are civilizations on other planets where the inhabitants do not need mechanical means to travel from one place to another but instead are able to use their minds to teleport themselves wherever they wish to go in the physical. Earth people can learn teleportation. Instant teleportation of a person from one place to another is possible both through the use of technology and also through the use of the human mind. Some humans can instantly appear in a different place from where they were before. (L)

The wheel is used for forms of transportation in other star systems. There are star systems in which the wheel is not used at all for transportation. They do learn to fly. They can fly and rise up and be in the sky and fly above. In Atlantis they did both. They flew and travelled on land. They have ground vehicles with and without wheels on other planets. The wheel is an invention on all planets.

On other planets electricity is not always a form of energy that is needed. Scalar energy is a major form of energy that is used throughout the universe.

Those on other planets measure such things as distance, weight, volume, energy etc. but in a different way from on Earth.

On other planets nothing has to be artificial such as lighting, heating and cooling, or systems for the disposal of rubbish. Technologies such as air conditioning are not necessary.

Others worlds have means for reproducing sounds, sights and visual activities including sound recordings, still photography, and motion pictures. They have the technology for all the trivialities you are talking about.

Some other star systems measure time based on their star, planets and moon as you do. You measure time on the rotation and revolution of your planet. Other star systems do the same.

Those on other planets do not measure time as you do; something comparable to your hours, days, weeks, months and years. They have no knowledge as to what you are talking about. Time is not important and therefore they don't have any instruments such as clocks or calendars. Today is New Year's Day on Earth but there is no such thing as New Year's Day on other planets. Holidays are manmade and are not what you think they are. They are not holy days. This is a manmade situation as your religion is manmade.

6. Work, business and leisure

Individuals on other planets do not enjoy the visual arts such as painting and sculpture etc. There are many forms of art. Music is also considered an art. It does exist on other planets if you wish to call it that. The arts do not exist in the spirit world either. They exist in one's mind if one has a mind but not everyone has. It is not the same on other planets. They look at us as ridiculous. Playing with dolls! Those on other planets are far more advanced than Earth people. People on Earth are one of the least developed cultures on the various planets. In fact, most Earth people are not so bright. They do not listen to their first thought, which is wisdom.

On other planets people do not have planned physical activities. They don't have bodies like you have or like I used to have. They don't need physical activities because of their bodies. They do not play sports. Sports are manmade as is religion.

Private ownership does not exist on other planets. They do not have the conditions you have on Earth but they are able to share ownership. They are more like the American Indians were. There is no private ownership of land. They are able to share.

On other planets, there is no need for specific places that house the various kinds of materials or goods that individuals may need where they can obtain them. They can initiate and make their own. Everybody makes themselves whatever they need. Since humans on Earth are the least advanced of any other planet, that means that entities on other planets can do much more than Earth people can do. They are more capable. They do not have any limitations as you put upon yourselves on this planet. I have been myself to this planet many times and I would say when I was on your planet, "I cannot do this." Life on this planet is more difficult than any other place.

Individuals on other planets travel for both work and pleasure. It is indeed a privilege to travel either way. It is pretty much the same as for Earth humans. You travel for work and you travel for pleasure and you travel for nonsense. It is the same on other planets.

Individuals on other planets have commerce as well as communication with those on various other planets.

Both work and leisure activities play a role in the lives of those on other worlds. It is very similar to your planet. It is not all work. It is also leisure and enjoyment. Work is also pleasure. Entertainment and activities for pleasure exists on other planets if this is what they seek. What is entertainment? It is comparable to humans. Those on other planets enjoy playing mental games with each other.

7. Miscellaneous

Gold is an element that is treasured throughout the physical universe. Gold, silver and platinum are treasured in other star systems.

Rare gems such as diamonds, emeralds and rubies are valued in other star systems but not the way it is humanized. They do not put a dollar sign on them. Sometimes they make use of the less rare gemstones such as amethyst, quartz, and jade. They are healthy and they will bring on energy from different sources. The way you use amethyst, for example, is for beauty and culture. You use it to bring about love but not everyone in the universe is aware. A diamond brings on love; the bigger the diamond, the more love. [This last sentence is an example of the guide's sense of humor which he used frequently in the answers to personal questions asked by the group's participants.]

There are multiple births on other planets, like twins or triplets.

In other star systems as well as on Earth, death is often preceded by pain.

Q. THE WORLD BEFORE BIBLICAL TIMES

1. The planet

The land masses of this world before the Great Flood were considerably different from the way they are today. Ocean levels were much lower than they are now, thus causing many coastal areas to be inundated. The total land mass of the earth was greater than it is now. The Nile River flowed into the Atlantic Ocean at the time of Atlantis. India and the area around it were not connected to the rest of Asia.

The Gulf Stream was engineered by intelligent entities, not a natural phenomenon, not the Atlanteans but by many extraterrestrials. The purpose was to keep the lands to the north warmer. (N)

Thousands of years ago a nuclear explosion created the Libyan Desert Glass but it was not caused by people. It was caused by gasses. It was natural.

A large asteroid that hit the earth millions of years ago caused the extinction of many of the huge animals that threatened the existence of humanity. This event was not engineered by extraterrestrials. It was a natural phenomenon.

A giant meteor hitting the earth followed by earthquakes and explosions triggered a climate change that caused the distinction of dinosaurs. The meteor was intentionally directed to Earth in part to get rid of the dinosaurs. Dinosaurs have shrunk to many little lizards. Lizards and many of the reptiles today were dinosaurs at one time. When that meteor hit the earth and the dinosaurs were destroyed, some animals survived underground. Some of those species are still in existence today. You have your ants and your frogs and turtles and little animals.

Since many ancient cities have been discovered beneath the water in the Mediterranean Sea, you can assume the sea was dry land before the Great Flood. It was the Great Flood that covered those cities. It was responsible, at least in part, for the creation of the Mediterranean Sea.

In the ancient past what is now the New York City area was located many miles from the ocean. Like everything else a long time ago it was much further inland and then the ocean rose. The ocean rose and then shrank and then shrank again. Alaska will be shrinking. This is a process that goes on repeatedly over and over again throughout history.

12,980 years ago a comet hit the earth and caused the coldest deep freeze ice age. The Great Flood and the destruction of Atlantis began when the earth began to warm up at the end of the Ice Age because of the rising sea levels. The comet was deliberately steered to the earth by extraterrestrials.

Earth pole shifts have been caused by nuclear explosions but explosions are not what caused Atlantis to become Antarctica. An earthquake is what caused Atlantis to shift and become what is now Antarctica. .

Although it was once a land with lush vegetation, the cause of the creation of the Sahara Desert was the storm. It was not an earthquake or a meteorite. It was the wind and the breeze and the shifting, a natural phenomenon.

2. Extraterrestrials and vestiges of ancient civilizations

Many of us masterminded the construction of Stonehenge. We had what you call architects. The extraterrestrials, the name you have selected to call us, are here now too. We are the bright ones, you know.

The prehistoric cave paintings throughout the world can be considered something like a key to your understanding of the history and future of mankind. There is hidden meaning in those drawings. The interpretation of those drawings tells of your history and your future.

The drawings of the caves of Lascaux in France are ways of communication, what we would say to you is writings by both Earth people and extraterrestrials. They are on this planet and they have not left. They have been here many a century. (N)

The ancient elongated skulls found in Egypt and in the Americas were of alien origin and some were a mixture of humans. The humans didn't try to imitate the aliens by forcing the skulls to become longer. They did it by having relationships. They had fun with each other. (N)

Lake Titicaca in Peru and its underwater city with sunken ruins were there eons ago. It was covered with earth and then with water. It was there before the Great Flood. Indeed an earthquake occurred and then water. The earth opened up here and allowed the water to overflow. I was not there but that is what I have been told. There were many cities that existed before the Great Flood and there are still remnants now.

You can explain the existence of the same type of hieroglyphs and cuneiform writings that are found in both ancient Sumer and near Lake

Titicaca in Peru the same way as in some caves or such other areas that were left. They were writings and messages left for the future. Some were left by extraterrestrials.

The huge statues on Easter Island were manmade products of people they worshipped and extraterrestrials were involved in the construction because they had more strength. The Lemurians played a role in the creation of the many large statues on Easter Island. The statues represented extraterrestrials and people that are of stature. The cause of huge statues on Easter Island to topple over and the population to be greatly diminished was because of the earth. The earth moved slowly and they toppled. It was more like an earthquake that occurred rather than some intelligent power causing them to fall.

The great pyramid at Giza was built for electricity before the Great Flood. It was a power plant to provide energy. Many Egyptians built it. The labor was made by humans and extraterrestrials too, as they are now with you. The extraterrestrials designed the pyramid and the humans built it using extraterrestrial technology. Slaves were forced to do the work. It was not fun. It was very difficult with slavery. Pyramids all around the world were built to create energy. That energy was not just for use on Earth but was also available for use in outer space as well as on Earth. The Cheops pyramid in Egypt was built by man power.

The architects and builders of the pyramids in the Yucatan and Guatemala were people that are striving from your past. They are reaching out and wish to serve in your future. They were actually built by those of another star system, the Pleiades. They also built the pyramids in Egypt and that is how they got to the top. The Pleiades are one of the most advanced groups. Our secret people were building your pyramids that they could reach from the top down. Humans provided a lot of the labor but extraterrestrials provided the technology. (N)

There validity and accuracy in the books called *The Pyramid Power* and *The Pyramid Prophecies* written by Max Toth. Max is here with me and he sends you his love. He is enjoying the pleasure of being departed and he has experienced his books. He is very comfortable now and glad to be here now and happy that you remembered him. You can rely on the information he gives to you.

The ancient rulers of various lands throughout the world have reptilian bloodlines as some of the ancient stone carvings seem to possibly indicate so.

There are extensive ruins of ancient civilizations that predate the continent of Atlantis beneath the sands of the Sahara Dessert. It is deep below the sands, much deeper below the sands. It will show the pavement of the sand. That is more than a hundred feet to forty miles beneath the sand. Those ruins will be discovered.

It is true, as David Wilcock says, that what you call the fallen angels were originally very tall inhabitants of the planet Saturn who disobeyed orders when they mated with Earth people and that their offspring were the Nephilim giants. Indeed, there were giants. There are still physical giants of male gender in Antarctica. You call them giants and they don't seem to like that name. They are the giants asleep in the various stasis chambers throughout the world. They go anywhere from ten feet tall to forty feet tall but they don't feel they were giants. The planetary influence on a physical being can help determine their height. For example, if they were on Saturn they might have been forty feet tall but when they come to Earth, the earth's atmosphere or influence after generations causes them to be much shorter. They will become much shorter and there are people that are the size of children that are adults. They have been recognized already by some intuitives who have seen them. In your Bible you refer to those tall people who were on Earth at one time as the Nephilim. Goliath was one of them.

The original pyramids in Egypt had a covering of white limestone that resembled marble and were very polished and reflected somewhat like a mirror. They weren't as they are now. They were beautiful structures that were highly polished and then the weather elements took care of breaking that down and making them look like they do today.

With assistance from extraterrestrials, the ancient Egyptians did invented hieroglyphs. That written form of language was given to them by more intelligent sources, extraterrestrials.

It was solely for extraterrestrial observation and their travel that the ancient humans placed so much focus on astronomy by building a great number of observatories throughout the world.

There was atomic warfare on Earth in ancient times before the Great Flood.

3. Atlantis and Lemuria

There have been previous human civilizations on this earth before Atlantis that were more intelligently and technologically advanced than your current civilization.

Antarctica was once the inhabited continent of Atlantis in the middle of the Atlantic Ocean. A natural shift of the crust and rotation of the earth and earthquakes caused it to be at its current location at the South Pole. It is the origin of the Great Flood. There are ruins of the ancient civilization beneath the ice in Antarctica. I have not been a witness to that but it is also told from previous lives that this existed. Atlantis was before the Great Flood. Although I myself had not had the pleasure, I have been told by many other entities that it was a beautiful town, country or civilization and very much advanced as you are today.

There were several breakups of the continent of Atlantis over a period of time caused by natural disasters. It was nature's harm or nature's good, not their technology. It was a question of being earthbound. It came from within the earth. It was like what you would call an earthquake.

When it was at its largest size, Atlantis was approximately the same size in total land mass area as India and China combined on the map they're showing me. The underwater rock formations north of Bimini in the Bahamas are remnants of Atlantis.

The Atlanteans were a hybrid race of humans and extraterrestrials as you are. They were meat eaters. Many of the oriental people alive today are reincarnations of the Atlanteans. (N)

The Atlanteans were not physically different from you to the point that you could easily see that they were not like modern humans. They were beautiful human beings. They did not resemble one of the current races more than the others. They covered many races, not only one race. There were different human races, such as those now on Earth, at the time of Atlantis. The American Indians were the closest to what many Atlanteans looked like. They had brown skin and they were beautiful souls. (K)

The Atlanteans had advanced technologies and they were interested in building and the mechanics of their building. They were very imaginative but you are doing quite well since the time of your typewriter. The Atlanteans and humans of long ago had medical knowledge that exceeded that which you have today. They had air travel but they did not need ground vehicles for transportation. Flying machines were much easier. They were powered by crystals. Cars were not important. You will find pyramids in Wyoming under water.

The architecture of the homes in Atlantis was similar to that of ancient Greece or Rome. They had no doors. They had big wide spaces and there was no structure. It was beautiful. It was freedom. And their tiles were artistically carved. Indeed it was a pleasant place to live.

The Bermuda Triangle is a vacuum on Earth. There are other vacuums on Earth as well. People disappear never to be seen again. They are joining us. Some of the crystals that the Atlanteans used to transmit energy are still in operation under the sea today in that area. They are the cause of the disappearance of planes and ships. They have power.

The two books that Plato wrote about Atlantis contain information that was to a great extent accurate. He wants you to know he's a good friend of mine. The destruction of the island of Santorini in the Mediterranean Sea by a volcano was related to the Atlantis that Plato described. Plato enjoyed life. He loved his territory. He loved the columns, the business in his life. He just loved life. He loved life and he loved Socrates. He wrote about the island of Santorini as being part of Atlantis; yet I have also said that Atlantis was a large land mass, a continent in the Atlantic Ocean that, when there was an earth shift, it slipped to what is now Antarctica. Antarctica was once Atlantis. Plato was not incorrect when he said that the island of Santorini was part of Atlantis. It was part of the land slide.

The role of the ancient Druids in England was to preserve the ancient Atlantean knowledge. They still exist and they uphold their quest for knowledge.

Atlantis and Lemuria never coexisted. They were different elements, different time. The Hawaiian Islands were once part of Lemuria. There are remnants of the Lemurian civilization that are on Earth today; for example, the statues on Easter Island. Some American Indians are the physical descendants of the later Lemurians. Some resemble what the Lemurians looked like. Earthquakes destroyed the continent of Lemuria.

The physical characteristics of the early Lemurians were different from Homosapiens. The early Lemurians were hermaphrodites, quite different from physical human beings. Before that they reproduced like starfish, cut off a part of them. There were physical humans on Earth before the Lemurians. Some of their bodies were as dense as your bodies are now and some were lighter. (K)

The writings of James Churchward regarding the continent of Mu are for the most part accurate, which is not completely true. You are going to have more information about the influence of the people of the land of Mu. There is information each day that is arriving and more appealing and understanding to you at this time. It will be given publicly but very little appreciation will be given.

There were many advanced civilizations on Earth prior to Lemuria and Atlantis. There are physical remnants of those civilizations visible today under water. They are very deep under water. For many centuries they have been under water. Some will be discovered in your lifetime.

The Atlanteans were originally both Earth people and extraterrestrials that came to colonize the earth and they are still working on such.

The Atlanteans, for the most part but not all of them, had elongated skulls such as we see with the Egyptian queen Nefertiti. Some humans alive on Earth today have similar elongated skulls. One or two of them are in the Vatican today. They are not noticeable, not obvious. The headdresses that many of those in the Vatican wear could conceivably conceal those skulls. Those with an elongated skull have a much larger brain and are more intelligent than you.

There were human/animal hybrids in Atlantis which were part animal and part human that Edgar Cayce referred to as the creatures. They were in existence. There were places in Egypt, as Cayce said, where they tried to normalize some of those creatures.

In addition to Atlantis and Lemuria, there is evidence of other past civilizations comparable to Atlantis or Lemuria. It is about to show itself. One of those past civilizations is submersed off the coast of Cuba. That even predates Lemuria.

4. Animals

It is not true that there was a time in the ancient past when animals, including humans, could mate with animals of different species, thus producing strange looking offspring.

There was a time eons ago when animals could mate and have offspring with animals of different species, as stated by Edgar Cayce, often producing. grotesque beings, part subhuman and part animal with weird appendages that Edgar Cayce described, actually existed and they still exist. [The above two entries appear to be contradictory. Perhaps

DNA manipulation by extraterrestrials is used for the meaning of "mate" in the second statement.]

The Atlanteans did not clone animals and humans to produce beings that were half animal and half human. They already existed as humans. The creatures that Edgar Cayce spoke about that he called the things were not created by the Atlanteans. They existed but the Atlanteans did not create them. [This entry also appears to contradict previous entries.]

5. Languages

The early physical humans communicated by telepathy. Spoken language gradually evolved and became their means of communication. Telepathy is much easier when we would read other people's minds and actions. Then there was originally just one spoken language rather than the proliferation of languages that exist in the world today. The proliferation of languages was caused by people going to different climates. Then we separated and went different ways. Language was given by those that were able to communicate by sounds and grunts and sounds of pleasure. We speak many languages on Earth. Your grunts are closest to the original language. (K)

More and more linguists are finding out that your languages are not that separate at all and that they are all flowing from an original language. Hebrew and Sumerian are very near to that original language and there was definitely one before, indeed before the Great Flood.

There is only one language that will occur in the future and that is no language at all. It is telepathy. You don't have to learn another language. Just think it.

6. Personalities

The early Egyptian pharaohs were either extraterrestrials or descendants of extraterrestrials. Queen Nefertiti in ancient Egypt was an extraterrestrial but she showed herself as an Earth human. The same is true of the Egyptian King Akhenaton. They are buried near King Tut's tomb but not in the same place. The ancient Egyptians tried to erase evidence to references that Queen Nefertiti and King Akhenaton ever existed because they felt that they had too much power and they wanted the dead to be deceased. They were full-fledged extraterrestrials, not hybrids. (N)

The Aztec Indians worshipped Quetzalcoatl. It was their god, what they call god. There was such a person. He is of extraterrestrial nature. He is with me now. He says hello. He can communicate with me. He is not on Earth. He thanks you for the recognition. (N)

The Amelius as mentioned in Edgar Cayce's readings was a high spirit such as I. He had a wife called Lilith. They were of extraterrestrial origin.

The spirits of the Nephilim giants of long ago still walk among you but you can recognize them only through different feelings, gut feelings.

Osiris, the Egyptian god of the underworld, was actually a robot. He was manmade.

7. Miscellaneous

Note: Information regarding Ancient Technology is included in Section X: *Science and technology*. Information on Humans before Homosapiens is included in Section K: *The Evolution of Humans*.

Cyclops never existed. We all make up stories. There are people who see more with one eye. It is nonsense.

The Java man found in Indonesia in the late 1890's was the remains of a giant with hair.

There is reality in the belief of the ancient Egyptians that there are five parts of the human soul; ren, ba and ka etc. There are five parts to the human soul including the soul.

The human population of the earth is greater today than it ever was in ancient history. There are many more people on your earth today than it was in the past, even in the time of Atlantis and Lemuria.

Throughout history there were plagues and epidemics that affected humans. These plagues were often preceded by a shower of red rain. The showers were related to the plagues and epidemics. They were caused by both what you might say a natural occurrence and by extraterrestrials.

The ancient Sumerian civilization was one of the first after the Great Flood to be advanced by extraterrestrials. There were other civilizations at that same time that were helped by extraterrestrials.

The early forms of writing such as the Egyptian hieroglyphs, runes, and the Sumerian alphabet were invented by humans at that time, some with input from extraterrestrials. After the extraterrestrials left, the humans came up with different ways of putting the events into writing in order to record them. (N)

Long ago ancient Anunnaki kings on Earth actually ruled for more than 20,000 years.

In ancient times, particularly in Egypt, it was thought that after a person died it was possible to bring the soul back into the dead body again and then the person would become alive. That is possible. You reuse eyeballs and all kinds of things, don't you? A dead person can be made alive again but not the complete person. Extraterrestrials have that ability. It is possible to revive someone who you think is dead but is not completely dead at that time. There are cases on Earth where people have died and were able to be revived. The soul can reenter the body.

In the ancient past there were humanoid beings as tall as forty or more feet. Some of those very tall beings have civilizations inside the moons in your solar system like your ant colonies. When you see ants, are they not of different sizes? Are not some larger?

The formation of comets came in part from the water in the oceans of the planet Tiamat when it broke up into many pieces and became the asteroid belt hundreds of thousands of years ago. It is not like water that is for healing.

Ancient civilizations, such as ancient Egypt, counted the days differently than you do now; for example more than seven days in a week. The whole thing of seven days in a week is not totally universal.

In ancient times there were warring groups of extraterrestrials in the earth's sky whose battles were witnessed by Earth people. Those scenes were often portrayed in drawings. A lot of your mythologies, whether they be the Norse mythologies, the Greek mythologies or the oriental mythologies were based on extraterrestrials that they observed. (N)

The direct descendants of Adam died by just by consciously willing themselves out of the physical body, rather than by diseases like modern humans die. It was like going to sleep. They did it intentionally. You do it at the subconscious level but they did it at the conscious level.

R. THE WORLD FROM BIBLICAL TIMES TO THE PRESENT

1. Noah and the Great Flood

The land masses of this world before the Great Flood were considerably different from the way they are today. Ocean levels were much lower than they are now, thus causing many coastal areas to be inundated. The total land mass of the earth was greater than it is now. The Nile River flowed into the Atlantic Ocean at the time of Atlantis. India and the area around it were not connected to the rest of Asia. (Q)

The cause of the Great Flood that is mentioned in your Bible and in the lore of other ancient civilizations throughout the world was the accumulation of weather that had formed. It was not an accident. It was precisely planned by alien intelligence to be helpful. The Flood was caused by the Anunnaki to purge the earth. It was not to rid of any specific species. It was a great cleansing. It was engineered by the Anunnaki. At the time of the Flood were there cultures throughout the world that survived by going underground. It was safer to be underground than above ground, as it will be in the future. Underground will be more positive for you. (IN)

There are monuments that predated the Great Flood. There were many, many floods before the Great Flood. There wasn't only one Great Flood. There were many floods over and over and over. They are correcting me to tell you "and over and over". There will be more Great Floods. The Sphinx was created before the Great Flood.

The Black Sea was not created by the Great Flood but the Great Flood did create new bodies of water such as lakes.

The Great Flood was orchestrated to turn over the earth, to rejuvenate the earth. It rid the earth of the Nephilim giants but a few of them did survive the flood. The Nephilim giants were cannibals who ate human beings. The very tall men nearly ten feet tall who were discovered on Easter Island in the 1700's were their descendants.

Although there are different theories about what Noah's Ark really was, it was actually a UFO. Animals were not actually put on what you call Noah's Ark, but rather it was the DNA of all creatures.

2. From Biblical times to the 18th century

When the Romans destroyed the ancient library at Alexandria Egypt, great numbers of the manuscripts were saved and taken to Rome and kept in the Vatican There are still there. (I)

Both the British royal lineage and that of Charles can be traced back to an Irish queen who was brought to Ireland by the prophet Jeremiah in the Bible. That Irish queen was the last descendant of King David. The remains of the prophet Jeremiah are in Ireland.

The Incan empire was created and influenced by extraterrestrials. (N)

Machu Picchu in Peru was abandoned after a hundred or so years because it was not very comfortable to live there. It was very high up in altitude. The climate and its past history had a tendency to have some reflection on those that are fearful of living there. Most of the people didn't survive because of the climate.

The Mayan Indians had settlements everywhere, not just in Mexico but also in many places in what is now the United States. Approximately ninety-five percent of the Mayan civilization disappeared more than 1000 years ago, long before the arrival of the Europeans because of earthquakes. There were earthquakes in Central America where the Mayans were.

There was assistance from extraterrestrials in the creation of the maps copied by Piri Reis about five centuries ago because when they stand on a higher hill, they see more of the mountain.

The origin of the system of priests in various religions was actually humans who were able to communicate with extraterrestrials and act as intermediaries between them and Earth people Aaron, the brother of Moses, was one such person; not well liked but Moses was well liked. I was on Earth at the time of Moses. (N)

The magician Merlin as portrayed in the Arthurian legends of England did not exist. It is made up again, stories concocted by human souls. The human soul is so good at making up a story, like Noah's ark.

The letter about Jesus supposedly written by Pontius Pilate to the Emperor Tiberius was a forgery written several centuries later.

Christopher Columbus was in search of a passage to the East. He was not interested in finding Atlantis. What he saw rising from the sea or was not a UFO. It was a natural phenomenon.

The Black Plague was intentionally designed by extraterrestrials for rats to reduce the earth's population. Poison gas was used. Everything was used. Right now we are working on that, decreasing the world's population by both physical disease and warfare.

Leonardo DaVinci's painting of the Mona Lisa is, in a way, a self portrait. It's part of him he's expressing in a feminine way. It is not a painting of a natural person. It was more a self-portrait he created. It was his smile.

Freemasonry was encoded in the design of Shakespeare's Globe Theater. The number 72 plays a significant role in its design. The number 72 is 9 and if you put it upside down it is evil. The design of the theater incorporates secret hermetic knowledge.

There is no connection between the Catholic Inquisition many centuries ago in which great numbers of infidels were killed and the current radical Moslem movement in which the infidels are killed. They are disassociated occurrences. It is not the same group reincarnating. They are similar but not the same but I have said that the current group of Moslem terrorists is the reincarnation of the Nazis. That is a fact. (I)

Centuries ago the Indians threw a great amount gold into the lakes in South America so the Spaniards could not take possession of it. There is still a lot of gold at the bottom of many of the lakes in South America.

The huge underground city which could house 20,000 people in Derinkuyu in Turkey was built by your slavery. That was built underground like the pyramids were built by humans that acted as slaves. It was not built by extraterrestrials. It was built to be a safe place. Humans built the city without any connection or advice from extraterrestrials.

There is historical basis for the existence of the city that we refer to as El Dorado. Lake Guatavita in Colombia has nothing to do with El Dorado.

The cause of the disappearance of the lost colony of Roanoke, Virginia in 1587 was what you would call an earthquake. The earth swallowed them. It wasn't unfriendly Indians. It was an earthquake like the grounds here that swallow up people.

Joan of Arc was influenced by extraterrestrials in order to avoid the negative consequences if the English won the battle against the French.

The cause of about 400 people uncontrollably dancing for many hours and days, some until they became very ill or even died, in Strasbourg, France in 1518 was certain plants beneath their feet. It was a hallucinogenic drug five hundred years ago. It was not marihuana but some other kind of drug.

In the Christian Bible, there is a description of an event which took place in what they called an upper room and suddenly everyone started speaking in Tongues. Most probably extraterrestrials were involved. Extraterrestrials speak tongues.

The Byzantine Emperor Constantine IV in the 7th century A.D. defeated the invaders by destroying more than one thousand ships with something called Greek fire. This was fire that could not be extinguished with water. Its formula was later lost and never rediscovered. Greek fire that would burn under water was actually oil.

Several centuries ago some French noblemen called the Knights Templar went to Jerusalem in search of King Solomon's treasure and brought great treasures of great wealth back to France. That treasure is hidden in both Scotland and Nova Scotia. The Knights Templar became the forerunners of the Freemasons. The Freemasons had a profound effect of the creation of our country. They were part of the Illuminati but since then the Illuminati have changed to become a negative.

Sir Francis Bacon was the illegitimate son of Queen Elizabeth I of England. He actually wrote most of the works that are attributed to Shakespeare. He was able to write and Shakespeare was not able to write. He assisted Shakespeare. If you wish, he could be considered as the father of Freemasonry.

Several centuries ago the Freemasons operated pirate ships to plunder gold from the ocean vessels of the various countries. That gold was to enrich the Illuminati.

3. The 18th and 19th centuries

George Washington had encounters with non-human intelligences during the Revolutionary War. He thought people were being misled. He appeared to think that people were going not well mentally. Extraterrestrials helped him with the war. While in the spirit world George Washington did not materialize so that humans could see him to help the North win the Civil War. It was another entity taking on the form of George Washington. (N)

The purpose of the street designs in Washington D.C. was that they could be seen from any angle, not necessarily from above but from below also. Below is very important, sir, not just on the earth but beneath the earth. There is activity going on beneath the earth and in the oceans, not just on the surface of the earth. It was a plan, my dear. It was a plan based on ancient wisdom. There are many intelligent beings on your planet.

It was not an experiment in democracy but rather a learning point that extraterrestrials were involved in the founding of our country for the purpose of establishing a new pattern for government for other countries. The American Revolution was originally an anti-Illuminati revolt. It did help raise the level of consciousness of human beings.

Some of the major founding fathers of this country were influenced by higher level conscious entities.

The Freemasons had a significant impact on the founding of your country. The source of the Freemasons' information was extraterrestrial.

Although some people believe that there was extraterrestrial or angel involvement in aiding the Americans in the fight against the British in the War of 1812 in regard to the manipulation of weather conditions, that is ridiculous. However, angels and extraterrestrials were always there to help the Americans. (D)

Napoleon Bonaparte and Adolf Hitler were the first two of the three antichrists that Nostradamus predicted. The third one has recently been born. [An earlier entry stated, "The third anti-Christ is still baking in the oven. In other words, he has not been born yet but is about to come into the physical. It is shown that he comes from another country.]

Abraham Lincoln was psychic. He used his first thought. He received guidance from the spirit world through a medium. Lincoln was a dear soul, a kind soul, and he wrote the Emancipation Proclamation himself. He was an intelligent man and he meant only well. He believed in extraterrestrials and so did his wife. He knew his life's plan and that he would die young through assassination but he didn't believe it, as we believe that we are not going to die. We always think that the other person is going to die. He is still in the spirit world. He has not detached. So he has not reincarnated because he is being held back here. His work in the spirit world is keeping him from reincarnating.

The assassination of President Lincoln was solely the work of John Wilkes Booth but there were other people involved. Booth held the gun himself but Vice-President Andrew Johnson was aware of what was going to happen. The assassination of Lincoln was a conspiracy and Andrew Johnson was in on the conspiracy. They were mentally disturbed people. It was a racial thing.

There were several dozen similarities between the assassination of

President Lincoln and the assassination of President Kennedy. Those similarities were not what you might call coincidences but rather an example of history repeating itself one hundred years later.

Although it has been traditionally believed that the inventor of the telephone was Alexander Graham Bell, the inventor was actually Elisha Gray but Bell had more publicity.

In 1892 Lizzie Borden actually murdered her father and stepmother with an axe. She enjoyed herself too. She was both demented and very angry. She was treated badly. She was getting even if you wish to call it that.

The artist Vincent Van Gogh did not cut off his own ear. It was cut off by sword in a duel by another person. It was a friend of his, the artist Gauguin. Van Gogh did not say anything about Gauguin because he didn't want to destroy their friendship. He said that he cut it off himself so he could maintain his friendship with Gauguin.

4. World War II and the Nazis

Was there a Nazi base on Antarctica during World War II. Indeed. They were all over. Everywhere, you know.

During World War II both the Axis and the Allied powers used psychics and channelers to assist them in their war efforts. There was assistance or influence from extraterrestrials. The Germans used everything imaginable. The Nazis received technology information from the extraterrestrials through reverse engineering of their crashed UFO's. There was influence from extraterrestrials. That is why they lost. They were deliberately misled. The United States government had an inkling in advance that Japan would attack Pearl Harbor and declare war on this country. They did not know the day.

Although there is speculation that Hitler escaped from Germany and died somewhere else, he died in Germany. He did not die a natural death. He was shot. He was killed. He did not escape and go on.

The Nazi's made contact with extraterrestrials living beneath the surface of Antarctica. They got some of their ideas for waging war there.

The German stealth aircraft existed during World War II but it was not successful.

Hitler played a predestined role and was guided by extraterrestrials. It was not the goal of that group of extraterrestrials to take over the world.

217

They were following his orders, not their own orders. This is the same group of extraterrestrials that is assisting ISIS today. We must get rid of them. You are on the same path with ISIS as you were with Hitler. They are a fungus. (N)

Hitler was definitely influenced by thoughts projected to him of extraterrestrials. He was not an evil man but he was just playing out a predetermined role in history. He got to where he was because he was influenced by thoughts projected to him.

The Nazis actually built UFOs in the 1930's. Not all of the UFOs that have been reported seen in the skies were extraterrestrials but [as to some being made on Earth] yes and no. That means that the Germans built the UFOs with help from extraterrestrials.

The Nazi's went into outer space. They developed UFO's in the 1930's. They established colonies or bases on the moon and Mars and much more. They are still there. They flew over the United States Capitol in 1952 when Eisenhower was president. Since the 1960's they have recruited millions of people, mostly highly intelligent people, to live on the moon and Mars.

5. The 20th century

It is interesting that Vice-President Andrew Johnson was involved with the assassination of President Lincoln and that the person involved with the assassination of President Kennedy was Vice-President Lyndon Johnson. He disliked Mr. Kennedy and he was jealous of him. He himself wanted to be president. It was just a coincidence that both vice-presidents were named Johnson. There was no foreign country involved in the assassination of President Kennedy. President Johnson was involved in the assassination. He was also involved a little bit with the assassination of Robert Kennedy. A very sneaky man wasn't he? By a little bit I mean that he knew it was going to happen but he wasn't involved more than that. He made it happen.

Lee Harvey Oswald was recruited by a government official in the assassination of John Kennedy. He was so but not successfully. He was not involved in recruiting Jack Ruby. Ruby was honest and faithful and loyal and stupid.

Our government found dead bodies of extraterrestrials in a UFO that landed in Roswell, New Mexico in 1947 and they still are finding more from that crash. They didn't find any live extraterrestrials. Perhaps they were human time travelers from your future, the extraterrestrials that you call the Grays. The Grays are humans of the future.

Your government performed autopsies on the aliens that died in a crashed UFO that crashed in Roswell, New Mexico in 1947 and they continue to do so. Some of those bodies are preserved in a vault today.

There were several UFO crashes discovered on Earth before the 1947 crash in Roswell New Mexico in 1947 but there was no publicity.

Amelia Earhart's plane crash made some delicious food for those in the jungle in that era. It did not crash in the ocean. It crashed on land. It crashed because the oil in the machinery did not work well. It got dry.

Princess Diana was accidently murdered. She was killed in the car. It was the fault of the driver who was speeding. He was under the influence of legal medication and not enough sleep.

The death of the actress Natalie Wood many years ago was accidental. She slipped and fell and drowned, not able to swim.

In 1949 did your Secretary of Defense Admiral Forrestal was murdered by the U.S. government because he had secret knowledge regarding Antarctica. He was disposed of because of his secret knowledge and he was not the only one. There were others too. Your government is wonderful.

Many years ago, in the 1940's, Admiral Byrd discovered advanced underground civilizations with people living underground at both of the earth's poles. There was a cover-up by your government regarding his expedition to Antarctica after World War II.

The five airplanes that disappeared in the Bermuda Triangle in 1945 went into a black hole, the mystery of life. They ended up somewhere else in the universe because there is a star gate in the Bermuda Triangle.

Princess Grace Kelly of Monaco was killed in an automobile which her daughter was driving. She was arguing with her mother and she was a young driver of perhaps the age of fourteen. It was an accident and it was hush-hushed that the daughter was driving. There was a rumor that the cause of the accident was that Grace Kelly had a stroke but the stroke was after the accident.

The murderer of the Jean Benet Ramsey was a lowly person who crept into the hall of the basement of that child and crawled into bed with her. He was a greasy old man who had been imprisoned. Overlooked, over minded, like many of the individuals that are on Earth. He is another earthworm hiding in the basement of their home. Crawling through the basement window of their home and remained there. She appeared to be as a young adult.

President Eisenhower and some of his advisors had face to face discussions with an extraterrestrial named Valiant Thor who said he was from Venus and who looked like a human, in Washington D.C. during the late 1950's. The man who looked like a human was actually manifesting himself as a human but was from Venus. They are among us always. I have said that extraterrestrials have far more abilities than you have since you are one of the least developed planets in the universe.

O.J. Simpson murdered Nicole Brown and Ron Goldman. He had no accomplices. He had himself and indeed he did murder and he is out to get another one. He was under the influence of drugs during the time of the murder. He did not confess to anyone what he did, not even to himself. At the present time he is out to kill another person. He is a very angry, hostile person. He is a fuse waiting to be ignited and he will do so.

NASA was aware that there were structures on the moon before they landed on the moon. There were not just natural things but things created by other intelligences all over the place. There are pyramids on the moon that were created by the same creators that created pyramids on Earth, the Anunnaki. They had a civilization on Mars and were everywhere. They established civilizations both on Mars and on Earth.

Saddam Hussein thought he was the reincarnation of King Nebuchadnezzar II but he was not the reincarnation of King Nebuchadnezzar II. Saddam Hussein was insane.

Tesla developed what was called a death ray. There seems to be some discrepancy in the knowledge regarding whether it was the use of the death ray that caused of the huge explosion more than 1000 times more powerful than the atom bomb that took place in Tunguska Siberia in 1908. We are not informed. It could possibly be the death ray that caused that huge explosion.

The Russian monk Rasputin was influenced by non-physical entities and he was also simply deranged. He was a little of both. He was influenced by from outside and he was very crazy also.

In the 1950's the CIA secretly injected LSD or some kind of drug which produced severe hallucinations and many deaths into the food supply in a town in France.

In regard to what happened to Michael Rockefeller in 1961 when his boat apparently overturned of the coast of New Guinea, he was eaten by scavengers. It was a horrible death.

The crash of the airplane in which John Kennedy Jr. was killed was an accident. It was not sabotage. He was blinded by the water. It was pilot error rather than mechanical failure and he was not a very good pilot. He was only thinking of himself. He was in an emotional state at that time with his wife. Although there is a rumor that John Kennedy Jr. was not killed in the plane crash but is still alive, that rumor is not true.

In 1947 President Truman established a committee called the Majestic 12 to investigate extraterrestrial activities in the United States. The findings of that committee were very accurate. If you were to read that report you could assume that it is true. It brought a smile to my face to remember those who have been there, too.

Frederick Valentich and his plane disappeared while flying over water in Australia in 1978. They were abducted by a UFO. He had gone where all the activities had been left with your Bermuda Triangle. He survived physically but not mentally. It will be indeed be difficult for you to reach him.

Dorothy Kilgallen is a dear soul who was correct when she wrote newspaper articles about a crashed UFO in England in the 1950's. A UFO actually crashed in England.

The bandleader Glen Miller's airplane that crashed in 1944 will never be found. It was ambushed. The plane has dissolved itself, disintegrated. It will never be located.

James Hoffa, the Teamsters Union leader, disappeared without a trace in 1971 because he became mashed. He was put into a tank that pulverized him. He was crushed. It was intentional. He was murdered. He was made to disappear so that his body couldn't be identified at all. They did not like him.

Mahatma Gandhi was visited by physical extraterrestrials.

President Reagan had face-to-face interaction with extraterrestrials, many which are not mentioned and not believable to the public eye. It will only be discovered when your dear president, and I speak tongue in cheek, will reveal in the future. The assassination attempt on President Reagan occurred to try to prevent him from revealing information about extraterrestrials. That was the main reason for the attempted assassination.

President Obama was born in the United States. Hawaii is part of the United States.

The Kennedy family was one of the thirteen families that were part of the Illuminati. President John Kennedy betrayed the Illuminati by going against what they wanted and was assassinated because of the betrayal. The same is true of Robert Kennedy.

There is a media cover-up regarding the death of John Kennedy. He was assassinated because he was going to reveal information about the illuminati. President Johnson was the one who was really involved with the assassination. He wanted Kennedy out. He was working in conjunction with the Illuminati. The assassination was an event that was predestined. Robert Kennedy was assassinated as a convenience, just to get him out of the way.

Although it is rumored that Jimmy Carter was the half-brother of John Kennedy because they have very similar facial features, that is not true. They were not related. Jimmy Carter is not working with the Alliance in opposition to the Cabal.

The Clintons ran a cocaine business in Arkansas in the 1980's and 1990's. It was clandestine and related to the Iran Contra deal. It helped Iran quite a bit. Vince Foster, who worked for the Clintons, committed suicide because he was going to testify against the Clintons and the pressure was too great.

The Clintons gave financial, industrial and military information to China for which they profited financially. This was done before Bill Clinton became president. He earned money for his own pocket. Clinton and his wife have been successful in adding money to their own pockets. I have said that Hillary Clinton is the reincarnation of Jezebel in your Bible. Regarding his previous incarnation, President Clinton is the cause of Jezebel. Hillary is interested in her pocket. She is not well mentally and physically. She will not try for another nomination to be president but she will be behind the scenes.

The Cabal was responsible for intentionally establishing the foundation for World War I and World War II to begin so that they could have greater control over the world. You could substitute the word Luciferians for Cabal.

The National Security Agency has designed bitcoins as a backup plan as a currency that cannot be tampered with and which will inhibit monetary control or corruption. The bitcoin is a positive thing. It will come into existence.

The Japanese in World War II captured a great deal of gold from the Southeast Asian countries. That gold is buried in huge bunkers in Southeast Asia. The Cabal controls the gold.

The bombing of the Oklahoma City federal building by Timothy McVey in 1995 was a test run for the destruction of the Wall Street Towers. His bomb was definitely too small to create such a large explosion. It was a controlled demolition by the Cabal. The explosion was orchestrated because all the documents for the Whitewater investigation were in that building. That was exactly what they were trying to destroy. The Clintons are very devious and you will find that out in the future.

In the 1980's the United States and the Soviet Union were secretly working on establishing a space program and extraterrestrial research. The United States is continuing research that you don't know about and they will continue to combine their research. Together they will achieve. They will join. Russia and the United States will continue to be friends.

In the 1940's the actress Heddy Lamar made inventions that made today's technology of Wi-Fi, GPS, Bluetooth and even the internet possible. She was a very amazing lady.

President Reagan was aware that the Iran Contra scandal money was used to buy arms for cocaine dealers. At the time he had some information but it wasn't expressed

Marilyn Monroe died of an overdose of medication. She herself caused her death. It was not someone else. She overdosed. The Kennedy family could not wait to get rid of her but they did not murder her.

Howard Hughes' mental decline or demise was very much hastened by an outside source. He received information from extraterrestrials. He obtained the Tesla patents that were sequestered by the government and then gave them to George Van Tassel who built a time machine. He paid girls to have sex with members of the Illuminati in order to have the girls get information to give to him.

The time machine that George Van Tassel built has been confiscated by your government.

During the Franco dictatorship in Spain, thousands of babies were stolen because their parents were opposed to Franco. Those babies were sold to other parents who supported Franco.

Most wars are intentionally created by the Cabal so that they can gain greater control. In some situations the cabal absolutely supports both opposing sides. The Bush family was involved with that. In World War II Preston Bush helped both the Nazis and the Americans.

There was a hidden reason for the Viet Nam war. It was not simply to stop the spread of communism. It was related to gold that the Japanese stored there during World War Two. Gold from Fort Knox is also stored there.

Of the eight United States presidents who died in office seven were elected in a year divisible by twenty from 1840 to 1960. This was a plan, not a coincidence. President Reagan who was elected in 1980 and was very seriously injured in an assassination attempt was able to escape the plan even though the plan was for him to die.

6. The 21st century

Note: Some current events regarding politics and world affairs are omitted from this section but are included in Section S.

There a government cover-up regarding the destruction of the World Trade Center Towers. They do not want to cause fear. When the airplanes hit Building One and Building Two in the World Trade Center, Building Seven did not collapse in the same manner. The collapse was because of poor structure, not explosives, the mismanagement of electrical wiring.

The government of Saudi Arabia was involved in the airplanes crashing into the Wall Street Towers on September 11, 2001. It wasn't just Saudi Arabians. It was the government that was involved.

Global warming is a natural phenomenon. It has happened many times before and will happen time and again. The earth is not hurting because of the greenhouses gasses created by man. Human beings can do nothing to stop or slow down the acceleration of the earth becoming warmer to the point where polar ice will melt, thus causing the inundation of many coastal areas, and the extinction of some animal life forms. It is the rotation of the earth. This is going to happen in many years to come. You won't be here. There's nothing you can do about global warming. That is the existence of your past and your future. The actions of humans are not harming the earth in ways that will result in bringing harm to physical humanity. The earth itself is not being harmed by mankind, not at all. This whole concern about global warming is ridiculous

Extraterrestrials are monitoring your nuclear facilities because they are concerned about the direction your civilization is taking. They are very concerned about these directions. They are very curious. They wish to be in control. They are not fearful of what you might do. They wish to control. They are seeking control. There may as well be a potential that there will be a nuclear war but it will not come to that end. You will wipe out Isis and you will come to the aid of Israel. Israel has forces as such that no man has created. The Jews have secrets. Indeed, Israel is being guided by a powerful extraterrestrial force. They want so much to be existing. (N)

The present groups of Islamic terrorists are reincarnations of the Nazis and are also the reincarnations of many groups throughout the history of your world. They come back again and back again and reincarnate. They travel as a group through their incarnations. The same group we call the Islamic Terrorists has appeared as a group at various times throughout history.

The spread of Lyme's disease was the result of experiments done with ticks by your government on Plum Island, N.Y. Much was spread in this special place on Long Island. Experiments taking place on Plum Island are dangerous for people. Other diseases have been created by your government, experimenting. Most of your hospitals in New York are filled with cancer patients on your North Shore. The experiments are causing cancer. That is the reason why there has been so much cancer on Long Island. That was explained to your wife. At that time she was aware on the North Shore.

This book you are writing, in which I give answers to the questions you ask, will be a worthwhile project that will be of interest to many people. Anyone who is closely tied in with religion will not accept this book. Not in control. It is control we are fighting. This book will be helpful to other people; very much so, and even those who slam it down and say "bull shit". It will keep the mind thinking. If you ever get it finished, it will be popular. I am always right.

It was solely because of his health and age as he stated, that Pope Benedict resigned. Anything that would cause health problems would be the reason he was resigning. It was only for health reasons and for gallbladder. It was because of differences of opinion. That can cause a gallbladder problem. That is why he resigned but he is there and will be of assistance. He is a dear, darling person, kind and genuine. (I)

The ten stones or commandments known as the Guide Stones in

Georgia contain coded messages for the impending apocalypse. The thinking of their creator was influenced by unseen sources. I want to go back to Stonehenge and Coral Castle in your neighborhood. They are elsewhere too. They are coded messages. The code will be broken.

Saddam Hussein discovered a star gate which he was planning on for nefarious purposes. He was interested in control, a very controlling person. That is why the Unites States invaded Iraq. They were aware that he had discovered a star gate. Your government is aware of star gates. They went after Hussein so he couldn't make use of that star gate.

U.S. technology now has an unmanned space shuttle that has been in orbit for two years and is capable of disabling enemy satellites. What is already in space can disable satellites. Disabling satellites has already been done. Ask Israel that made the satellite. They know what to do with their satellite. The unmanned satellite has to do with North Korea's satellites misfiring. You are protecting yourselves through that satellite.

Cuba's economy will be restored to a level of prosperity and the lifestyle of its citizens will be greatly elevated. The Castro regime will end with the departure of Raoul Castro after a while. It will take time, just as it took time to get this way. It will become less socialized. It will become more democratic. They need a chance and they will have a chance.

Nikolas Cruz, the mass murderer of high school students, said that for years he was tortured by demon voices in his head that told him to kill. It is true that he heard such voices. He was deranged.

The Nazi's still have influence, power and bases. They are all over. They have bases under the ice in Antarctica and in other places in the world also.

Both President Obama and President Trump were taken to see the civilization under the ice in Antarctica. In a way, the presidents were threatened with extinction if they exposed this. Obama is keeping quiet but Trump will expose many things. This has a basis for Trump establishing a space force. Trump is aware of extraterrestrial activities on Earth. Donald Trump's established a Space Force because he has information about extraterrestrials that the public does not know.

The main reasons that Supreme Court Justice Kavanaugh was so violently opposed by the Democrats were that he opposed abortion and that he was in favor of military tribunals for civilians accused of treason.

Politicians in your government profited financially from the sale of uranium to Russia in 2010. The Clintons are to be blamed. They profited from that sale. They love money. Money will be obsolete someday anyway. We will not have paper. You will not have coins. The concept of bitcoins or something similar to them will be replacing money.

John McCain's career was not built on lies and deception as some people say. He did not broadcast anti-American propaganda to the Vietnamese people over the radio. He was such a loyal man and such a giving man and such a kind man. We can twist it anyway we want to make it into a negative. John McCain was actually murdered. He was killed. He was poisoned. He was honest to the best of his ability.

Anthony Scalia's death was self-inflicted. He chose to go.

Admiral Jeremy Boorda's death was natural

There is much hidden information about the town Paradise, California which was recently completely destroyed by fire. Extraterrestrials from Alpha Centauri had some kind of treaty with humans there that permitted them to have a safe haven and live there peacefully because they were kind people and were nearly identical to humans. The fire was created and enhanced by laser beams by the Cabal to destroy the Centaurians because they were on the verge of disclosing their existence to the public and the public was fearful. There was a connection between the fire and the shooting incident in which several people were killed when a gunman opened fire at a restaurant in Thousand Oaks, California. (N)

In 2011 there were hundreds of thousands of dead birds and fish found ashore. Those deaths caused by or HAARP facility in Alaska to defend underground facilities. Some kind of waves generated by the HAARP facilities is what killed the birds.

There is a ridiculous theory that no one in the planes that crashed into the Wall Street Towers in 2001 was killed and that the passengers were secretly taken off that plane and taken safely to an underground facility where they are secretly living today and that the crash was orchestrated by our government with a remotely controlled plane.

Your government was involved in the airplanes that crashed into the Wall Street towers in 2001. It is covering up things about the Wall Street Towers crash. Nuclear weapons that emitted very little radiation were used to destroy the Wall Street Towers in 2001. Some of the first responders died of radiation. The Bush family was involved in the destruction of the towers.

The cause of the death of Robin William's was influenced by an outside source. There seems to be a tremendous pressure here. I would say it was murder as well as many other places [situations].

It is true regarding John of God in Brazil, that more than 600 women came forward and accused him of raping them. A person can actually do what you call miracles such as healing a person from disease and yet perform evil acts. That goes on all the time, right before your nose. Let's see you pick the next president. A person can be evil and yet do good things at the same time. (L)

Your government does not still store gold in the vaults at Fort Knox. The gold has been transferred. Heroin or dangerous drugs, instead of gold is stored in Fort Knox. The gold that was stored in Fort Knox has been transferred to various underground places in Southeast Asia.

The two opposing groups at this time are the Deep State, or the Cabal or the Luciferians or whatever you want to call it, and the Alliance. The Wiki Leaks were intentionally promoted by the Alliance for the good of mankind.

The percentage of the members of both political parties in our congress is more corrupt today than it has been in the past. It is ignorance that makes it corrupt.

Jeffrey Epstein actually committed suicide but he received assistance in doing so. The Clintons were indirectly involved. The Clintons will be revealed and she will have a problem.

Thirty years ago your wife said that the most important presidential election would be that of 2012. Although it appears that the 2016 election was the most important, she was correct. It was really 2012 that set the groundwork for being the most important presidential election. Obama was supposed to lose that election but the Democrats were able to manipulate the elections. The Democrat party was slippery as they are now. Both the 2012 and the 2016 election were equally important.

S. CURRENT SOCIAL, POLITICAL, ECONOMIC AND NEAR FUTURE EVENTS

The last channeling session of the Coral Springs Metaphysical group was held on March 1, 2020. No information in this book appeared after that date.

1. The Cabal and the Alliance

Two opposing forces are now working to gain control of all facets of human life on Earth: the Cabal and the Alliance. The Cabal includes factions such as the Illuminati, the Deep State and the New World Order. The Alliance includes the Elohim and other factions which work for the upward evolution of humanity. It is the constant struggle of what you might call good and evil. The Cabal is currently frantically struggling to gain total control of society in a negative manner. The Alliance works for the good of mankind. At the present moment the Cabal is strongly exerting its influence but in the end the forces of good will succeed. It is the constant struggle of good and evil.

The media in your country are mainly under the control of the Cabal. The media have absolutely conspired to produce fake news as Donald Trump claims. It is true that they are making up fake news against Donald Trump. He is not so innocent, you know, but they do make up stories.

The media in the United States are as controlled, dishonest or biased as some people portray it to be. The media in this country do not know how to tell the truth. There is an awful misconception in your country. They keep secrets. Everything is a secret. The media are not honest and actually does provide fake news. I don't want to take sides but at this moment Trump is telling the truth for a change. It is not always his truth. The press does not tell you all sides. The press is one-sided and tells you one side.

The five major media companies are somewhat controlled by the Illuminati. Even the Fox news channel is controlled by the Illuminati. They cannot be trusted the way you would like to trust them. No news source can be trusted.

Social media programs are manipulated by their creators to be of assistance to the Deep State. It is all manipulated.

The media will not eventually be more accepting of Donald Trump. They need an enemy. The media will not change. They will still be against Donald Trump until his demise, until the end but he will prove himself over and over. It's like banging his head against a wall. He was sent here to do that and he is doing that. He was preordained to become president. Preordained as a cuckoo man but he is not but he is. He is sly like a fox if you wish to term it that way. He doesn't know what he is doing. It's like cooking something when you throw in the extra salt when it's needed. I am saying that he is absolutely relying a great deal on his intuition rather than his knowledge. He was selected for that, because of his intuition not because of his knowledge.

There currently CIA operatives in the media. It has always been that way.

You know that there is currently a great deal of fake news about your country, but is there also a great deal of fake news about the history of your country since its founding. A lot of what you read in your history books, including the founding of our country, is inaccurate, made up. It was fake news that George Washington chopped down a cherry tree to make history a little more embellished.

2. Popular Culture

The media are very much controlled by the Illuminati. Many of the current popular music stars, including the popular singer Lady Gaga, are instruments of the Illuminati. The same is true of movie and TV stars. They all get together and make your simple laws. You have something to fear from the Illuminati. You should ignore them or oppose them. Be strong and know what is better for you, each one of you individually.

The lyrics of pop music perpetuate American idiocracy. The IQ level of the lyrics has dropped dramatically within the past generation. The mentality of those with you has been very short limited. There are forces that are part of the dumbing down of America and they are part of that. The reason for that is so they can get control of people. They are doing a good job. The same is true of the movies that come out. That is the mentality of the people. Television programs are dumbing down people too. Hip-hop music was created or used to promote criminal behavior.

You Tube is used by the Deep State to lead people into their way of thinking and belief system. The same is true of Google.

The Illuminati, the Cabal and the One World Order are dark forces which your government should seek to eliminate. Your government is very deceitful to you. Your government does not tell you all that is true. There are both Republican and Democrat elected government officials who are instruments of the Illuminati. It is not just one party. It is both parties. Both are to blame but one will be eliminated. The one that will be eliminated is the Illuminati.

The Illuminati are working toward the dumbing down of America. It is brainwashing people and practicing mind control through popular music and other forms of media entertainment such as the super bowl commercials, the Grammy Awards and ballgames. All work of the simple people. The most simple people will be ignited by the Illuminati.

The Illuminati are very much engaged in your government. For many years they are there to erupt and will continue to erupt and be that way. Your government is controlled by the Illuminati but the people in the country are not as controlled as much as the government is. There seems to be a war underneath it all but no war will come from it with your president at peace.

The information that Edward Snowden provides about the Cabal and the Illuminati is aiding in the downfall of the Illuminati and other factions of the Cabal. He wants to discourage it. He has a great deal more information that could shake your political scene. Your political scene is shaken already. He has secret information about the activities of extraterrestrials on Earth. Everything is secret. The government is hiding because they do not want to cause any fear. And another thing, they want control.

The information that David Wilcock provides about the Cabal and the Illuminati is mostly accurate. I have said that David Wilcock is a dear soul. He possesses knowledge for which the Illuminati would like to assassinate him. His lifestyle and actions prohibit the Cabal from harming him. There are no plans to assassinate David Wilcock. He will not be assassinated. He is not of extraterrestrial origin. He is extremely honest and accurate in his findings. And wise.

The Euro is a creation of the Cabal. It would assist them to have control humanity.

General Flynn was unjustly targeted by the Mueller investigation. The reason for that is that he has much information that the Deep State does not want disclosed.

There is currently corruption or influence from the Cabal on the United States Supreme Court.

The Alliance is causing the price of gold to go down for the purpose of diminishing the power of the Cabal. It is a good thing that the price is going down because the Cabal is your enemy. It will go down and it will go up again. It is a constant struggle between good and evil.

The worship of the god Baal in the Bible that was introduced by Jezebel continues today as part of the cabal. In other words the god Baal is still worshipped in the Deep State. I have previously said that Hilary Clinton is the reincarnation of Jezebel.

The current administration in your government is part of a secret international alliance to fight the Deep State. The Deep State will be defeated but it is not close to being defeated. Those in the Deep State realize that they are being defeated. The Deep State is structuring situations that will eventually force or encourage our country to go to war.

4. Donald Trump

Trump was destined to become president for the purpose of combating the Illuminati. All was planned. Trump will be successful in combating the Illuminati. He will not only be successful. He will be very successful. Do not worry about his mouth. His mouth will confuse you.

The origin of the hatred some people have for President Trump was embedded into the DNA of the ancestors of those people hundreds of generations ago by extraterrestrials. The great amount of hatred that people have toward Donald Trump is because they are not knowledgeable. They are not aware that your president will go down in history as a well informed man. He is a little whacky but he is a nut like other people are.

Donald Trump is aware of extraterrestrial activities on Earth, very much aware. Your government is secretly taking money and investing it into space programs with the knowledge of elected officials including your president. Unlike what some people have said, no people are being drafted into the secret space program without their desire or consent.

There is major significance in President Trump's establishment of a sixth branch of the armed forces for space or extraterrestrial exploration. He does he have information that the public is unaware of regarding our space program and knowledge of what is occurring in outer space. He has sensitive feelings. Other countries will have the same.

Pedophilia is a serious wide-spread problem among our elected officials. Aborted babies used to be sacrifices to their god known as Baal. You have an intelligent blind man leading your country and it is given to us by God and you did it. If you wish, you can connect the two when you say that this man was given to you by God and that God works in mysterious ways.

Donald Trump can trust Jared Kushner. Jared Kushner is absolutely not working against him. He has been beneficial in helping. He is kind and sincere. He will have a successful role regarding Israel in bring peace. I see the possibility of an accord or peace between the Palestinians and Israel in the near future. They are both wrong.

President Trump will order the release of information that has been classified for decades. With his big mouth, he loves to tell you everything. If he doesn't tell you he blurts it out. He is going to release information that has been kept secret to a point. This man is not a dumb man. He is not a stupid man. He may act dumb but he is not.

The conviction of George Papadopoulos was a set up by the FBI intended to assist in the destruction of the Trump presidency. Everything is against Mr. Trump and he is following rules, his rules. He is receiving assistance from extraterrestrials and from angels. He is not only receiving assistance. He is being told what to do. He is being told what to do as Abraham Lincoln was told what to do. Then you could say that he is not as smart as he thinks he is but he is getting good assistance. He is able to do. He is not a politician. He is an actor following his role.

There was no collusion between Donald Trump and the government of Ukraine to get information regarding Joe Biden in exchange for help from our country but Joe Biden was guilty of helping his son Hunter of getting underserved money from Ukraine and China.

Donald Trump will not be impeached. They can't figure a thing he did wrong. They don't talk about what he did right. He didn't do anything wrong. You don't like Donald Trump but he will be a winner. He will end up a winner. You might not like the way he smells but it is only when he opens his mouth

Angels protect people by projecting thoughts into their heads, what we call telepathy. Donald Trump is not as intelligent as he comes across but he receives a lot of information from angels and extraterrestrials. When he follows that advice he will come up with the right answer. He is a buffoon but he will continue to follow the advice that is projected into his thoughts. He is determined. He will be reelected.

Your president that exists at this time will be able to stop the war that is programming. Remember that he is a liar. He is charming. He is an actor. He will be able to be successful. Donald trump will stop the war from occurring. Do not worry. You will not be affected by a war. Remember he is an actor and he does a good job. If he follows his script, in other words the thoughts that are projected into his head, he can become powerful; but as a personality he is somewhat lacking.

Donald Trump will complete his second term as our president. His second term will in some ways be more successful than his first term. In the end Trump will go down in history as a hero. As negligent and ignorant as he may appear, he is not stupid. He loves women.

Donald Trump will be elected to a second term and the ridiculous attempts to impeach him will continue throughout his second term as they did throughout his first term. Shame on them.

In regard to the presence of UFO's on Earth, President Trump will acknowledge it but in a sly shaking manner. It won't be completely understood but it is kept quiet.

President Trump is truthful in what he says about his telephone conversation with the president of Ukraine. Trump is honest in what he tells the public but not completely honest. In other words, he does not always tell the whole story.

After President Trump's reelection, there will be further attempts to impeach him but of course it is done by the wrong people and they will not be successful. At this time after his reelection Mike Pence will continue to be the vice-president for a short time but it could change. It is not yet finalized.

President Trump is sincere when he says he wants peace but he wants peace his way.

5. Forces influencing our politics

There is always voter fraud. You should go back to counting of the ballots. Much voter fraud could be eliminated if more people were to use paper ballots instead of the use of the computer. George Soros owns much of the software that is used to tabulate computer voting. He is fooling around with those results. More than that, he is trying to control the outcome of elections by creating voter fraud. That is true. The company that makes computers is involved. Everyone has some pull. When it comes to money, it is like having bullets. Your cash is stronger than bullets.

Your government is not becoming increasingly corrupt. It has always been corrupt and it always will be corrupt.

Other countries are covertly influencing American politics at this time. Everyone is busy. One of those countries is Russia. Americans are very confused and not together. They are split. They should join each other.

Extraterrestrials are influencing American politics. Different extraterrestrials are influencing one party and other groups are influencing the other party. Your politics arena is a contest between different extraterrestrials groups.

There was some voter fraud in the 2016 presidential election, but not much. It was under control. It was particularly more prevalent in California than elsewhere. When I said some time ago that the Republicans would win but the Democrats would squeeze in I meant that they do not let go. The person that won was supposed to win. That meant that in California there were more votes for Republicans but because of voter fraud it showed that there were more votes for Democrats.

President Obama was not knowledgeable about a spy being placed in the Trump campaign. There was a spy, or whatever you want to call it, placed in the Trump campaign to get the dirt on Trump. But there is no dirt on Trump. He shows you his dirt.

Many of the large corporations in your country have negative intents regarding the direction or future of your country.

The promoting of political correctness is an attempt to stifle free speech to the point that people can be controlled.

There are factions in your government that have amassed a great deal of information about thousands of people in your country, information that they will use as a form of blackmail to keep them in line.

I have said that history repeats itself in cycles of a specific number of years. The Biblical time of Ahab and Jezebel is being replayed now with Bill and Hillary Clinton. Bill is the reincarnation of Ahab and Hillary the reincarnation of Jezebel. Jaylu the warrior in the Bible came in to fight Jezebel. The role of Jaylu is now played by President Trump. There is no connection between Jaylu and President Trump.

6. Political, social and economic unrest

It is sometimes true that the current social unrest and humans disregard for other humans is related to the effect of planetary alignments but the current unrest is not related to the approaching of the planet Niburu.

The origin of your current political unrest dates back to the time of Atlantis or even before that time. The agenda of the Republican Party is influenced more by the Alliance and the Democrats are influenced more by the Cabal. (Q)

There will be increasing civil unrest in your country. Many lives will be lost because of the unrest. It is occurring at this moment. Civil unrest will become so bad that martial law will have to be imposed in some parts of the country. That will be just as bad as it was during the time of your Civil War. That is my opinion. Many people will be killed. They should not be here anyway. It will be their time to go. If they are killed, they were supposed to go. It is mostly between black and white.

In the near future there will definitely be an economic collapse in the U.S. similar to the economic setback that occurred in 2008. It is coming to that. It is always good to have money handy. Make sure you have money handy because your banks won't let you take any out. You should keep as much cash as possible on hand. You should not cash in your stocks. You will be able to ride out this economic collapse. It will be less than seven years, shorter than the last economic collapse.

If you wanted to invest your money in a safe and advantageous way, I recommend your buying silver coins and then not keep them in bank safe deposit boxes but instead kept safely in y our homes. It is a very good idea. Buying silver coins is better than investing your money in a bank. The value of silver will go up and make it profitable.

What you call the Alliance or the Elohim is supporting the use of bitcoins in a way. They are supporting bitcoms such as what is now being used in Africa. That is a positive thing. It can replace the use of world currencies.

As some people say, the physical activities such as earthquakes that are happening in California right now come from the thinking of the people in that state. There is a connection between the level of consciousness of the people and the level of destruction. It is a way of pushing the wheel. Yes, the wheel is being pushed.

The rise of anti-Semitism in this country and the world has risen dramatically especially when you have congresswomen that make nasty remarks about the Jews and Israel and are really not rebuffed by other politicians if the same things were said about other minorities. The future of this sudden rise of anti-Semitism is that you always need someone to hate. You never point guns at yourselves. You always point them at someone else that doesn't look good to you.

You're living in another civil war based on race relations in your country it. It is and it isn't the same kind of civil war. It is right now. Now you are living through it. There will be great fires in cities such as Chicago and New York. There will be as much devastation as there was in our great Civil War. If you have gone to Baltimore, that will tell you about the destruction of the big cities. That will spread. Do something about it and stop it right now. Race is ridiculous. Everyone is the same. People only wear different colors. People are the same. They have blood. Any blood given to you is good.

There will be several indications of mass shootings in your country but not in Orlando or Atlanta.

It is ridiculous that a million people are planning to force their entry into Area 51 in Nevada in September. Some people will try to get in. It is only a news item. Fake news. It is an item that will sell.

The United States is not involved in a recession at this moment but in the future there might be a problem. It depends on the makeup of your next election, which means that Mr. Trump will be elected again.

The so-called trade war with China will be reconciled before the next election. It will be no problem. Remember that your president is an actor and he will solve problems that cannot be solved.

In the 2020 election, it is not decided yet which party will gain control of the House of Representatives.

In the election of 2020 the Republicans will not take back the House of Representatives from the Democrats. Nancy Pelosi will continue to be the speaker of the House of Representatives if she doesn't die of a heart attack first. She bites off too much. [The previous entry was channeled in a session prior to the latter entry.]

People who are now elected officials in your government who have committed crimes will be found out and punished, mainly those in the deep state.

Joe Biden will be found guilty of quid pro quo but it won't really make any difference. He is not of mental health.

In his leadership role in the process of impeachment of President Trump, Adam Schiff knows he is manipulating. There is nothing whatsoever to impeach President Trump about.

The Democrat nominee for president will be both a man and a woman. It will be one of the current top contenders, not someone relatively new on the scene.

The goal of the Deep State is not just socialism but communism also.

The Democrat National Committee computer was hacked by someone within the Democrat party who went to their computer and transferred the information to a memory card.

The stock market will drop more and then it will rise high. It will drop more but then hold on because you are going up. Gold will go high. It is better to buy silver rather than gold at this point. It is less expensive.

The Coronavirus was created by an individual. The creation was sort of both intentional and accidental. It was not intentional but then it was developed to be intentional. It was not an experiment that went wrong. The experiment went right. It was a success. I cannot answer who created it. The virus will continue to spread for some time. It is controlled and holds fear. It is a controlled virus. By that I mean that it could be stopped if the powers to be so choose. Millions of people will die because of it. It will not end soon. It will end up closing schools and banks in Florida. Get the money out of the bank. A vaccination already exists.

7. The USA in the near future

This country is going to get more than two political parties. A new party is just at your threshold waiting to be discovered. There will be a third party because one of the two parties will break up and split into split into two.

There will be changes or modifications made to the second amendment of the U.S. Constitution regarding guns. New laws will be passed regarding the use of guns but the answer is not correct. The answer is improper. They should not have. There will be many guns that are not legal but there will be better control. The control on guns will be more.

The outcome of all the immigrants on our border will not be successful at first but it will be at the end. The end is what counts. There will be many deaths and bloodsheds mainly because of the ignorance and stupidity of some of the people; some of the immigrants and some of the Americans.

There will not be a widespread electrical blackout in your country but blackouts are occurring. Another country will get into your computer system that controls your electricity. I do not see war coming to your country but that could be considered a form of warfare but it is not dangerous and not controlling.

The new Supreme Court will forbid abortions but abortions will continue. They will not be legal but will continue to be performed illegally. There will be different attitudes toward abortions in different states.

The debts that our government has incurred will be lowered by reductions in Medicare and Social Security in the future. You will all be taken care of.

At this time the Republicans and the Democrats will not arrive at an agreement for a health insurance bill. What you call Obama Care will continue for a time. There will eventually be a new health care bill. All will be taken care of. A great deal more people will be suffering because of the lack of health insurance than are suffering now. Many people will be going without health insurance for a time. It will be short lived.

In the next few years it will be resolved for people in America to get affordable health care for preexisting conditions. It will be helped and Americans will be able to get health care. The preexisting situation will occur for all. It will benefit for all.

In the near future there will not be trials in our country in which thousands of government officials and workers and elected officials will be sentenced to prison. That will not occur. There will not be many people sent to prison. It looks like there is a temptation to, but it is not going to happen. They will not tear down your presidency.

Michelle Obama could seek to run for a political office, for presidency but remember, dear people, remember her past. Before she came into the limelight she went to that church and how much she spoke against the disaster of America. She and her husband talked about that church and the disaster of America. The Democrats would like a woman that is not of her past. A woman is most likely to be desirable for the Democrat nominee to run against Donald Trump and really negative like Elizabeth Warren.

There will be a recession or a depression in the near future. It will not be because of your Republican Party. It will be because of the other party that is making issues look bad. The recession will be as great as the recession that began in the year 2008. To prepare for the recession you could invest in silver right now but don't forget about gold.

A serious recession will occur after the Democrats take control within the next twenty years or so. You should buy silver to prepare for it, either silver that you can actually keep in your possession or silver that you purchase on the stock market.

In the 2020 election, it is ridiculous for Hillary Clinton to be nominated as a candidate. She should be jailed.

Alexandria Ocasio-Cortez and the three other women that you call the Squad in the U.S. House of Representatives will not continue to have influence in the Democrat Party. The Green New Deal is not of interest but it will not fade away. It will become more dominant.

8. Other countries now and in the near future

The people in North Korea do not want to die. They do not want death. They are rooting for their mates in South Korea to be with them. I see the North Koreans using an atom bomb but not on you; not on another country but in the ocean. They do not want war because they don't want to die and they know that this nut who is ruling your country, who is a very kind man, has different problems. The North Koreans are bluffing as much as your president is bluffing. They are both bluffing. They are both enjoying the stage. You will all live through the current president's term of presidency. You will survive it. Nothing is going to happen to the leadership in North Korea. They just blow wind. Your president has really scared the hell out of them. They are going to mess up and not go near America. Your leadership is a bulldog and he will be strong.

Relations between the United States and North Korea will improve. They can open the door and talk verbally. All the threats that were made will be dissolved. There will be no war or banging on doors. North Korea will never detonate a nuclear bomb on another country. It will backfire on them.

North Korea and South Korea will be reunited. I see that occurring within the lifetime of those here. I see North Korea and South Korea being united within the next twenty years and they will become one country. North Korea will become friends with your country.

The leader in North Korea has a mishap in his brain. He is a young man who is really in love with himself. He will last as a leader and he will not be that successful. But Mr. Trump feels he will become friends. He is very good at manipulating. He can manipulate anybody to be his friend or his enemy. He will manipulate the North Korean leader. He has every intent to do so.

Prince Charles will become the king of England, but for a very short time; just a moment or so. He is a weakling. I see his son, Prince William, absolutely being a good king. Eventually he will be king for a long period of time.

There is no concern about Saudi Arabia running out of oil. This is not going to occur. They do not tell. They are not honest. You do not trust them. OPEC will continue to exist but there will be another name. Much more oil will be discovered in your country but it is not needed. The United States and Israel are energy independent now.

The economic situation in Venezuela will get worse before it gets better. Due to the current political unrest in Venezuela, Russia will try to get involved in trying to dominate that country but will not succeed. Venezuela is not going to be invaded. There will be peace coming like that of the United States which wishes to build a wall around their freedom. Venezuela should have done the same. Nicolas Maduro will be in power as much as he can be. Madura in Venezuela will stay in power longer than appreciated. He will not win.

The Russians are now planning an expedition to the moon and they will tell you that there are extraterrestrials on the moon waiting there. Extraterrestrials are among you now, even in your audience. The Russians will expose them to the world. They will have no need any more to disguise themselves. They will expose who they are. They won't frighten the hell out of you.

Russian president Putin is not a secret ally of the United States. Russia has used chemical weapons on people of other countries at times and haven't you? Teresa May, the British prime minister, was justified in expelling Russian diplomats recently for that reason. A lot of countries are justly retaliating against Russia.

There is a cold war between the United States and Russia. Not a war but a cold war. Russia and the United States will be more closely aligned in the near future. They will be friends and they will exchange architecture. Mr. Putin is not completely aware of the Illuminati.

China is making a lot of inroads into Africa and they are taking over some of those countries.

Politically whichever way America goes, liberal or conservative, other countries in the world will follow.

Iran is experimenting with manipulating people's DNA so that those people will work against the enemies of Iran. They are so used to being sneaky but that is their way of life. At the time that President Obama gave more than one billion dollars to Iran he was working with them.

Individuals who have political views similar to those of President Trump will be coming into leadership positions in other countries throughout the world in the near future. They think like him and unthink like him. They are just as confused as here but he makes the right choices.

The islands that the Chinese are building in the sea do not have anything to do with star gates but there are UFO bases in the China Sea. The Chinese are doing much more than your government in regard to the exploration of space. They are way ahead of the United States. Their involvement with space exploration will help the Chinese inherit the earth. Extraterrestrials will help the Chinese. They are at this moment. (N)

China is building islands in the water to extinguish America. They are getting ready like Japan did on the American troops. The Chinese are getting ready to do same. Similar conduct, this is true. You will increase your knowledge of water. The sea and under the sea we will have troops which we already have. It is not above the land. It is below the land that we must be mindful of.

China secretly owns a lot of natural land resources in the United States like New York and oil fields and things like that.

Iran is being directed or assisted by the lizard headed extraterrestrials called the Draco. Iran has a problem. Iran opens its mouth and its mouth will be closed by Israel. No matter what, Israel will not give in. The extraterrestrials called the Draco are for you dangerous but they are influencing Iran. (N)

The huge wildfires in Siberia are just another way of scaring about global warming. Going back in time to the beginning of man, you did not have guns but you had fire.

Iran was directly responsible for the recent attacks on the oil fields in Saudi Arabia.

9. Miscellaneous

In the year 1139 an Irish priest, Saint Malachy Morgain, had a vision about the Catholic popes. He said there would be 112 more popes and said things about those popes. Pope Francis is the 112th pope. The vision of Saint Malachy was correct in a way when he said that the 112th pope would signal the end of the power of the Vatican. The Catholic position is getting less in control but is very powerful. Pope Francis will be the last pope but the Catholic Church will continue for some time. The downfall of the Catholic Church is already in progress, but it will continue in a different way. The Catholic Church will continue to be good and continue to have control. It is control even without the Pope.

The ancient prophecies are correct when they say that Pope Francis will be the last pope. You are in the middle of the last pope. The Vatican has connections with extraterrestrials. It is partially true that the Jesuits wear headdresses to cover their elongated sculls because they are extraterrestrials.

By moving so far to the left and by exhibiting such hatred for President Trump and everything that he is trying to accomplish, the Democrat party is dissolving itself. It will dissolve within a couple of years. There will be another party coming through that will be much stronger. They are fearful. They know what is happening and they're trying to make best. They are thinking of this idiot who is running the country. He is not such an idiot. It will not be anything like the progressive Bull Moose Party that Theodore Roosevelt tried to establish. It will not be a progressive party. It will be a more centrist party like the original Democrats, a much kinder; a much more stable party is coming through.

Your government and the governments of other countries are building huge or numerous underground cities.

People are being kidnapped for the purpose of having their organs harvested. That is for profit, not research. It has always been true. It is not new.

The massive amount of plastic garbage that is disposed of in your oceans is having a negative effect on humans as well as on animal life.

The United States will see proof of UFO's soon.

The crash of the Bowing 737 airplane in Ethiopia with several United Nations officials aboard was not an intentional crash that was controlled remotely. It was simply a mechanical problem, not a human error.

T. THE WORLD OF THE FUTURE

1. Planet Changes

A major earth shift will occur within the next century. The areas least affected will be all the places not near water. As Edgar Cayce said, I still see the Virginia Beach area as safe. I foresee a major Earth shift in the next thousand years, such as when Atlantis virtually disappeared, but not in your lifetime.

Global warming is a threat as many politicians say but it is a natural occurrence. There is little that humans can do to prevent it but they can help to delay it a little. When you talk about global warming or weather changes you are going to have colder weather. You are coming into a disastrous weather issue as far as weather is concerned. There will be more terminal nasty weather for people on your planet, meaning Florida, New York and the globe. The answer to global warming will be solved within the foreseeable future in a different direction from where you are going now. There will always be arguments when people don't agree. Although global warming is a natural thing that is going to occur no matter what, you can slow it down. Reducing what you call the carbon footprint can retard or slow down.

In regard to global warming, sea levels will rise to the point that many east coast cities of the United States will be inundated with water. One of the areas of the world that will be most seriously affected by the rising levels of the seas and oceans is Florida. But there will be others. Japan will be affected. It's a good idea to buy land in South Florida because you will be here. Although it is true that the water will rise, I do not have dates about the water rising. It will not be in your lifetime but it looks like the rising of the water is eminent in Florida. Water from the rising seas will intrude into your community in the next century. Florida will be underwater but not at the turn of the century, not in your lifetime. The effects of the rising sea levels will not be within the lifetimes of anyone in this room. It will be later.

The forthcoming solar flash that has been predicted is not the actual basis for the extreme concern about global warming expressed by some people. You can worry about global warming and do nothing about it. It will occur anyway. By watching your actions, humans can help delay or mitigate global warming. It is something that is going to happen yet you can delay it.

The most powerful volcanoes on Earth today are in the United States but those volcanoes will never cause a major effect on the development of humanity.

In the future when Earth experiences severe cataclysms and changes, a sizeable portion of the people will be rescued and placed aboard UFO's. You can assume that it will be many centuries from now but that is not true. It will be sooner than that. It will not be in the lifetime of anyone in this room now.

I agree with Steven Hawking when he said that you have only about another hundred years on this planet and you will need to find somewhere else to go. You will go on to different planets. A few of you will remain.

A huge emission of methane from thawing Arctic permafrost beneath the East Siberian Sea is a possible threat to mankind, not in the near future but it is controlled.

The ice covering Antarctica will begin to melt in a couple of thousand years.

Photographs of the sun show that there has been a reduction in the number of sunspots. The last time that occurred was in the 1600's when there was a mini ice age. There is a possibility that you are going into a phase that might offset some of the global warming. The sun is facing another direction at this moment but it won't be forever.

The earth is likely to be struck by an asteroid or some manner of extraterrestrial body in the near future but it won't have any affect.

You will not see the rise of Atlantis during next few years.

An increasing number of members of the United States congress say that they believe that life on Earth will end in twelve years if we do not take drastic steps to control our climate. The belief is accurate but the words, the matter, are not accurate.

2. Warfare and terrorism

China will dominate the world within the next century. The people of China are smart and intelligent. They continue to build and will someday inherit the earth. They are currently working with extraterrestrials regarding their plan to overtake America. There will be economic warfare with the United States. The Chinese will win. They will dominate the world within the next century. I cannot answer if it will be in your lifetimes. Other countries in the world will be involved in this, including ISIS which will fail. Russia and China will be on the same side. The European countries are confused. The African countries will join in on America's side. I do not have an answer for South America. The conflict between the United States and China will not lead to a third world war but Isis will lead to a third world war.

It is true that you will be going to war with China but that will not be a physical war, more economic control. At this moment there are other countries that you are in disagreement with but there will not be any action such as you perceive as war. There will indeed be nuclear war between other countries. There will be mismanagement of opinions. Iran is insignificantly not knowledgeable regarding the detonation of an atomic bomb. Regarding atomic weapons, the country that you have most to fear from is yourselves. North Korea is very limited.

There will be many wars between man and woman on this earth. People fight all the time. There are mean people among us. Future wars may not involve uniforms. World War II taught people lessons. The wars to come will be different.

There is peace in Israel but there is also war and that is religion. So as long as you have your religions you will continue to have war.

World War III will not be a world war and it will not be immediate. It will not be as other wars that you have presented. It will not be a world war as you perceive a world war. It will not be a war as other wars. You have a world war right now on your streets. The enemy does not wear a uniform. You have a war among yourselves right now. It could be your neighbor. There is a world war right now. You are fighting that war now. It is not a war like a war in the past. In the past the wars wore uniforms. The uniforms are not worn today. There is a war now, even your racial war which is nonsense, absolutely nonsense. People are fighting each other for no reason. That is why we call it ignorance.

There are countries or groups of people who are definitely making plans to use atomic bombs. You have most to fear from North Korea. Iran will attempt to use atomic warfare but they are very slow and very ignorant people, you know. They are not a people of stature. Russia will not consider using atomic warfare. China would use atomic warfare. They will inherit the Earth. They are the brightest culture of all. The United States will use the atomic bomb again. That will be in the lifetime of some here today. That depends on how long they are going to stay. It is not in the near future but much further off.

There will not be a bomb dropped on the United States within the next five tears. They do not wish to alarm you about a bomb dropping. They are saying no, not in your educated mind. You are at war at this moment but you won't have to worry about nuclear war. You won't be here anyway.

The radical Muslim movement is making a good point of its generation and more radicals will prove with time. It will still be here in twenty years and it will progress to be more of a threat. This will not come to an end soon. It was always there. It is a very serious situation with Syria. Eventually there will be an end to the threat. Fifty years from now there will be more peace on Earth after more destruction. (I)

There is an alarming number of mass shooting these days, some of which are terrorists and some domestics. It will only get more. It will only be bigger.

There is no country outside of America that will be safer during the time when terrorism strikes. At this moment there is no such thing as safe. It is not safe when you get up in the morning. It is not safe when you go to sleep in the evening. There is not such a thing as any complete safety. What is predicted is predicted.

There will be a devastating war in your country, caused by the invasion of other countries, in which more than a million people die. It is arising now. Now is the time to stop this evil force. ISIS is a crisis.

With all the confrontations you are having with North Korea, Russia and China is there is eventually going to be some kind of military action. It will take time for this to be in progress. It is a meeting of the mind.

Iran will not team up with North Korea for a nuclear ballistic-type missile. They will never hit the United States or another country with any kind of missile. They will try to hit another country with a missile but it will not and has not been successful. They are aiming towards Japan but actually the U.S. is their objective. They want to hit from behind and sneak up on the United States which they will not be successful. They will go for Seoul South Korea but it will not be of any success. So you need not worry for your own being.

There will not be a war between the U.S. and North Korea. There will be a war between North Korea and other countries such as Japan and Russia. Their stupidity will show itself. They will make an error. They will make a very big error. Do not fear about North Korea. They are a little country with a little brain. Rocket Man is a loser and your government is a winner. So it is this wonderful man that is full of stupidity that you have elected to be in judgment who is fooling Rocket Man, the Korean who doesn't have a functioning brain in his body. But China will win. It is the Chinese that will inherit the earth.

It seems that every couple of days somebody takes a gun and shoots a lot of people. Some of these tend to be the result of religious convictions and others don't. This is not going to cease and lighten up. It will progress and even more so. So look forward to confusion. Confusion is the reason for it.

In your future extraterrestrials will prevent some countries from using nuclear weapons for warfare. They will get directly involved to stop some countries from using nuclear warfare. I do not see a nuclear war coming in the future. Extraterrestrials will prevent humans from ever using nuclear weapons. They will not allow it. It is coming close, really close to be discovered. There is a nuclear war now but there won't be the end of time. It is not considered the end of time that does not exist. Fear not. It is not the end of time. [This seems to contradict previous statements.]

About thirty years ago China and Russia almost went to war with each other. They will not be adversaries again. They will be together.

Iran will use nuclear weapons on Israel but they will not be successful. They are too backwards. At this moment it is not foreseen that Iran will be on friendly terms with the United States

I do not see any war with China. I do see Russia and the United States combining. I see part of Russia becoming part of the United States.

Guantanamo Bay prison in Cuba will be used to house numerous people who will be charged with treason in military tribunals. The answer is not yet shown to me whether that will occur during the Trump presidency or after the Trump presidency.

The United States will not go to direct warfare with Iran. Iran will in part continue to conduct proxy warfare through Hezbollah and Hamas. They will attempt to take over the government of Iraq. There is sort of a revolution against the Islamic regime in Iran taking place right now. The regime will continue to exist. It will not be dissolved.

No other country will ever use nuclear weapons on Israel and Israel will never use nuclear weapons on another country.

3. America and international relations

Of all the present major world countries the most stable currency for the remainder of this century will be the U.S. dollar. There's nothing like the U.S. buck. Is that not true? The Amero or something similar will be an accepted currency in the United States within the next two generations. The dollar, the piece of paper will disappear. They have already proceeded and will continue to do so.

Speakers of Spanish will someday comprise more than one-third of the population of the United States especially in your region [South Florida]. Your country will have an official language and that will be no language. In other words, you will be able to read thoughts. That will not really be a long time off.

The European Union will exist at least for several more generations but will be broken up in different ways. The Euro will not decline in value. It will increase.

America will remain a dominant force in the world for a long period of time in the future, at least until the end of this century until China takes over. China and Russia will be a strong force. Not in your lifetime.

In regard to the international political situation, America will be very strong and very opinionated and will succeed. America will be successful. It will be difficult but it's what's in the end that counts.

There is a cold war between the United States and Russia but it won't be any worse than it has been. There isn't any war coming in. Russia and the United States will eventually become allies and no longer be considered enemies. That will be in the lifetime of some of the people in this group. The younger people will be able to see Russia and the United States being comfortable friends. China will straighten them out.

The United States will not continue to exist as a country for several more centuries. It will not be dissolved. It will be created to a bigger flourish. A new country will begin. You will add more territories to your country. The United States is going to be the new Atlantis in many different ways. It will be more powerful and controlling. The physical Atlantis is now the continent of Antarctica. That continent and the physical features that remain from the time of Atlantis will indeed submerge from the ice. In a way, the people in America will take on the qualities of the ancient Atlanteans.

Some states in your country will make efforts to secede from the

United States as several did states when Lincoln was president. There will be many, many, many changes. Each state will have its different rules. States be successful in attempting to withdraw from the union and will consider themselves to be another country. That will come but not in your lifetime. States will be divided. There will be another war within the states. As they're showing now, the war has begun and it is very slowing coming within states. The confusion is, as you can see now with your president, the difference within the states. The states will not be attached. They will be divided. New Mexico will be one of those states that will withdraw from the union. Florida will take the same route as New Mexico. Florida has already separated in different ways. Florida is starting to separate from California. States will separate and show anger as with your politicians. The confusion will rise and be more. The guns are not the problem. It is the people handling the guns that are the problem. The drugs are not the problem. It is the people eating the pill.

California will eventually split up to become more than one state in the far future. It is aiming in that direction as you can well tell by the voting of people. The United States is now breaking up as a country. Parts of this country will not become a totally different country.

[Since this statement appears to contradict previous statements, perhaps both are correct but the question of timing must be considered.]

Wiki leaks will expose many Americans who are supporting the work of the Deep State.

4. Society and religion

There will not come a time when there will be peace throughout the world and wars will be a thing of the past. Man was put upon Earth to outdo each other. When I was on Earth I was fighting to survive but I was better than you, stronger than you, more intelligent than you. I look back and think about what you call "what a dummy". There will always be confrontations, always confrontations from the beginning of mankind.

At some point in the future women will become the dominant gender. Your wife will. Women will take more leadership roles in different areas of the world. Do not fear if it will be in the relative near or distant future. (K)

The time will come when there will be large numbers of designer babies created; that is, selected DNA from more than two parents or even a community of parents. That is available at this moment. I see them. That will increase in numbers. That happens on other planets also.

Human society will never get past the point where the one with the most money rules and makes the rules and oppresses those that have less money. It has always existed. Money is a god.

Although some people believe that human nature is the reason that socialism as a form of government will never endure, it will continue to exist in the physical realm.

The time will come when Christians, Jews and Moslems will coexist peacefully without confrontations or warfare but in your lifetime you will still have wars. Religion causes wars. Religion is very good for those who are not knowledgeable. It is a safety guard. It is very strong for those that are not knowledgeable. They take advantage of religion. There will be religion after many, many, many failures and many deaths. Religion will no longer exist centuries from now. It will slowly dissolve and it is coming about showing you now very slightly how it is dissolving. The big churches that you perceive will become less and less. Fighting over religion is ridiculous. It does not matter what you believe. It's all one. (I)

Racial discrimination in your country will continue to exist for a long time in the future. It has always existed. You always need war, something to fight over. Racial integration such as in Brazil will not occur in your country. Peace will not occur. It is ridiculous but it will continue not only over race but religion also and thoughts and opinions. Racial discrimination is by ignorant people. It will continue for everyone who is alive on Earth today. Racial discrimination is decreasing but will continue. There will always be havoc. When you don't have someone that is like you, you wonder what is wrong with them, not what is wrong with you. Don't look for them but look at yourself first.

In the near future I see major changes taking place in the churches of many religions, not just the Catholic. In a way the Cabal exerts influence over your churches. The churches are being controlled by forces that are not necessarily beneficial to humans. They are not necessary because there is too much negativity. I see the churches going in a more positive direction. They will become more meaningful. (I)

There will be Marshall Law in your country to combat civil unrest in certain parts of the country, not the entire country. There seems to be a problem with discrimination. That still exists. It is amazing to me because you are all black. Even though some are white, you are all black.

The human race was originally black and in Africa. Because of where you went that had an influence on the development of the races. In a part, Mr. Trump will be considering it. At this moment he is thinking of it. He is in control and sometimes the issues are not correct but he will come to the right conclusion on how to deal with it. His attitude is in the right direction. His mouth is in a different direction. He is getting words from the Russians. The Russians are communicating with him and so is China right now. He is a very intelligent man even though he is stupid.

If a civilian (a non-military or non-government person) is charged with treason, there will be some trials by military tribunals. I see courtrooms and judges. I see judges taking over. It is much easier to move on things by military tribunal rather than going through the slow process of civil court.

The world is going to be more orderly and united in the future. You are going in the direction of the one world order that is propounded by the Illuminati.

People in your government will be accused of treason. There will be all kinds of issues before that but no one will actually be charged. I think the Clintons have enough money and security to bow out.

The third Jewish temple will be built in Jerusalem replacing the second temple that was destroyed in the year 70 A.D. It has to be. President Trump will not play an instrumental role in this. It is further down the road.

There will be more and more biracial couples. The world will be biracial. The black race will inherit. Remember that in the beginning everyone was black and then you separated and went to different parts of the earth. Some came out orange. Some came out yellow. Some came out pink. In regard to whether biracial couples will have problems, it is people that don't like people who will have problems, not the biracial couples. That will be the climate of the world. Everyone, even now, is biracial. You are all black.

5. Science and technology

The genetic manipulation of human DNA to create a more advanced human being by your scientists will become a reality in the near future. It is already in progress definitely and they are experimenting and this also will come to light in a very short time. The danger in what they will create is another person. It is not being developed for negativity. It is being developed to be used in a harmless way but everything harmless turns out with some negativity. (K)

Humans will be able to travel to the home planet of the extraterrestrials that helped build the pyramids. It is coming shortly. They will travel the same way they arrived. I am not able to give the information about how humans will travel but with your mind you can do so much. So many of you have bright minds and you don't use your minds. We have so much to offer and so much to give. So we come therefore to give more help. Open up your minds and you will get there. (N)

Physical humans will be able to time travel. Time is manmade.

Scientists will rediscover the means of counteracting gravity. That has already been put to use but it is not publicized. That technology was from extraterrestrials. Earth people got some of it from crashed spaceships.

The Doomsday Vault in Norway which stores the seeds of various varieties of vegetation will never be used in the event of an Earth catastrophe. It will be successful for humans to have this but it is not needed.

Humans will discover and take advantage of more abundant sources of energy than they now have. There are many energies coming to them. Their lifestyle will be very different. You will not see this in your lifetime but you will come back and see.

Automobiles without wheels will run on your streets and highways in this century. Airplanes will have another engine. It is necessary for your airplanes and helicopters to have another engine for safety reasons. They have ground vehicles with and without wheels on other planets. The wheel is an invention on all planets.

Within the lifetime of those alive today, the United States government will require microchips to be implanted in the skin of all newborn babies. Like animals, people will be micro chipped. That will be for control and identification. The birth certificate will no longer be needed. Instead there will be microchips. This is an action indeed influenced a little bit by the Illuminati, one world control. All will be chipped. You don't have to worry about that.

In your future, mechanical robots will increasingly take over the functions of many activities that are now performed by humans to the point that human life will be very different from what it now is. That could be in the future of those who are alive today and it is already successful.

The time will come when artificial humans will be virtually identical to biological humans but that will not be while you are around. It will be in the future. It will be robots almost indistinguishable from humans. Women won't need men and likewise men won't need women. The time will never ever come when human-like robots will be self-reproducing.

The internet will continue to exist for many years to come. It will change radically from what it is now in your lifetime. Your government will be taking increasing control over the internet. The internet access will not be free. There will be different charges that will take place like your telephone bill. It will cost less money than it does now just like telephone bills are less than they used to be. There will be more mind reading, messages. There will be telepathy and that will be in your lifetime. It is already occurring with the new generation that is coming through.

Free energy is slowly coming into existence but will not be accepted easily. As you Earthlings know, you are not quick in your learning experience.

Humans will be implanted with devices under their skin that will directly connect them with the internet. They are doing that now. Your government is keeping that secret from you.

6. Miscellaneous

There are major forces at work in many countries to create a one world government. There will be a one world government in time but not in your time. In another era there will be a one world government. It takes much time, centuries from now.

The time will come in the not too distant future when you humans will have visual physical contact with extraterrestrials that are very recognizably different from you physically. The neighbor next to you is questionable if you wish. That will be in the lifetime of people already here. There are people in your world who have already seen these extraterrestrials.

As Edgar Cayce has stated, there is a chamber under one of the paws of the sphinx called the Hall of Records that contains a full account of the pre-history of mankind. The contents of that chamber will be exposed to mankind. I see that occurring within the lifetime of some of those alive today.

Truth is the only important word. The truth is the only word that is important. The truth is your answer to everything. And many of us do not follow the truth. Is that not true? It will regain the respect that it deserves. That will come in the future.

There was a connection between the 1917 Spanish flu pandemic in which 50,000,000 people died and the event at Fatima, Portugal in which three young girls were visited by an entity they called the Virgin Mary. There is a connection now that is coming through with you state of Texas that people have passed through. Disease will come from this and death and be careful of touching and kissing. You must be very careful of disease. Anyone who dies as a result of what happens in Texas was meant to die at that particular time. There is nothing they could have done to prevent their death. It was their time.

There will be a time when the thirteen crystal skulls that are located throughout the world will be brought together and tremendous changes will occur because of that. There is something very powerful about those skulls and when they are all brought together, something will occur to be helpful in elevating the level of humanity. It will grow and you will learn to respect each other and not murder any more.

Predictions of future events sometimes do not occur as predicted when unpredicted events occur before the time of the predicted future event. It is because there is no such thing as time and you insist on putting time in your interpretations of predictions.

The Kurds in Iraq will eventually get a country of their own and the Kurds in Turkey will join them. It will not occur in the near future.

There will be a New World Order dictatorship but not in the lifetimes of those alive today.

The prophecies of Mark Taylor regarding the future of our country are worthy of your consideration.

UFO's that can hold as many passengers as your largest airplanes will come to your planet. At the time of great upheavals on Earth, UFO's will come to Earth to transport large numbers of people from Earth to elsewhere in order to save them from the catastrophes occurring on Earth. That will not be in your lifetime. It will be in five hundred years.

In regard to the U.S. Federal Reserve Bank which is currently privatized, there will be problems with U.S. currency. I think they are beginning to arise. If you take money out of the bank and put it elsewhere, it will make it worse. In that regard, I still see the dollar being replaced by the Amero or something like it. The Amero will be used in countries other than the United States, like Mexico and Canada. The paper dollar bill will dissipate itself and be replaced by what they call the Amero.

The time will come that money is no longer needed because you will be able to materialize all of your needs, but it will be time away, not when you are available. For some people this is so anyway. It is that way on other planets. They don't need a monetary exchange. They just create things with their minds. The intent of the Cabal in ancient Sumer was to establish a monetary system so that society could be controlled by the people in power.

Guantanamo prison in Cuba will be used to house hundreds of those in your government who have been convicted of treason or other crimes against or government. That is why Trump is keeping Guantanamo open. My dear friend Trump is trying to do the best he can do. He is mishandling his tongue. His tongue tells you one way but the enemy is the other way. Mr. Trump is aware of the evil. He is very intuitive.

I do not see what you would call a collapse in the real estate market as there was several years ago. It will continue to play that real estate is important but people are not investing in real estate. At this particular time real estate is not working. It will turn better but it will take time. Money is an issue. At this time real estate is at a plateau. It is not real estate that is moving but apartments. Condos would be a much better investment at this time.

Within your lifetimes, the banks of our country will put negative interest rates on your savings. Are they not now charging you for them to save money for yourself? The better route to take is to not put your money in banks. As gold was the first investment silver will be the next. It will be more valuable than gold is now. Silver is used in so many components of your technology that there is going to be such a demand for silver that it is absolutely good to invest in silver now.

As has been prophesized, in the very near future more than twenty different extraterrestrial species will be simultaneously introduced to you. Your government is keeping it a secret because they don't want to frighten you.

The New York Times will gradually shift toward supporting the Alliance. It will shift away from the Deep State and more toward the Alliance.

Within your lifetimes, will there be a relatively peaceful transition to a new financial system making your current system irrelevant but not at this particular time. Economic capitalism in your country will continue to exist in the future in favor of socialism.

The Palestinians will have a country of their own but territory wise it will be a very small area. That country will eventually become a member of the United Nations. It will be a little more than twenty years from now.

You will see a woman president but not immediately.

Greenland will never become a possession of the United States. That is completely ridiculous, complete nonsense.

The United States Treasury is not going to replace the Federal Reserve. Nothing will replace the Feds.

The small particles of plastic that have been found in the fish around Antarctica will not be a problem for people. It is no bigger than it was before.

Although all humans started out in the black race, in the far future I the human races end up to be only one race. The black race will not be the dominate race. It will be a combination of all the races.

U. HEALTH, HEALING AND PROTECTION

1. Healing devises and external aids

Any object whatsoever that a person believes to have healing qualities will be effective in healing. If you believe so, no matter how nonsensical it may be, it is true if you choose to believe. The following healing devices can be effective if one believes in them: the Grounding Pad, the Body Shaper, the E-Power machine, and the Aura Ring.

Irving Pheterson's invention, the Body Charger, will provide the healing benefits that he claims. It is worth using if the mind wishes to use it. It will work for other things, not for what you wish.

Scalar energy is an effective healing modality that has to be looked into. No question that it should not be avoided. To some degree the Aura Ring is. Scalar energy is effective for healing.

The wearing of a battery powered wrist watch can be of healing benefit in some cases. The same true of magnets. Sometimes 'tis true they will bring anything to the victim. It depends on the magnet.

When you believe in it, the E-power healing machine will be an effective healing modality at times. If you don't believe in it, it won't be effective.

There is no truth to the theory that, because of modern technology, humans are being excessively bombarded with positive ions and this is having a negative effect on their health. Devices that are imbued with negative ions are not of benefit to your health. Such devices are not of importance.

The wearing of gold can be of benefit to the health of the human physical body. Although you have heard that if a man wears a fourteen carat gold ring on the ring finger of the left hand he will be more susceptible to lung problems, there is no truth in that. It's ridiculous.

Much of what is said about various kinds of crystals being able to aid humans or to bring healing is correct. When one's soul wishes it to be of assistance, when one believes that this will be, it will be. When you hold a religious article, or what you call religious, it will be. It is very easy to be. When one wishes, what is true will be true. When you believe in good, it will be good. When you believe in bad, it will be bad, or not good.

The use of castor oil packs for health reasons as described by Edgar

Cayce will be effective if you believe in them. They will not if you don't believe in them. If you don't take it, it won't be effective.

It is therapeutic for people to be in the ocean water. It is relaxing and you will find that you Earth beings will be more aware of the ocean. There is more to come of the ocean. The ocean will be something that humans will be relating to; no longer a mystery as it has been in the past.

Using a laser beam on water or food before it is consumed can be more beneficial to a person's health than if the laser beam had not been used. The same is true of using a laser beam on the meridian lines of the body to promote healing. You can say that the instrument that Jeff Starkman presented to you is of value to you.

In the 1930's Wilhelm Reich invented the Orgone Box. That device could actually have some healing effect on the person inside of it if they believed it. Whatever you believe will be.

The use of the royal scepter used by kings is related to the ancient Egyptian use of the staff that was said to be able to restore human life.

The Quantron Resonance System is an effective healing modality, indeed, very valuable.

Sitting in a salt room will help improve some health problems. The salt room that you visit is a place that will help many people. It will be very successful and even for animals.

Acupuncture will absolutely help macular degeneration.

2. Foods

At times genetically engineered vegetables such as corn are harmful to your health. It will improve in the future because they will use less germicide.

Eating meat is a reflection of lower level consciousness. You can definitely raise your level of consciousness by avoiding red meat. Eating red meat is not beneficial to your health. The time is coming slowly that the great majority of humans will no longer eat the flesh of animals. Eating fish is better for you than meat. It is healthier for you. Seaweed is a food that would be beneficial to add to your daily diet as long as it is not moving.

For those of you who continue to eat meat, it is better for your health to eat the meat of animals that have been fed organically grown food. If you insist on continuing to eat red meat, the meat from buffalo is less harmful to your bodies than the meat from cattle. When I said that eating red meat was not good for your health, I was referring to the meat of all four-legged animals, not just cattle. I have said that it reduces your level of spirituality by eating meat. Fish and fowl are preferable to eating the meat of four-legged animals.

Eating organically grown fruits and vegetables is significantly better for your health than eating most of the fruits and vegetables that are sold in supermarkets. For years and centuries before, we Earth ones were eating fruits and vegetables and survived. So now we give it a new name, organically grown. Now you use a lot of chemicals and fertilizers to make them grow better. You would do better to eat fruits and vegetables that haven't been treated by chemicals. It is better to eat food that has been grown near where you live rather than to eat food that comes from far away if you are referring to fresh food.

There is a danger in drinking filtered water because doing so will leach out essential minerals and trace elements from your body. Drinking filtered water is not really a good thing. It is silly. It is ridiculous. Although many people believe that drinking bottled spring water is better for your health than drinking the water that is piped into your homes that is not correct. Water is water. You don't have to buy any water. It is ridiculous that bottled water is more healthful than city water, Coral Springs for example.

It is possible for humans to exist on a type of green algae for nutrition, but not solely. There are grasses that will help you.

For many people, drinking a glass of wine each day would be beneficial to their health. I would advise a glass of wine and a glass of water also.

For food intake, all is good except for the amount of being excessive. Sugar is not good for your teeth.

In regard to whether raw plant based foods can help cure cancer and other diseases more effectively than cooked plant based foods, It depends on the individual. I would not suggest a diet of mainly raw plant foods for most people. It is not always good to eat raw mushrooms that are poison. At least cook the poison out.

Regarding whether drinking alkaline water is good for your health, it depends upon who is drinking it. It will help some bodies to be less acidic.

For the past several decades, wheat has been used as a weapon by the Cabal. It has been genetically modified to affect the thyroid gland so that people become less productive and more easily controlled. That is why you (Charles Zecher) become very sleepy after eating wheat. Other foods have also been modified for similar purposes. It could it be of your benefit to eat organically grown foods.

3. Herbs, drugs and supplements

Vitamin B12 is one that would be good for the improvement of your memory. It is a little bit of nonsense that simply inhaling the fumes from vitamin B12 is much more effective that vitamin B-12 pills. B-12 must be injected. Medications are not my advice to you. Be careful of medications. Vitamins are medications.

Health supplements such as turmeric, green tea and aloe are healthful to the body. So is water, just plain water. It is very needed for the body to be good.

Herbs found on Earth and other natural remedies absolutely exist for curing all human diseases.

Ionized air can be of benefit to your health. It depends on who is asking for it. For some people, yes and for other people, no.

I have said that it is not good to stand in front of a microwave oven while in use but I also would say that eating food or drinking a liquid that has been heated in a microwave oven can also be detrimental to your health. You should avoid heating things in a microwave oven if possible. Don't stand in front while you press the buttons so you don't get the electricity. Standing three feet away is not far enough away. Three feet away is dangerous,

There is absolutely a great deal of truth to what you have seen on television about hemp oil or marijuana helping with cancer. It is real true but the government does control and that is why you selected your government control.

There can be very limited use of marijuana for people who have illnesses where you wouldn't be smoking enough to do any damage to your lungs. One doesn't have to smoke. It is only a plant and all medication comes from plants. There are different parts of marijuana that are good for some illnesses. The use of marijuana can take a person to a higher level of thinking or to a lower level. Even a controlled or limited use of marijuana can be detrimental to a person's health as smoking cigarettes is. If you smoke marijuana it will have the same effect on your lungs and arteries as cigarettes but then there are stages that marijuana is helpful.

261

Mind expanding plants like magic mushrooms, peyote, San Pedro, Iiboga etc. are useful for expanding the level awareness of humans. You can actually increase your level of consciousness with all your drugs; like other plants, like your marijuana and different plants. The use of mind-altering drugs can enhance a person's creativity or mental abilities by connecting the person with a higher level form of intelligence for a moment. It is for the moment. The use of mind altering drugs can make a person temporarily creative. Both drugs that come from natural plants and chemical pills are medications. You can expand your consciousness with synthetic substances, not just the plant based.

The ingestion of DMT (Dimethyltryptamine) can cause meaningless hallucinations and it can also help in making connections with higher intelligence beings. There are certain groups that use it in Africa. Some of you think marijuana does the same. Sometimes it can take you to meaningful connections with higher intelligence and sometimes it is meaningless hallucinations.

There are certain types of coffee that you should avoid and there are some that are okay. You can drink coffee that was not triggered with some liquid. The coffee that stimulates the growth is very healthy for you because it stimulates the veins. Starbucks coffee contains nicotine. That is why people need their fix in the morning. Be careful not to overdose. I would have a little drink now and then. The nicotine is fine to open up different arteries and is necessary to open up the arteries. Sometimes it is made positive. It is a drug that is positive. Forget about decaffeinated coffee. No decaf.

If a person uses a lot of artificial sugar in his diet, there could be an increased likelihood that the person will develop cancer. It depends on the health of the person whether much artificial sugar will lead to cancer. Sugar substitutes such as Sweet & Lo are not harmful to your health if you don't overdo it. Nothing is harmful if not in abundance. In some conditions artificial sugar is not helpful. If a person has bad teeth, it is not going to make the teeth any better. If a person has bad teeth, it is preferable to use artificial sugar.

A pill called Prevagen which is widely advertised as being helpful to aid a person's memory is effective in some cases, but detrimental in others. It depends upon on where it is performed. I would suggest to you [Charles] that it is a good thing to try. It would not be detrimental to you if you were to take it, but not to extreme.

In some cases the fluoride that has been added to your drinking water is harmful to your health but in most cases it is not. I may answer you that the plastic is more harmful to you people. The plastic does more deterioration to your foods.

The cannabis industry will grow quickly over the next several years.

Scientists have invented a pill that will erase bad memories especially those memories related to post traumatic stress disorders. That information is correct. It has existed for several years. It is very much effective but not effective for everyone but on most people.

4. Protection

A person can endow any object to serve as an effective good luck charm or an object of protection if they believe in it. If you think that something is a lucky charm for you, it can become so. It can actually be effective if you feel that way. I think you are limiting your potential if you do not believe in good luck charms. The only good luck charm is you. You make your way.

Physical objects such as a statue of St. Jude placed on the dashboard of your car or a mezuzah placed at the doorway of your home or amulets are not imbued with special powers, such as for protection or healing. It is only for comfort to those who believe. (D)

Water can dissolve negativity that is potentially harmful to humans. Water is water. It is not holy. It is no more effective if it has been blessed by a priest than if from out of the faucet. Water is water from the ocean, from the sea. It can keep fire away. It can extinguish fire. It can extinguish hotheadedness, heat. It can cool off and experience no longer having heat. Placing a glass of water on your nightstand will help keep negative energy away at night. Do not use if for nurturing yourself. It will keep evil spirits away as they are fearful of water

Making the sign of the cross with your hand in front of your chest as done by the Catholics does not actually bring assistance or protection to the individual doing so but it does give them peace of mind.

You can we protect yourselves from negative energies. Don't think negative. Don' let it enter your mind. Change your negative to a positive.

5. Visualization and channeling energy

When you visualize surrounding someone with white light 'tis true that can be of actual benefit to that person. White light can be beneficial to most.

A person can send healing energy to another person merely by his thoughts.

If you are weak and cannot resist the flow of negative energy, it is possible to take on someone else's disease or problem when you are channeling healing energy to them.

Healing energy can be passed on from one person to another when one person touches another person but the healing energy that is transferred will be decreased if more than one person at the same time touches the person who needs healing. It will be an energy that has decreased. I recommend that only one person at a time touch the person that needs healing.

If a person visualizes that he is physically exercising, rather than actually performing physical exercises, that could have a positive effect on the physical body. Does not your wife do that? However, Charles will have to do more than that. He will have to move his ass. It is not easy. He will have to work.

Humans can definitely remove physical pain from their body by treating the pain as if it were a conscious entity and telling the pain to go away just as Sondra does.

6. Diseases: diagnoses, causes and cures

There are known cures for cancer but your government is creating a cover-up. Your physicians do have a cure. There are many cures for cancer. That cure will become public in your lifetime. It is already public. In different aspects cancer is controlled. They are here among you. There are many kinds of cancer and there is a cure.

There has been research where they are curing cancer with viruses like measles and cold viruses. In a way, these therapies are going to become cures.

Epidemics or plagues that have affected humans have been caused by microbes on meteorites and asteroids that have hit the earth. Some were deliberately sent by extraterrestrial entities to the population.

Some diseases afflicting humans in today's world were caused by extraterrestrials. They meant no harm. It was not intentional. It was experimental. Those diseases are neurological in nature. (N)

Physical ailments are frequently the result of emotional disorders. Many of them are, such as a headache.

People sometimes make the choice at the soul level to have a particular disease or physical problem so that they can advance more rapidly in their spiritual evolution. If you wish, at the subconscious level, a long painful death, such as from cancer, can help resolve karmic debts. (G)

The cause of the 2014 Ebola virus outbreak was a natural occurrence, not manmade. No more fear than a cold in your atmosphere. It was not something that was intentionally started.

The sound of a person's voice when he speaks will indicate specific health problems he might have. That technology is available to you now if you wish for physicians to take knowledge.

You can stop yourselves from having fatal illnesses by understanding that something is wrong in your life and by changing it. You can do it but mainly, attitudes are very important. We can say that the material written by Louise Hay can pertain to your question.

The Zika mosquito can be used in some manner for the improvement of a person's health, such as stopping the growth of cancer. It will be found to be able to halt any more growth of tumors. The injections will be made and they will be made to be a positive use. It's not all negative, you know. I see that they can make use of it after science and the doctors find out. The Zika virus has not been caused by the use of chemicals on agriculture. The mosquitoes have often good to offer. It will be put down as something we will be grateful for when used properly. The children infected with the Zika virus will have something injected into their system to offer for a chemical for different viruses affecting other people.

What appears as defects, such as blindness or deformed body, has been intentionally created by those conscious entities responsible for the construction, growth and maintenance of your physical bodies rather than such conditions occurring just by random chance. There is no such thing as random chance. It is a learning ability. If a person is born with some kind of defect whatsoever that was intentionally done in the creation of that person's physical form.

A cleansing of the body or elimination of toxins will help cure sleep apnea. Throat exercises are also an approach to cure obstructive sleep apnea. Having any suggestions of the body being influenced by medications, getting rid of different medications, indeed it would help to a degree. The mind isn't so busy where you are constantly just going and moving like when on drugs that will cause such an illness. Sleep apnea is caused by an overactive mind. Certain throat exercises will also help cure obstructive sleep apnea. It would actually make you feel better and safer and make you feel like you are accomplishing something. Throat exercises and eliminations of poisons in your system are both important to your system. Concentrate on what you are doing, one thing at a time not two, three or five things.

There is a complete breakthrough for Alzheimer's in existence but it is not recognizable. It was derived in another country but it can be used in your country. Alzheimer's can be detected through the investigation of your DNA. If you were to examine a person's DNA, that could be used to predict the onset or possible onset of Alzheimer's. There is currently a cure for Alzheimer's disease. It has already been announced.

It is possible that a person's DNA can be altered so the person will permanently be prevented from having specific diseases such as cancer, Alzheimer's, Parkinson's etc. It can be altered but it is not being altered at this time. There is no knowledge of them being able to do this before birth but they will do it after birth. Humans will do that on a regular basis, not just experimentally.

Stem cell implants are a healing modality that is worthy of continued injections and further research. Implants are very worthy when given the correct stem cells. They are experimenting with animal stem cells for humans. Rather than rabbits, pigs would be better. They are more like humans than other animals.

The paradigm of medicine as we know it today will shift drastically.

Schizophrenia related to the malfunctioning of the pineal gland. Schizophrenia, what you call the third eye, comes from the pineal gland not functioning properly. One of the symptoms of schizophrenia is that people often hear voices in their heads that others do not but you cannot assume that the cause of schizophrenia is the influence of negative non-physical entities.

HIV developed naturally and it was also an engineered virus. It was not done to reduce the earth's population but for different reasons.

The government has a cure for almost every human ailment and they are intentionally keeping it from the public.

Cancer can be cured by pumping more light into your DNA. Eating a few apricot pits a day can increase the light in your DNA, like walnuts would. It is ridiculous that drinking water that has been stored in a pyramid can do that also. There are many different elements of cancer and there are cures available at this time but they do not want to be known. There are common foods that you could eat that would help cure cancer.

There is a relationship between chicken pox and multiple sclerosis Chicken pox can make a person more susceptible to or lead to multiple sclerosis. Chicken pox is a very delicate question. It is prone to many other diseases that are not available. It is not good to have chicken pox or measles. It is dangerous to the human body.

There is a possibility that the current outbreak of measles could develop into a very serious health situation in our country. It could, but it won't. It will be under control. The government is very stingy in their information and will not allow anything that will be sensational. The outbreak of measles is designed like the gun is designed. It is designed to kill.

Humans are prone to certain physical problems because of extraterrestrial having tampered with their DNA. Many extraterrestrial groups have spliced their DNA with human DNA.

There is most definitely a connection between autism and vaccines given to children.

7. Miscellaneous

The cause of different blood types is the cause of different people. What caused you to be a male or your wife to be a female? She (Sondra) chose to be a female and she chose her blood type. Some blood types are negative and some positive. It is just a spin of the wheel and it does not matter. An individual's blood type can indicate which kinds of food are best suited to that individual as described in the book *Eat Right 4 your Type.* The information in the book is administered to you by a dentist who gave you the information that he found out. There is some correct information to a degree in that book. The food mentioned for your blood type would help you to a degree. All that is written is not 100% correct. There is some basic core of correct.

There are times that organ transplants and blood transfusions can affect the recipient in more ways other than just on the physical body.

This can occur on the emotional and mental levels at times. When the recipients are sensitive, they can pick up the memories of the donor since memories are stored in the cells of the body.

Sleeping with your body aligned with the polarity of the earth, that is your head facing north as some people believe, will be of health benefit to the body if that is what your mind thinks.

The intentional provocation of an out-of-body experience could be detrimental to an individual's physical health if they do not protect themselves.

I have said that the length of a person's life is predetermined but not cast in stone, but being of service to others will help prolong a person's lifetime. So all of you get out there and help other people. You will live longer if you help others. You will be happier.

When an amputee feels pain where there was once a leg, that person can feel pain in the leg that is no longer there. This is because the leg is always there in what some call the etheric body and has never gone away. The etheric body remains even when the physical leg is gone. Pain is located in the etheric body, not just in the physical body.

There is sometimes a danger if a person is cremated too soon after dying because there is a possibility that the etheric body may not have fully separated from the physical body, thus causing the entity to feel pain. You must wait two or three days before being cremated. When a person is cremated, the soul evolves no differently than if the person were buried in the ground. If you are cremated it will absolutely not hurt the soul. (A)

To a degree living near high tension electrical lines or a radio transmitting tower can affect a person's health. It can also claim more energy from a person's psychic or medium abilities. They can deteriorate from such ability as well as experience more. It will also be determined that standing in front of a microwave will affect a person's health. 'Tis true to a point that you should not use the microwave oven so much.

The use of cell phones that so many of you carry can interfere with your sensitivity. It is not good for you to have as much electromagnetic radiation radio waves going through or bodies all the time. Cell phones can indeed affect your health.

Saying "I want to stay well." is much stronger than saying "I don't want to get sick." In other words, I am saying that when you pray or when you think or visualize something, you should think in the positive, not the negative. The positive is heard. The negative is not heard. The negative brings a judgment cost among you people. The positive brings the happiness.

Sondra's illness (multiple sclerosis) has happened to her for others to see so she can help others. The illness that she has is to help others.

Although it appears that there is an increase in the incidence of neurological diseases, it is not an increase but you are just becoming more aware of it. It is more recognizable.

When people are born deaf or blind or in some way deformed, the reason for that condition is not necessarily something they have chosen at the spirit level. It could be the result of karma or something that was chosen for their own advancement. It is very similar with animals. (G)

People are now living to be in their nineties or over a hundred. The cause for that has been a change in diet and a change in living. There is a change in mind control. People will live to be a hundred and fifty. That will be the new young look. A hundred and fifty will be the new age for those that are a hundred.

Humans will be able to survive if a pig's heart is transplanted into them. It has been achieved so far. Many pigs are very much like animals that are on Earth. You don't necessarily need a human heart donor. It is possible to transplant a pig's heart into a human.

When a person is what we might say "out of their mind" and, for example, screaming that there are hundreds of bugs crawling all over their body when that is obviously not true for those with that are with him, it is preferable to tell the person that there are no bugs and is it not better to go along with the hallucination. Honesty, the truth, will always be there. The truth is very important. Even though it may welcome a fight or argument between the two, it is better to tell the truth rather than to try to be nice and go along with them.

People do not subconsciously choose to acquire physical ailments for the purpose of helping them change their habits. They do so, to change their wisdom, not habits, but their wisdom. Sometimes you choose at higher level to have ailments to advance. It is wisdom that is being learned. You inherit a lot of your personality traits from your ancestors.

Memories are also sometimes passed on in the genes in your body. Memories are also sometimes passed on from when you were in the animal stage of development before you incarnated as humans. You have memories from when you were animals. You have both. Some of you have not changed yet and still act as animals and look the same.

The Chinese meridian lines on the body that show the body's parts have been accurate for thousands of years and they have been helpful in many, many ways. You don't have to use only acupuncture needles but pressure points also help.

Physical health problems are not the result of mistakes made by those conscious entities which are responsible for the construction, growth and maintenance of our physical bodies. They are not mistakes. What you see as mistakes is intentional. They are learning points.

In a way, it is true that children who grow up playing in dirt and with animals and who are not overly protected from germs develop a stronger immune system than children who grow up in a more sterile and protected environment. It is correct except for those who are not protected. It depends on the immune system of the child. Sometimes a child can be overly protected.

Several years ago there was a report of a terminally ill nun who survived for eleven years without eating anything. Instead of eating, her body was covered with olive oil every day. There is no truth in that report. That is fake news.

There will be medical breakthroughs this year and next. They are pending now. In that regard I have already told you more than two years ago that the Zika mosquito would be used to cure cancer and now you have read in the news recently where they are finding that would be true in the kind of cancer that John McCain had. It will release ammunition from the brain and then it will go on to be used not only for the brain but for the mobility. There will be more uses for the Zika mosquito. It goes to the brain immediately and that is the connection to the mobility of mankind. It is the connection of the nerve cells in the brain.

Living in a home that has Wi-Fi might be detrimental to your health, such as causing headaches, perspiration or physical pain but most of the time people will do that. I am not aware that using a cell phone can do that.

The original use of the appendix in the human body was to take nutrition from the liver and reintroduce it into the small intestines. The functioning of the appendix was deactivated through manipulation of the DNA by extraterrestrials because if it weren't deactivated, humans could live to be nine hundred years old. Within time, it will be reactivated.

I have said that male circumcision originated not for health or cleanliness reasons but rather to show that the man belonged to a specific tribe. However, there is more to it than just that. Extraterrestrials do not have foreskins. The original reason was that the Earth people involved wanted to show that they were the descendants of extraterrestrials rather than the original inhabitants of Earth.

Biological science will reach to point that will enable humans to re grow a limb that has been lost. Science will reach a point that it will teach an organ to regenerate itself.

As some doctors now say, with every birth there is a twin that vanishes in the womb and is absorbed into the mother's system. The twin that vanishes has a soul. It can remain in the spirit world or it can reincarnate while the surviving twin is alive. A condition known as situs inversus, in which all of a person's internal organs are reversed, is related to the vanishing twin syndrome.

Although at the present time modern medicine appears to have no interest in curing diseases because they are more interested in making money, in the future I that will be a thing of the past.

V. ANIMALS, INSECTS AND NON-HUMAN CREATURES

1. Evolution of animals

Extraterrestrials have influenced the development of mankind and they also have had an influence on the creation or the development of insects and animals on Earth. (N)

At times animals have soul groups, much the same as humans do. They feel as we do and at times karma plays a role in their world. (H)

Whales and dolphins do not have a higher level connection with humans than that of others animals. They can reincarnate as humans. The level of consciousness of dolphins and whales is closer to that of humans than the level of consciousness of other animals.

Animals can incarnate in a variety of species before evolving into a human. Some do but some can be just one species and then evolve into the human kingdom.

Insects in their evolutionary journey can eventually evolve into angels. They can also sometimes evolve into animals or birds. Birds and flying insects can evolve into angels As far as I know; they do not evolve into elementals.

Animals, including insects, fish and birds cannot exist that are not part of a soul. Each animal has a soul, even insects, even an ant. They do not have awareness and sense when they are going to be stepped on. All forms of physical manifestations are part of a soul, any kind of soul.

Animals are very intuitive, much more intuitive than humans are.

2. Animals and reincarnation

All species of animals can incarnate directly into the human kingdom. There is no chain of evolution among the animals. There are some animals that will become humans on their passing, such animals as cats, dogs; closer to humans. All animals will evolve to the human state. It will be eventually in time.

Certain kinds of animals are not more likely to reincarnate as humans than other kinds but domestic animals are more likely to reincarnate as humans. They have bonded with their human masters are more likely to reincarnate as a human than are wild animals. Are they not more like humans? You have a cat that is like a human. You have a dog that is like a human. They understand the human race. When a person has a pet they are very attached to and the pet almost acts as if it were partly human, that animal is likely to reincarnate as a human.

Humans first incarnate as animals before incarnating as a human but it is not possible for a human to reincarnate as an animal. It is not completely true that there is no going backwards. Some humans never outgrow being an animal. They can be human but act like an animal. Many of you are pigs, snakes or elephants. Animals reincarnate differently from humans. A cat won't always reincarnate as a cat but a human will always reincarnate as a human.

If an animal died in a fire, it is likely that the entity might have fear of fire when it incarnates as a human. That is very possible and likely such as one drowning. It can transfer from the animal to the human if it was a fear.

Animals reincarnate the same as humans and can live in parallel lives; that is live many lives simultaneously.

When animals are about to cross over to the spirit world, they are aware of that. They know when it is going to rain before it rains. They are much more sensitive than humans. When I was a human, I was not as sensitive as my animals were. Animals are very psychic and know ahead of time when things are going to happen. Some come back as humans.

There are times that domestic animals are predetermined to be with their owners. Some owners are like parents. They are not easy. Sometimes animals do not wish to be like your children. Some children we bring up are not easy and are enemies. Sometimes we bring up enemies and we call them children.

When a species of animals becomes extinct on Earth, that does not affect the evolution of those animals. That soul will reincarnate in a different species. When animals reincarnate, they don't always reincarnate in the same species.

Animals have karma. It is the same type of karma that people have, not like a group-type of karma. (H)

Animals have spirits. Animals are like people. After many incarnations at some point they will become humans.

Animals can reincarnate more rapidly than humans. They can come back as soon as they arrive. If a close pet dies, there is a possibility that the pet will reincarnate to return to the same owner in the same lifetime or to a similar ownership in order to fulfill their karma.

3. Human and spirit connection with animals

Animal totems that are said to hover over each person's head are a reality. They are part of a composition a build-up of strength to help the individual gain strength. (D)

It is a human decision whether or not mankind should endeavor to protect endangered animal species whose endangerment is not caused by mankind. Why not keep all the bugs alive? They will come and sting you. It really doesn't matter whether we try to keep them alive. What purpose does it do? What is the purpose to keep alive all the humans that have passed away?

The time is coming slowly that the great majority of humans will no longer eat the flesh of animals. Eating fish is better for you than meat. It is healthier for you. Seaweed is a food that would be beneficial to add to your daily diet as long as it is not moving. (T)

Animals are sensitive to the thoughts and emotions of people. They are very sensitive and can smell you a mile away

Sometimes it is true that apes are the errant genetic descendants of humans rather than the reverse.

You can help your cat who is getting older as far as her health goes. Talk to your cat and tell the cat how much you love her and how much you care. She will hear you and she will understand you. Cats know far more than you do.

Humans or spirits can have memories or emotions that developed from the time when they were incarnated as animals before they became humans perhaps such as certain fears.

When an entity reincarnates from the animal kingdom to the human kingdom, the species of the animal can have an effect on the personality of the new human but will have very little effect on the physical aspects.

Spirits can communicate with animals in the physical world as well as with animals in the spirit realm. They can Influence animals too. (B)

Animals in the spirit realm can show themselves to humans much the same as do the spirits. Your dog that is now in my realm could show herself to you as do the spirits in my realm. Your dog Lady has appeared quite a few times.

Since entities in the spirit world can create what they want with their mind, it is possible to create one of the person's animal pets who were on this plateau when they were here.

4. Non-human creatures

Creatures are part human and part animal. They act in animalistic ways. They are what Cayce referred to as the "things". They came into existence as through part development, not through genetic manipulation. It was development. They are among you right now. The grotesque beings, part subhuman and part animal with weird appendages that Edgar Cayce described actually existed and they still exist. The strange creatures that have been reported seen throughout the centuries are not the offspring of a human and an extraterrestrial.

Mermaids never existed. There never were beings that had the upper part of a woman and the lower part of a fish. There is no basis for the legends about vampires.

There are creatures in the sea that are larger than the largest mammals, indeed larger than any land mammal or any whale or octopus. The underwater beings that you refer to as Telchines actually exist. You will all be going underwater.

A monster or creature of some kind exists in the waters of Lake Champlain It could be the size of people, too. Not humongous. That creature is related to the Loch Ness monster but the monster has passed on. The Loch Ness monster has died but at one time there was a Loch Ness monster.

Creatures of extraterrestrial origin exist on Earth today. The huge human-like footprints found in the Himalayas were made by one of the creatures that we call Bigfoot or Sasquatch that are seen throughout the world. They were created by extraterrestrials. They have a brain. They have some of the abilities that humans have and also some abilities that humans don't have. They are mystical beings. They have been around for ages and they continue to propagate.

Large monsters that you consider mysterious live in the sea today.

5. Miscellaneous

Note: Information on animals of the past was included in Section R: *The World Before Biblical Times*

Animals have intuition as well as instinct.

Animals can be possessed by evil spirits and they can be earthbound and not cross over. (C)

There is what you might call "mystical" connection to the scarab beetles portrayed in ancient Egyptian beliefs or drawings. They are a happening of the past. They were extraterrestrials, what I would refer to as reincarnation. The ancient Egyptians drew them and revered these beetles.

There is factual historical significance to the American Indian mythologies which often portray beings that are part ants and part humans. Such beings did exist and they still exist on Earth. (N)

Extraterrestrials were the cause of the numerous mutilizations of animals across America in recent years in which certain organs had been surgically removed. It happened for experimental reasons for research. (N)

Memories in animals can be passed on through the genes from one generation to the next. The same is true of some humans but not all. Theoretically, you could have memories of your ancestors. That is what makes confusion.

Animals have free will and when love is expressed by the human the animal will respond with love. [Speaking to the woman who asked the question]You should not feel guilt about the animals that you just had put down. Your animals are happy to be free and relieved. So do not feel despair because you have done them a favor so they can go on.

Although dragons play a prominent role in Chinese drawings they do not exist. What the Chinese depicted in their ancient drawings as dragons were actually spaceships. There were no animals involved as dragons but that is how the Chinese interpreted what they saw in the sky.

Earth humans are not the only humanoid species in the universe whose physical bodies were created or modified by extraterrestrials. There are humanoid beings and animals on other planets whose physical bodies were modified. There are animals that are more human that are so much not to be taken for granted, like your dogs who know the weather. They know the future.

W. GOVERNMENT COVER-UPS, CONSPIRACIES AND SECRET SOCIETIES

1. Secret societies and covert influences

It is true that there are secret societies composed of human beings that control much of the activities on the earth. There is much power with money, both benign and malevolent. Your country is run by mostly by certain behind the scene powers. It really does not matter who is elected president.

The Illuminati are a group of people that want to control and take over. They don't want to let go. They leave and come back again. We don't care for them particularly. They are back again. I don't know if the individuals are conscious of being part of the Illuminati. The Illuminati absolutely have control or a strong influence on the popular music industry. Many of the current popular music stars, including the popular singer Lady Gaga, are instruments of the Illuminati. The same is true of movie and TV stars. The media are very much controlled by the Illuminati. They all get together and make your simple laws. You have something to fear from the Illuminati. You should ignore them or oppose them. Be strong and know what is better for you, each one of you individually. As many people believe, George Soros is involved with the Illuminati. We all are in different ways. The Illuminati are succeeding in taking control of our society as they been in the past

There are major forces at work in many countries to create a one world government. There will be a one world government in time but not in your time. In another era there will be a one world government. It takes much time, centuries from now. (T)

The Freemasons had a significant impact on the founding of your country. The source of the Freemasons' information was extraterrestrial. The Society of Freemasons exists with the idea of creating a one world order. Everyone likes control. I cannot answer about their purpose but I would say "absolutely". We all like control. (R)

There is a secret private organization for space exploration that is not connected with the government of any country. It is all secret. Everything is secret. Your country is a secret. This organization will be successful. They will attempt to control.

The Priory of Sion is both a hoax and has truth in it. It manages to promote the marriage of Jesus to Mary Magdalene and their descendents to prove a secret bloodline of the Merovingian dynasty on the thrones of France and the rest of Europe. It is proving that the kings of France are the descendants of Jesus.

I have informed you that there is an organization in Bohemian Grove California that is composed of select individuals who are those who decide who the next president will be but that Donald Trump was not selected by them. I said that he was selected by the people instead. The Bohemian Grove is an arm of the Illuminati. They are against him. This group is an extension of Skull and Bones of Yale University.

Some of the pirates who plundered gold from many ships several centuries ago were members of the Knights Templar. The gold that was plundered was used to fund activities of the Knights Templar. The Illuminati come very much into it and it was a negative situation there.

It correct to say that the Luciferians are what you call the Cabal and that the Elohim are what you call the Alliance. The conflict between the two is manifested in your current political conflict. There is some truth about extraterrestrials promoted by the Cabal in many of the current science fiction movies produced in Hollywood. The Cabal is currently regrouping and rebuilding and moving troops from your country to South America.

Planned Parenthood is indeed a manipulation of your society by the Cabal. The aborted fetuses are not always discarded. They are used by certain groups in their ceremonies if you wish to call it that, but they will be used for perfection, meaning they use them for experimentation and research.

In a way, Lady Gaga will change direction and seek to expose the Illuminati and the harm they have done to her soul. It's like she sold her soul to the devil. She needed to be noticed. They promised her and they made her a star where she would not have got to the point where she is now if not for the Illuminati. I see the number four. I don't know if it's four years or four months. What you mean when you say selling your soul to the devil is allowing another entity or group to take over you.

The universities in your country are being used to promote the One World Order. They are trying so hard. This is also true in the public school systems throughout the country.

The Cabal is in charge of our secret space program. It is managed by the Rothschild family. It is controlled. The Rothschild family is one of the thirteen families that are controlling the behind the scene powers.

Queen Elizabeth plays a significant role in what you call the Illuminati, the Deep State or the Cabal. The thirteen families that compose the Illuminati are really the behind the scene controllers of world events. For that reason, the royalties of the various families tend to intermarry to keep the blood lines pure. They are gradually losing control if they are no longer intermarrying.

2. Our government and aliens

All paragraphs in this section, except the last two, have appeared in previous chapters

NASA is withholding some very significant information from you regarding the universe and extraterrestrial life. There is secret cooperation between your government and aliens. Your government has been spending much money each year for secret facilities and searching for extraterrestrial life. The amount is not for public airing. NASA has a secret space program in addition to their publicized program. You know that in America everything is a secret. They have secrets regarding the planet Mars. NASA is doing things on Mars that they are not telling anybody about. Your government is not without an odor. (N)

The reason for the intense secrecy surrounding Area 51 in the air force base in Nevada is that security is needed. Your government chooses that. They wish that it is a secret. They are hiding information about aliens, UFOs, equipment and things like that. They're hiding it without too much success, you know. (N)

Some people in this room will meet face-to-face with people that look like me, but not me, and actually see them. A lot of those beings are housed in Area 51 in Nevada beneath the ground now and in other places in the United States. They look totally different from humans and live mostly underground. They can change. Your government is aware of that. The government has shown it. They have presented it. (N)

The HAARP facility in Alaska to control weather is a potentially dangerous experiment to the earth and mankind. You cannot control anything that's going to happen regarding the weather. The danger will be when the people doing the experiment drown. There is no extraterrestrial involvement at this time. There will be a time that others will need help but at this time, no. Your government is using the HAARP facility in Alaska for nefarious purposes, such as mind control. There is secrecy about the HAARP facility that the government is not publicizing. (N)

Some of your technologies have been achieved through the analysis of equipment found on crashed UFO's. They have been there for years. What is so different? There is nothing different you know. The United States government is involved in programs of reverse engineering of alien spacecraft or other alien technology. They are examining things they found and then cover it. (N)

The formation of the numerous crop circles throughout the world has been caused by extraterrestrials who are attempting to communicate with the people on Earth. Mathematics is used as the basic form of communication because it is easier to use mathematics. (N)

Your government has direct communication with many different kinds of physical extraterrestrials from several different star systems. It will come to light in a very short time. They are being heard at this very moment. There are some currently on Earth. Some live underground mysteriously but not in the way that you present it. I see full disclosure of the alien presence coming soon. They have been there and they are there now.

Within the lifetime of those alive today, the United States government will formally proclaim the existence of extraterrestrials in your country. The government does not want you to know how crazy they are. Extraterrestrials that look different from humans will be seen by many people. There are extraterrestrials here now who look like humans and you cannot tell the difference. Some are among you here.

3. Government withholding information

The Amero or something similar will be an accepted currency. It will be an accepted currency in the United States within the next two generations. The dollar, the piece of paper will disappear. They have already proceeded and will continue to do so. (T)

There is a government cover-up regarding the destruction of the World Trade Center Towers. They do not want to cause fear. They had nothing to do with it. (R)

There are known cures for cancer but your government is creating a cover-up. Your physicians do have a cure. There are many cures for cancer.

They are here among you. There are many kinds of cancer and there is a cure. (S)

There was a conspiracy and a government cover-up regarding the death of Marilyn Monroe. The CIA was involved, if you want to call them that.

There wasn't a cover-up regarding Dorothy Kilgallen's death, not that much but because of her loud mouth. She died of an overdose as reported in the news. It was self-inflicted also. She was a drinker, you know. It was drinking and medications.

There is indeed a government cover-up regarding the *Blue Planet Project*. The information in its publication is not too accurate, but somewhat accurate. There is some truth behind every lie.

In 1949 did your Secretary of Defense Admiral Forrestal was murdered by the U.S. government because he had secret knowledge regarding Antarctica. He was disposed of because of his secret knowledge and he was not the only one. There were others too. Your government is wonderful. (R)

Many years ago, in the 1940's, Admiral Byrd discovered advanced underground civilizations with people living underground at both of the earth's poles. There was a cover-up by your government regarding his expedition to Antarctica after World War II. (R)

Many years ago, a man named G. E. Kincade found artifacts in the caves in the walls of the Grand Canyon and then the Smithsonian Museum removed them and denied their existence. They are fearful and do not understand and they fearful that others will not understand. Those artifacts were of ancient human origin, not extraterrestrial. They were leaving their customs behind, a writing of their history for later humans to discover and learn.

The information in the book *Majic Eyes Only* by Ryan Wood is informative but not accurate.

Although the media have reported in the past few years that scientists have recently discovered planets around other stars, in reality, they have known about the existence of extraterrestrial planets for many years. It is not a new phenomenon.

There is a media cover-up regarding the death of John Kennedy. He was assassinated because he was going to reveal information about the Illuminati. President Johnson was the one who was really involved with the assassination. The assassination was an event that was predestined.

Robert Kennedy was assassinated as a convenience, just to get him out of the way. (R)

The government has a cure for almost every human ailment and they are intentionally keeping it from the public. (U)

Of all the secret classified documents in your country, those regarding extraterrestrials are of the highest classification and the most important. That information will probably be coming to light in your lifetime.

4. Secret government activities and places

The spread of Lyme's disease was the result of experiments done with ticks by your government on Plum Island, N.Y. Much was spread in this special place on Long Island. Experiments taking place on Plum Island are dangerous for people. Other diseases have been created by your government experimenting. Most of your hospitals in New York are filled with cancer patients on your North Shore. The experiments are causing cancer. That is the reason why there has been so much cancer on Long Island. That was explained to your wife. At that time she was aware on the North Shore. (R)

There is a hidden city beneath the earth near Dulce, New Mexico in which thousands of extraterrestrials live under the cooperation and observation of the United States government. There has been a pact between you and the aliens. These extraterrestrials experiment on humans there. They share their technology with you. They keep up to their part of the agreement, sort of. In addition to the installation in Dulce New Mexico, there are others that house extraterrestrials. There are more secret underground military installations in the United States. The government installation in Roswell, New Mexico is still the home of aliens. (Laughing) I must see my family there. I am not able to share [the information regarding a secret government installation beneath the Denver airport.] (M)

There are a number of secret installations where extraterrestrials live in your country. The greatest or largest secret government installation for extraterrestrials is Area 51.

Some of NASA'S activities are kept secret from all elected government officials of the United States. NASA is doing covert activities that neither the president nor the senators nor anybody in the government that is elected knows because they don't want to frighten the public. They are also keeping them covert because they don't want other countries to know. They are doing more covert activities on the moon and on Mars than you could imagine.

The United States government regulates the price of gold, silver and diamonds.

You would be correct in fearing what the pharmaceutical companies are doing to mankind. They need the money and they are making the money. They want power and they have the power. They are misusing the power for humanity. Indeed, they are not fair to humanity to mislead them in the wrong direction and they know it. The pharmaceutical companies exert influence on politics. Indeed, more knowledge must be given. They are very controlling, your organizations.

Project Mercury of the National Security Administration actually records telephone conversations of a large majority of Americans. They are recording the conversations of some of the people in this room. Particularly there are special people in this room that are being recorded. They [those with the Guide] do not wish me to reveal [who are being recorded]. I would say that you should be more careful of what you say in your telephone conversations and your thoughts also. A wired phone in your home is not safer than a cell phone.

Your government has been able to erase certain memories from people, especially memories of secret government projects on which they have been working. Indeed, your government has the power to tamper with your memories. As in the movie *Manchurian Candidate* years ago, you will, in a way, be mind controlled by the government. Your government uses mind control to cause people to do nefarious acts. Many people do. If the government wants a crime committed, they can put thoughts into a person's head to perpetrate that act.

Your government is experimenting with modifying the DNA of humans in a manner similar to what the Anunnaki have done. They are secretly experimenting with changing the DNA of humans.

The United States absolutely does have military bases beneath the ice in Antarctica.

In the 1950's the CIA secretly injected LSD or some kind of drug which produced severe hallucinations and many deaths into the food supply in a town in France. (R)

In the project Stargate of the United States government, some people are successfully being trained to do remote viewing. Your government is recruiting and training people to do remote viewing. You have always done that. I have been to Russia many times, you know. The Russians are well known for doing remote viewing but you are doing it also.

Your government has a spy satellite that circles the moon in order to monitor the activities on the far side of the moon. Your government has many secrets. They don't think the people are intelligent enough to understand. The back side of the moon is teeming with people and has so many structures that it looks like Manhattan. The astronaut Buzz Aldrin was taken by a UFO to the far side of the moon where he saw many structures and much activity. It is true that he said "Holy shit" many times.

In 2001 Donald Rumsfeld said that more than two trillion dollars from the Department of Defense could not be accounted for. That money was secretly used for your involvement in space.

There are Americans now on several planets and moons in your galaxy and that have not been recognized. There is a lot that your government is keeping secret from you and your president is keeping it undercover also. He is aware but he was never told. He has much knowledge about that. That is why he established the space force. Watch what his actions are. Don't think about what he is thinking. His interest is in making America great again. He will do so even though he is not agreeable. There are Americans on several planets in your galaxy. That could be interpreted as outside your solar system also. You have already gone that far regarding your technological advancement.

In the 1980's the United States and the Soviet Union were secretly working on establishing a space program and extraterrestrial research. The United States is continuing research that you don't know about and they will continue to combine their research. Together they will achieve. They will join. Russia and the United States will continue to be friends. (R)

In your government and military there are as many as thirty-five levels of secrecy above that of the president. There are many secret activities taking place which are even kept secret from the president and other elected government officials. A secret is no longer a secret when you tell one person. There is much going on that even the president does not know. That involves a lot of space exploration. Some of those activities have to do with your exploration of space. Some of what I have told you in the past is actually mind boggling. You actually have bases on the moon and on Mars.

Both your navy and your air force operate UFO's. Some of the UFO's that you have seen are actually your government's UFO's. There is no less influence of the Cabal on the Navy than there is on the other branches of the armed sources as some people believe.

Your government intercepts applications for patents before they are sent to the U.S. Patent Office to prevent certain inventions from becoming a reality such as those for free energy or for cures for diseases. If you just continue reading your columns on Dick Tracey you will find out the rest.

Time travelling machines have been discovered periodically and then confiscated by your government. In the crash of the UFO in Roswell, New Mexico in 1947, they were able to reconstruct a time machine. Time travelling machines have been discovered here and there. The Nazis had a bell shaped one. It was time travelling that got me from my homeland to here.

The use of magnetism to create space travel at near the speed of light is secretly being used by your government. They are now. You will never find out all the things they are keeping from you. They are doing a good job of that [keeping things secret]. They don't realize how much you are able to handle.

Your government does not still store gold in the vaults at Fort Knox. The gold has been transferred. Heroin or dangerous drugs, instead of gold is stored in Fort Knox. The gold that was stored in Fort Knox has been transferred to various underground places in Southeast Asia. (R)

The CIA experimented with mind control in the Montauk Long Island Project in the 1970's to make people behave like zombies and they are still doing it. It was one of those secret projects of the government. At that time children were temporarily kidnapped for research in this project.

5. Miscellaneous

The assassination of President Lincoln was solely the work of John Wilkes Booth but there were other people involved. Booth held the gun himself. Vice-President Andrew Johnson was aware of what was going to happen. The assassination of Lincoln was a conspiracy and Andrew Johnson was in on the conspiracy. They were mentally disturbed people. It was a racial thing. It is interesting that Vice-President Andrew Johnson was involved with the assassination of President Lincoln and that, as I have told you, the person involved with the assassination of President Kennedy was Vice-President Lyndon Johnson. He disliked Mr. Kennedy and he was jealous of him. He himself wanted to be president. It was just a coincidence that both vice-presidents were named Johnson. There was no foreign country involved in the assassination of President Kennedy. President Johnson was involved in the assassination. He was also involved a little bit with the assassination of Robert Kennedy. A very sneaky man wasn't he? By a little bit I mean that he knew it was going to happen but he wasn't involved more than that. He made it happen. (R)

Recently it was announced that astronomers are getting a signal from a planet that is nine light years away from ours. That is the voices that I have been addressing you to. Scientists are now backpedaling on that because there is a government conspiracy to shut that up. It is control.

In regard to your space program, your government has not gone back to the moon because something was discovered on the moon that has caused your country fear to go back. The government hates to take you in that direction. Your government conceals much of its awareness.

Time and space travelers exist. There are many of them on Earth now. Some of the current members of your government are from your future. They are planted everywhere. Some of your leaders are actually from your future.

In addition to providing health care, Obama care was designed by behind the scene powers as a means to control society. The Illuminati are controlling the scene there. The belief is that if the government can control your health, they can control many facets of your life eventually, like even where you live or what kind of work you do. You are being manipulated. It is to your advantage to resist that manipulation. Manipulation is not a positive thing for you but it will be controlled.

Your government has the technology that could replace fossil fuels, such as gas, oil and coal, as well as nuclear power for creating energy that could be used for electricity. That knowledge was gained from reversed engineering from the crashed UFO in 1947. Your corporate and financial community has been powerful enough to keep that secret from government officials including the president.

Your government has a secret space program whose activities and achievements most people would find too incredible to believe.

Nickola Tesla was able to create a UFO by discovering the key to overcome gravity. He was brilliant. Magnetism is important in overcoming gravity. Your government knows the secret of overcoming gravity but they will not discuss it with you.

John McCain was murdered by the Cabal. They actually provoked the brain cancer. Michael Jackson was murdered for similar reasons but in a different way.

Jesse Ventura is on the right path with his conspiracy theories. There is some basis or truth in most of the conspiracy theories that are circulating. It wouldn't hurt you to listen but you don't have to do. It's not what you say. It's what you do. (R)

Monsanto is using many chemicals in your weed products and many people are now allergic more than ever. They are slowly killing you. That is true. That is done with nefarious intent. They intend to do it. It is not accidental. Some extraterrestrials are involved in that. It is a purposeful plan or way of lowering the population.

X. SCIENCE AND TECHNOLOGY

1. Ancient technology

In ancient times there was a global wireless energy network throughout the world. It was used by extraterrestrials and it was used by previous civilizations of Earth peoples. All star systems need similar kinds of energies. The energy system that was on Earth was used in other parts of the universe. Other star systems picked up on the energy that was on the Earth. It was created on Earth but used in other star systems.

There have been previous human civilizations on this earth before Atlantis that were more intelligently and technologically advanced than your current civilization.

The Atlanteans had advanced technologies and they were interested in building and the mechanics of their building. They were very imaginative but you are doing quite well since the time of your typewriter. They had air travel but they did not need ground vehicles for transportation. Flying machines were much easier. They were powered by crystals. Cars were not important. (Q)

Humans of long ago used the power of sound, taught to them by extraterrestrials, to accomplish such feats as moving extremely heavy objects. Sound was used in the construction of some of the unusual ancient monuments we find throughout the world. It was used in the construction of the great pyramids. It was also used when the Israelites went around the walls of Jericho and made the walls crumble. It was the frequency of the sound. Edward Leedskalnin used sound to raise those heavy stones to build the Coral Castle in Homestead Florida. That is the same way you have seen opera singers break drinking glasses. Sound was also used to move stones at Stonehenge.

The Ark of the Covenant in the Bible produced energy. There is an Ark of the Covenant that still exists today. Indeed, it will comfort you and you need to have that. It is hearsay that it is in Israel. It contained alien technology, energy producing technology. There were several Arks of the Covenant. They were all used as weapons. In Biblical times, the Philistines stole the Ark of the Covenant and then suffered the serious consequences of its effects. After the return of the Ark of the Covenant from the Philistines, many people, perhaps as many as seventy, actually died when they looked at it. The technology encased within the Ark of the Covenant was instrumental in bringing down the walls of Jericho. It was amplified sound waves of the blowing of the trumpets that caused the walls to fall. Loud noises can jar anything. The Biblical account of this event is accurate for the most part, and you know how interpretations get misconstrued. The ancient temple of Solomon did not house the Ark of the Covenant. (I)

People were knowledgeable about the creation of and the use of electricity in Biblical times. Was there not lightening at that time? They were able to harness that. The pyramids were used to create electricity. There was electric lighting in the ancient tombs in Egypt. They made use of other electrical devices, something that begins with the letter R with protection of wiring in the tombs. The tombs were wired. (I)

Antigravity technology exists today. It was used in the construction of ancient structures if you wish to call it that way.

In ancient times were there occasions in which great numbers of people were killed by radiation from atomic explosions caused by intelligent entities, perhaps such as in Mohenjo-Daro Pakistan. Your ancient times might even be referred to as now.

The ancient Egyptians were able to perform brain surgery. That was taught by extraterrestrials in a way yes and in a way no. They had some assistance from the aliens but they were able to progress on their own.

The ancient Egyptians were able to create gold by the transformation of other minerals in the pyramid at Giza. You will never learn that secret. It is only God given. He gave it to the Egyptians. When I say God, I mean the extraterrestrials.

The ancient civilization in India possessed information about aviation that was more advanced than that of today. That is so true. If you went back and studied some of the ancient Sanskrit writings, you could learn to advance your knowledge of aviation.

Highly sophisticated robots existed on Earth in the ancient past. They will exist again and they do exist at present.

Some of the ancient structures on Earth were built by melting rock and then reformed by putting it into molds.

To a point, some of what the ancients viewed as magic was actually advanced technology.

Laser technology existed in the ancient world.

2. Involvement of the spirits and extraterrestrials

Throughout history the majority of great scientists have been influenced by extraterrestrials. Their creations were not necessarily emanating from their own minds but their minds are being influenced by the external and being controlled. Thomas Edison, for example, received a lot of his information from other sources. He had information on what we call electricity. He channeled the information from extraterrestrials. The extraterrestrials are having a great deal more influence than you might think on the thinking of humans because they can project their thoughts. They were not recognizable but they have always existed. (D)

Einstein used his psychic ability to develop the Theory of Relativity. His work was attributable to both his high I.Q. and assistance from extraterrestrials in developing that theory. Steve Jobs, the founder of Apple Computer, received information about his inventions from extraterrestrials and he took it with him. He couldn't explain it. It was given to him. He still has the information and that is why it is not publicized. Nicolai Testa received advice regarding electricity from many of our spirit friends. He got his information from those in our world. Many of us have contributed. Lightning has been able to be shared with him.

During World War II both the Axis and the Allied powers used psychics and channelers to assist them in their war efforts. There was assistance or influence from extraterrestrials. The Germans used everything imaginable. The Nazis received technology information from the extraterrestrials through reverse engineering of their crashed UFO's. There was influence from extraterrestrials. That is why they lost. They were deliberately misled. The United States government had an inkling in advance that Japan would attack Pearl Harbor and declare war on this country. They did not know the day. (R)

Some of your technologies have been achieved through analyzing equipment found on crashed UFO's. They have been there for years. The United States government is involved in programs of reverse engineering of alien spacecraft or other alien technology. They are examining things they found and then cover it. The development of the transistor in the 1940's came from reverse engineering of objects found in crashed UFOs

There is currently technology that was retrieved from UFOs in the hands of nations which we consider your enemies, such as Iran, Russia, China, and North Korea. Some of that technology is dangerous and could lead to warfare. You are in war now. You have war on your hands now. For example, North Korea has gotten some of their technology from UFO's that have crashed.

Spirits can be knowledgeable about technologies they never knew during their lifetimes in the physical. Not all of us are advanced but we are aware. We have been knowledgeable about the future, have we not? All modern communication technologies (computers, Wi-Fi etc.) were inspired to humans by spirits who previously experienced embodiment on more advanced worlds. It was all here before you simple souls appeared. My good friend Plato had all of these like your electricity. (D)

The earth has been visited by machines that humans believed were biological entities. There have been robots on Earth that were thought to be humans. They were from extraterrestrials. They are not visible to your eyes but they are here. Highly advanced extraterrestrial civilizations have absolutely been able to imbue robots with sentience or some level of consciousness.

The melting of the ice on the west coast of Antarctica and the growing of the ice on the east coast is the result of energy being produced beneath the surface by intelligent beings.

Liquid mercury was used in the propulsion systems of UFO's to counteract the effects of gravity.

Extraterrestrials have placed artificial satellites that orbit around the earth. Those satellites are for your protection. They are also giving them information about what is happening on Earth. They are not afraid of the miserable man who has no brain. The Van Allen radiation belt that surrounds the earth was placed there by extraterrestrials. There is a satellite traveling around the earth from pole to pole that was not placed by extraterrestrials, but rather by humans. They are still travelling, from pole to pole. (N)

The Nazis actually built UFOs in the 1930's. Not all of the UFOs that have been reported seen in the skies were extraterrestrials but [as to some being made on Earth] yes and no. That means that the Germans built the UFOs with help from extraterrestrials. (R)

3. Energy

Scalar energy has the potential to provide much of the world's energy needs and thus relieve humans of their dependency on fossil fuels. It will be much more possible in the future. The time is not given but it is in the process. Not in your lifetime. You needn't worry. Scalar energy is an effective healing modality that has to be looked into. No question that it should not be avoided. To some degree the Aura Ring. Scalar energy is effective for healing. (U)

Pyramids all around the world were built to create energy. That energy was not just for use on Earth but was also available for use in outer space as well as on Earth. The Great Pyramid at Giza was used as a hydrogen power plant to produce electrical or scalar energy. It was a hydrogen power plant.

Electricity can be broadcast wirelessly as Tesla thought. Tesla was right. The many ancient obelisks throughout the world were used for broadcasting electricity wirelessly. You will transmit electricity wirelessly through the air, on a large scale, as Tesla tried to do. That technology was used in the time of the Atlanteans or before. There are people with their present attitude that are strong enough to do that. It is possible that electric lights can be turned on without wires. That technology was used in the time of the Atlanteans and even before that.

The liquid mercury that was found in the pyramids of Teotihuacan in Mexico was used for UFO propulsion. It was used for fuel. You have developed that technology. The government is keeping that secret from you. Your government secretly operates UFO's if you wish to call it that.

Your government manipulates the weather to be used as a weapon against our enemies if you wish that but it is not important.

4. New and future technology

The technology exists for making cloaking devices to make objects appear invisible to the human eye. It also exists for developing prosthetic gills for humans so that oxygen could be extracted directly from water for when they are under water. It will become economically viable to turn salt water into fresh water in the next twenty-five years.

The technology exists that will transfer an individual's thoughts to another individual. What is known as the "God Helmet" does this. There are times that with the God Helmet it is possible to transfer one person's thoughts to another. You can put a thought into another individual. It doesn't say that you can put the will into another individual but you can

292

put a thought. You cannot control another individual but you could inject a thought.

Although alchemists have tried for ages without success to transmute common elements into gold, the secret to doing so will be taken very seriously. The secret to making gold will be the mixing of minerals. There will be many types of gold as there are now.

Electro-magnetism will be used to counteract the force of gravity. It can be used on a wide scale to overcome gravity. To a point you will be able to witness that but you will not be able to overcome gravity in your lifetime.

Star gates can be created through the use of technology. Your government has that technology now. Your government is very well aware. They are not trying to create star gates now but they have created star gates.

The large Hadron Collider in Cern Switzerland will not present a potential serious danger to your planet. It could open up a portal that will allow entities into this physical plane.

Automobiles without wheels will run on your in this century. Airplanes will have another engine. It is necessary for your airplanes and helicopters to have another engine for safety reasons. They have ground vehicles with and without wheels on other planets. The wheel is an invention on all planets. (T)

The flying car invented by Paul Moller in California and other such cars will become more and more popular each year. Cars in the future will be more flying and also be used as a boat.

Within the next two or three generations the majority of cars will not continue to use solely gasoline as power. They will use little fragments of oil, something that does not exist now.

Within the next century there will there be a proliferation of robots that are practically indistinguishable from humans created by your technology. Some of those robots will be designed to serve as sexual partners for humans. They will look just like humans but will not be biological. They will be very popular. There will be a time that robots will take place for breeding. This is already in existence at this time. Robots will become your friends and they will be very useful in the future. The time will come when artificial humans will be virtually identical to biological humans but that will not be while you are around. It will be in the future. Women won't need men and likewise men won't need women.

It is not possible that robots of the future will have the ability to reproduce themselves. (T)

Technology will reach the point where nearly all of the internal organs of humans could be replaced by mechanical means. Are they not now? A mechanical heart could be installed inside a person; a liver and other organs, too.

Scientists will clone the bodies of human beings. They have already done so and they will continue to do that. They will be able to clone a human brain and place it in a cloned human body. The human brain can be replicated and this will be done by mechanical means such as advanced computers or something like that. That is very much off in the future.

You will have the capability of transplanting the head of a person onto the body of another person as they have done with monkeys. It can be done but it may not all be successful. It is not possible to put the head of one species of animals onto the body of another species.

U.S. technology now has an unmanned space shuttle that has been in orbit for two years and is capable of disabling enemy satellites. What is already in space can disable satellites. Disabling satellites has already been done. Ask Israel that made the satellite. They know what to do with their satellite. The unmanned satellite has to do with North Korea's satellites misfiring. You are protecting yourselves through that satellite. (R)

You now have remotely controlled flying drones which take photographs or move small objects from one place to another. That technology will develop to the point where drones will be used on a widespread scale for moving people from one place to another. That will be in the lifetime of the people here.

Scientists will develop plasma beams so they can be used in a way similar to laser beams. That will be in your lifetime but it will not be used for good.

The internet will continue to exist for many years to come. It will change radically from what it is now in your lifetime. Your government will be taking increasing control over the internet. The internet access will not be free. There will be different charges that will take place like your telephone bill. It will cost less money than it does now just like telephone bills are less than they used to be. There will be more mind reading, messages. There will be telepathy and that will be in your lifetime. It is already occurring with the new generation that is coming through. (T)

What you refer to as materializers exist. That is, there is technology which can replicate objects such as UFO's and things like that, like printing machines that can actually print 3D objects. They are working on that technology at the present time. Not only in your country. A few others are interested.

There have been reported UFO sightings that are not alien spacecraft but are UFO's made by Earth people. They were experimental and you took them as UFO's.

In your future, mechanical robots will increasingly take over the functions of many activities that are now performed by humans to the point that human life will be very different from what it now is. That could be in the future of those who are alive today and it is already successful. (T)

Gravity can be tapped to provide an endless source of energy. It is not necessary at this time that your scientists be aware of how to provide an endless source of energy. It would create chaos and would disrupt the world if there were an endless source of energy. That is why it is not necessary.

The use of magnetism to create space travel at near the speed of light is secretly being used by your government. They are now. You will never find out all the things they are keeping from you. They are doing a good job of that [keeping things secret]. They don't realize how much you are able to handle. (W)

Time travelling machines have been discovered periodically and then confiscated by your government. In the crash of the UFO in Roswell, New Mexico in 1947, they were able to reconstruct a time machine. Time travelling machines have been discovered here and there. The Nazis had a bell shaped one. It was time travelling that got me from my homeland to here. (W)

Howard Hughes' mental decline or demise was very much hastened by an outside source. He received information from extraterrestrials. He obtained the Tesla patents that were sequestered by the government and then gave them to George Van Tassel who built a time machine. He paid girls to have sex with members of the Illuminati in order to have the girls get information to give to him.

You have the technology for time travel and the technology also exists for regressing a person from, for example, the age of forty to the age of twenty. Do not think that it will not be possible.

Artificial intelligence does not pose a serious threat to humanity on

Earth. It will be an aid to humanity. There has been much in the news lately about A.I. Robots will indeed be a help to humanity.

Biological science will reach to point that will enable humans to regrow a limb that has been lost. Science will reach a point that it will teach an organ to regenerate itself. (U)

Electronic devises can be constructed to interfere with a person's consciousness. For example, an electronic device can be used to remove certain memories from the person if you wish.

It is currently it is possible to search the internet by using your voice with a computer. It will be possible for technology in the future to pick up your thoughts to allow you to search the internet rather than speaking into a computer. It will also definitely be possible for the responses to your thoughts to be able to be transmitted directly to your brain rather than by a voice from the computer or a computer screen. This technology is not far off. It is around the corner. They are experimenting with that right now. Your brain can be a computer receiver that connects directly to the internet.

5. Miscellaneous

The Bermuda Triangle is a vacuum on Earth. There are other vacuums on Earth as well. People disappear never to be seen again. They are joining us. Some of the crystals that the Atlanteans used to transmit energy are still in operation under the sea today in that area. They are the cause of the disappearance of planes and ships. They have power. (Q)

There are many more elements on Earth (such as iron or calcium etc.) that have not yet been discovered by scientists. Wait until you visit the other planets. In reality you will find more for your use. Gold is an element that is treasured throughout the physical universe. Gold, silver and platinum are treasured in other star systems.

There is no truth to the theory that, because of modern technology, humans are being excessively bombarded with positive ions and this is having a negative effect on your health. Devices that are imbued with negative ions are of no benefit to your health. Such devices are not of importance. (U)

Helena Blavatsky's writings had a significant influence on Einstein's thinking. He thought of her constantly.

The thoughts and feelings of humans have an effect on the properties of water. Water is very important. If there is a glass of water in front of you, your thoughts and feelings have an effect on the properties of the water.

At times there are conscious entities overseeing that what are considered to be the laws of science, such as the Law of Gravity, are implemented automatically whether by angels or some other kind of entities.

The German stealth aircraft existed during World War II but it was not successful. (R)

There are subatomic particles smaller than quarks that we would call waves. I would call them dangerous waves.

Major weather events, greater than just rain or snow, can be manipulated by the use of technology.

Humans have been taught that there are three states of matter: solids, liquids and gasses but now scientists say that there is fourth state called plasma. As the Theosophists believe, there are three more subtle states of matter. It has always been such. There are seven states of matter.

There is technology on Earth today that can destroy UFO's. Your government has that knowledge. They keep it secret. Everything is secret with your government.

Since time and space do not actually exist, they are on the same continuum as some scientists speculate. There is a point where time becomes space and space becomes time. Time and space are fluid and flexible as proposed in Einstein's Theory of Relativity.

Your government has the technology that could replace fossil fuels, such as gas, oil and coal, as well as nuclear power for creating energy that could be used for electricity. That knowledge was gained from reversed engineering from the crashed UFO in 1947. Your corporate and financial community has been powerful enough to keep that secret from government officials including the president. (W)

Your government has a secret space program whose activities and achievements most people would find too incredible to believe? (W)

As some scientists now believe, light can be created by using sound.

Nickola Tesla was able to create a UFO by discovering the key to overcome gravity. He was brilliant. Magnetism is important in overcoming gravity. Your government knows the secret of overcoming gravity but they will not discuss it with you.

Although the media have reported in the past few years that

scientists have recently discovered planets around other stars, in reality, they have known about the existence of extraterrestrial planets for many years. Where do you think they have been informed? It is not a new phenomenon. (W)

The more advanced a society is, the less they have need for technology. It is not necessarily true that the greater your technology, the more advanced your society is. In fact, the opposite is true.

George Van Tassel built a time travelling machine. That machine has been confiscated by your government. (R)

What you refer to as shape shifters actually are not biological entities but rather mechanical robots that have artificial intelligence and are designed to look like humans.

After the death of the man who built the Coral Castle in Homestead Florida papers that he had written were found stating that magnetism could be used as an anti-gravity device to lift heavy objects and that he used magnetism to life many stones weighing several tones each. Your government knows the uses of magnetism to reduce the pull of gravity.

The Death Ray that Tesla spoke of was some form of laser.

Y. THE EARTH: THE PLANET, MYSTERIOUS PLACES, ANCIENT STRUCTURES AND ARTIFACTS

1. Mysterious places

Places exist in the physical world that you call wormholes, black holes or star gates where you can go through some kind of portal and emerge in faraway places in the universe. Not only through one's mind but in the future. You can go into the future and into the past. They are what you may call black spaces. It is available to you. There is a network of underwater portals used by extraterrestrials. There are many star gates within the borders of your country but they are mostly in the water. The earth is made of water. Those that are on land are not mostly on mountain tops as some people believe. We look above but we do not look below. We must look below. Some are in your lakes and oceans and they are near here. As according to your scientists there is a black hole in your galaxy that has a white hole at the other end of it, thus causing a tunnel that aliens could travel through. (LM)

Nature has a lot to do with the creation of star gates. There are hundreds of them on Earth. Extraterrestrials have not created them on Earth but they live among them. The cause of the disappearance of so many ships in the Sargasso Sea is that there is a black hole in the earth. The same is true of the Lake Michigan triangle. When something goes through a specific star gate, it does not always arrive at the same place somewhere else in the universe. So if a ship goes through that star gate it can arrive at different places in the universe but it is all the same anyway because there is no such thing as time or space. Most of the time, a ship appars somewhere else in the universe when it is caught in a black hole. It goes on to another black hole. Henry Deacon used a star gate when he worked on Mars.

There is a gateway to other worlds at the Vatican. Mount Graham International Observatory in Arizona is a star gate used by the Vatican for contact with extraterrestrials. There are many places like that, as sincere as that. Not only one place. The Vatican is always secretly researching space. They are always secretly doing things. They are secretly in control. The observatory in Arizona is actually a star gate or wormhole that you can go into and end up somewhere else in the universe. The Vatican is making use of it but no one controls it. Representatives from the Vatican can go into it and end up somewhere else in the universe. (I)

When a ship is caught in a black hole, such as the Michigan Triangle, that ship appears somewhere else in the universe. If there are people on that ship they will remain alive somewhere else in the universe. You say alive. They are not what you refer to as dead. It is similar to the Bermuda Triangle. The Bermuda Triangle is a vacuum on Earth. There are other vacuums on Earth as well. People disappear never to be seen again. They are joining us. Some of the crystals that the Atlanteans used to transmit energy are still in operation under the sea today in that area. They are the cause of the disappearance of planes and ships. They have power. (Q)

Ghostly spirits are not the cause of so many people committing suicide at Aokigahara located at the base of Mount Fuji in Japan. Japan has its own influence and has been inundated by much water. The concern there in Japan is the water, the overflow. There is very little truth in ghostly influence. They are committing suicide because they are mentally disturbed and they are in fear. (C)

There is a connection between the Grand Canyon and star beings as thought by Native American Indians in that area. Star beings are from the Grand Canyon and are imbedded in the Grand Canyon and remain so for protection. (N)

There is a large magnificent underground civilization on Earth that is inhabited by humans and extraterrestrials.

There are human or humanlike civilizations beneath the surface of the earth. There are entrances at both the North Pole and the South Pole. The bodies of those entities need air. The world beneath the surface of the earth resembles yours in many ways: such as having sky, rivers, mountains etc. The Nazis entered this world. They are also part of the ISIS. The same group of reincarnated Nazis is now ISIS members. What you have to fear from the civilization beneath the surface of the earth are the animals. There are currently people living beneath the surface of Antarctica. There is life but they are not like you or me.

The prehistoric paintings in caves throughout the world were drawn by people from a more advanced Earth civilization that preceded those whom you traditionally think of as nearly savage cavemen. The cavemen were not savage either but they were addressed as savage because they were learning. They were not coded messages left for you. They were writing their own history before they left. You may have to study the messages in order to understand what they mean. They are more than what meets the eye. It was not meant for code. It was their way of expressing themselves. They had no other way to speak English.

The serpent mounds in Ohio were a naturally occurring blister. It was not some conscious entity that created them.

The area of St. Augustine is a power place. 'Tis safe and it is covered with many human abilities protecting it. In other words, there are ghosts waiting.

The creation of the Valley of Death in Siberia was a vibration of the earth. People become ill there. First of all it starts off to be mental stimulation and when people are fearful, that will contribute to their fear.

There are no animals or insects in what is called the Dead Zone in the Algerian desert. An atomic explosion happened in the past is the reason that no animal life can be there. There is a certain kind of radiation.

There are what could be called evil places on Earth; that is, places with negative energies. There are negative places and also negative people as well as positive places and positive people.

There are ruins of whole cities on Earth both on the land and in the waters that were built by extraterrestrials.

There is a large system of caves in the state of Washington in which a lot of people from other planets live. The caves were put here many years ago. (N)

The island called Hy-Brasil of the coast of Ireland in the Atlantic Ocean that has occasionally been reported seen by sailors but which you have been unable to locate is not a true island. It is something that has been created by extraterrestrials. That is why it can come and go. That island is very vague at times and can disappear and reappear.

There a gold treasure secretly buried beneath Remy Chateau in France and there is gold buried in quite a few other places also as well as in your oceans.

Although in the 16th Century Ponce de Leon spent many years searching for the fountain of youth, such a fountain of youth does not exist. There is no such place. The fountain of youth is in your head. It is not how old you are. It is how old you think you are that counts.

There are twelve locations on the earth in which there are large areas of aluminum isotope 26 under the surface of the land. Those areas hold a threat to mankind. They are destructive. Your government is withholding information about them because they are not really very knowledgeable about them. I do not have an answer as to whether their occurrence is natural or the work of extraterrestrials but I have a feeling to give to you that the answer would be both.

Lake Guatavita in South America has a great deal of gold at the bottom that will be recovered but not in your lifetime.

Stasis chambers do exist. That is, there are several places around the world in which ancient technology has been used to slow down time in small areas in which there are giants that have been in hibernation for thousands of years. President Lincoln saw one such giant in a sarcophagus in a cave in Ohio. It will come out that questions that are kept secret will be belonging to the public. Those giants are taller people than you with larger brains. They will be awakened. Their brain will be connected. They are both humans and extraterrestrials.

There are still many ghosts in the city of Pompeii Italy which was destroyed by a volcano in 79AD. Some people can sense their presence.

2000 years ago about 960 Jews in Masada Israel committed suicide rather than being captured by the invading Roman army. That area is haunted by the ghosts of those people today. It is another place where there are many ghosts.

2. Mysterious structures and artifacts

Note: All but the final entries in this section have appeared in previous chapters.

Most of the mysterious ancient structures found on Earth today were built by extraterrestrials for their own activities rather than for the use by or the good of humans. (N)

There are monuments that predated the Great Flood. There were many, many floods before the Great Flood. There wasn't only one Great Flood. There were many floods over and over and over. They are correcting me to tell you "and over and over". There will be more Great Floods. The Sphinx was created before the Great Flood. (R)

Lake Titicaca in Peru and its underwater city with sunken ruins were there eons ago. It was covered with earth and then with water. It was there before the Great Flood. Indeed an earthquake occurred and then water. The earth opened up here and allowed the water to overflow. I was not there. (Q)

That is what I have been told. There are many cities that existed before the Great Flood. There are still remnants now. (Q)

Thousands of years ago the Libyan Desert Glass was created by a nuclear explosion but it was not caused by people. It was caused by gasses. It was natural. (Q)

You can explain the existence of the same type of hieroglyphs and cuneiform writings that are found in both ancient Sumer and near Lake Titicaca in Peru the same way as in some caves or such other areas that were left. They were writings and messages left for the future. Some were left by extraterrestrials. (Q)

The huge statues on Easter Island were manmade products of people they worshipped. Extraterrestrials had an improvement in them because they had more strength. The Lemurians played a role in the creation of the many large statues on Easter Island. The statues represented extraterrestrials and people that are of stature. (Q)

Aliens were involved in the construction of the Coral Castle in Homestead, Florida to help Edward Leedskalnin. He was too little to do this himself. His ability to communicate was remarkable. (N)

The Dogu (Dogoo) statues found in Japan represent aliens in space suits. (N)

The purpose of the numerous very long lines, drawings of animals, geometrical shapes and mathematical diagrams in South America that can only be seen from the air was for those that were up high in the sky so they could read it easier when above the land it is written on. I am talking about extraterrestrial UFO's. They were constructed by extraterrestrials for the purpose of providing instructions or information to the people of Earth. The same could be said about the various crop circles that have been appearing throughout the world. They are messages or instructions to Earth people from extraterrestrials. They are in your face. They are right there. They are trying to assist you and aid you. They are trying to be heard. (N)

Extraterrestrials have imbued thirteen crystal sculls with special powers. They have been cleansed and are very clever and very intelligent. If they gather together that will be a tremendous powerful force, a controlling force. When those glass skulls are brought together power will occur, power to the extraterrestrial groups that made them. They are extremely powerful. There are other objects located on Earth that are endowed with powers, such as you humans have power that was endowed by extraterrestrials. Humans will be using the crystal skulls relatively soon to communicate with extraterrestrials. There will be a time when the thirteen crystal skulls that are located throughout the world will be brought together and tremendous changes will occur because of that. There is something very powerful about those skulls and when they are all brought together, something will occur to be helpful in elevating the level of humanity. It will grow and you will learn to respect each other and not murder any more. (S)

Extraterrestrials were involved in the formation of the Devil's Tower in Wyoming. We have been there and we created it. Extraterrestrials are still involved in the Devil's Tower. We are everywhere. We have been here for centuries. (N)

Some of the ancient structures on Earth built by melting rock and then reformed by putting it into molds. (X)

The St. Louis Arch has an effect on the weather in that region. Extraterrestrials were instrumental in providing information for its design. They want to know if they were good designers. Part of the purpose was to affect the weather. (N)

The prehistoric cave paintings throughout the world can be considered something like a key to your understanding of the history and future of mankind. There is hidden meaning in those drawings. The interpretation of those drawings tells of your history and your future. (Q)

There are inscriptions written in the ancient Sumerian language in Tiahuanaco Bolivia as well as in ancient Sumer because the Anunnaki visited both places. It is like Americans. They are everywhere. (N)

There are stone wheels carved into the earth in Syria, Jordan and Saudi Arabia that are older than the Great Flood, They were again leaving their announcements that they were here. It was a way of sending a message telling you about them. You have yet to learn the secret of how to read them. You are trying to interpret them now. They are trying very diligently to inform you about the past.

There is a deep mysterious pit in the ground on Oak Island in Nova Scotia in which the Ark of the Covenant is buried. It was hidden so many years ago, before the Europeans settled America. A lot of your answers will come out. Some of you will be alive when they get to that, not just the younger ones. It doesn't matter how old because there are people who will be alive who were not aware that they would live so long. Life will be much longer for them as you well know. Life will be much more. There are many more people above a hundred, many more who exist. I see the average lifetime of humans being 120 years. And with new medications coming out, many diseases will be conquered and people will live to be over 150.

Although I have said that the Ark of the Covenant is buried on Oak Island, Nova Scotia, it is not true that six people have died trying to get to the Ark because of a curse and that after the seventh person has died the Ark will become accessible. It just happened to be. There is no such thing as a curse. It just happened that six people have passed on because of different reasons. There is no such thing as a curse. You cannot be cursed by another soul. That is not possible. The soul would be cursed themselves if they wished to put a curse on you. They would be receiving the curse that they are putting out to you. Be careful and do not wish any ill on somebody else. It will come back on you. Curses do not exist. Curses from the Egyptian tombs in the pyramids do not exist. It is all coincidental.

There is knowledge left by the Atlanteans under a paw of the sphinx inscribed on tablets of gold. Gold is used because it is virtually indestructible and desirable. That knowledge will become available to you in the future, not that near but it will be exposed within a hundred years.

A man named R.C. Christian constructed the Georgia Guide Stones. His motivation or intent in creating them was to teach. The Guide Stones will tell you the source of the information. The Rosicrucians were involved. The Rosicrucian beliefs are in the Guide Stones. Those stones do not contain hidden coded messages. The messages are direct.

Regarding the many large standing Carnac Stones in France, the cause of the field of high energy magnetism that surrounds them is the environment. The stones transmit energy.

The fabled city of El Dorado in South America actually exists in brief parts. It has been discovered but it has not been publicized. You are being controlled.

The head of the sphinx was originally that of a lion or an animal of some sort but was later cut down in size to be shaped to appear as the head of a man. The sphinx is much, much, much older than what you believe. There are many more sphinxes under the ocean. There will be new elements found under the ocean. The sphinx in Egypt predates the great flood. There were many Great Floods. It predates Atlantis also. It is more than a hundred thousand years old. Henry Deacon is a man who lives in the United Kingdom and commutes to work on the planet Mars on a daily basis. I know this is difficult for you to believe. This is one of those secrets that are being held from you. In a building in England he goes down a corridor or tunnel and at the end there is a door. He places a key in the lock and when he opens the door he is on Mars. He also says that there are many Earth people working on Mars.

There are many huge heads carved in stone in Mexico that they call the Olmec heads that are depictions of both extraterrestrials and Earth beings.

3. Pyramids, obelisks and Stonehenge

The great pyramid at Giza was built for electricity before the Great Flood.

It was a power plant to provide energy. Many Egyptians built it. The labor was made by humans and extraterrestrials too, as they are now with you. The extraterrestrials designed the pyramid and the humans built it using extraterrestrial technology. Slaves were forced to. It was not fun. It was very difficult with slavery. Pyramids all around the world were built to create energy. That energy was not just for use on Earth but was also available for use in outer space as well as on Earth. The Cheops pyramid in Egypt was built by man power. (Q)

The various ancient pyramids strategically placed throughout the world were created by extraterrestrials for radiation, lightening and experimenting. They created them to produce energy. The earth's energy was given throughout the universe. That is why they are placed all over the place. That means of producing energy is already no longer a secret. There was no danger. It was just exploring, learning and growing.

There are pyramids beneath the ice in Antarctica. They had to do with the continent of Atlantis. It will come out to be. Antarctica once was Atlantis and the earth shifted and pyramids were on Atlantis.

The architects and builders of the pyramids in the Yucatan and Guatemala were people that are striving from your past. They are reaching out and wish to serve in your future. They were actually built by those of another star system, the Pleiades. They also built the pyramids in Egypt and that is how they got to the top. The Pleiades are one of the most advanced groups. Our secret people were building your pyramids that they could reach from the top down. Humans provided a lot of the labor but extraterrestrials provided the technology. (NQ)

The purpose of the many ancient obelisks is the same as we are told all over the world where everyone is being shared. That is to produce both communications and energy.

There is significance to the fact that the Washington monument is in the form of an obelisk. It is not for me to express more about that. There is a reason based on ancient wisdom why the monument is shaped as such. It is correct because it was interpreted in that form. The interpretation was given to mankind.

When I said that the purpose of Stonehenge was to provide shade, I was referring to the shadows caused by the stones as the sun moved through the sky. The shadows were like a clock and a calendar. That was the way of telling time. I was involved with the building of Stonehenge. Stonehenge was basically not for healing people. It was basically for telling time. Stonehenge was also used to be an extraterrestrial spaceport. Stonehenge and some of these other recently discovered structures predated the Great Flood. He's telling me that it was a clock. It was like telling time.

Humans of long ago used the power of sound, taught to them by extraterrestrials, to accomplish such feats as moving extremely heavy objects. Sound was used in the construction of some of the unusual ancient monuments we find throughout the world. It was used in the construction of the great pyramids. It was also used when the Israelites went around the walls of Jericho and made the walls crumble. It was the frequency of the sound. Edward Leedskalnin used sound to raise those heavy stones to build the Coral Castle in Homestead Florida. That is the same way you have seen opera singers break drinking glasses. Sound was also used to move stones at Stonehenge. (Q)

4. The effects of humans on the planet

What you call global warming is more than just the earth getting warmer. It also involves extreme weather and climate changes that are apparently coming to your Earth. What you call global warming is not manmade but is exacerbated or accelerated by man. Humans should stop being angry with each other and by stop having war, so all together you can think the same. You can slow it down by watching your disposals of garbage, the gases etc.

Although mankind has been blamed for climate change, that is a very incomplete picture. There other cases or reasons for climate change other that Co2 and other stuff in your environment but there is hope that you can do something about it.

Global warming is a natural phenomenon. It has happened many times before and will happen time and again. The earth is not hurting because of the greenhouses gasses created by man. Human beings can do nothing to stop or slow down the acceleration of the earth becoming warmer to the point where polar ice will melt, thus causing the inundation of many coastal areas, and the extinction of some animal life forms. It is the rotation of the earth. This is going to happen in many years to come. You won't be here. There's nothing you can do about global warming. That is the existence of your past and your future. The actions of humans are not harming the earth in ways that will result in bringing harm to physical humanity. The earth itself is not being harmed by mankind, not at all. This whole concern about global warming is ridiculous (R)

Planet Earth is well taken care of as you may well know. It has many successions and will have again many successions. Planet Earth will continue to multiply. We will continue to eat and defecate on your planet Earth.

The health of planet Earth is affected by the way people treat one another. If you treated each other better, your planet would be better.

There are programs underway right now to thin out the population of the earth. The Illuminati believe there are more people now on the planet Earth than can be successfully sustained; too many people to feed and shelter.

Cremation is a most efficient way to dispose of human bodies that will help the soul and the earth at the same time.

5. Earth changes

A major earth change will occur within the next century. The areas least affected will be all the places not near water. As Edgar Cayce said, I still see the Virginia Beach area as safe. I foresee a major Earth shift in the next thousand years, such as when Atlantis virtually disappeared, but not in your lifetime. (T)

Edgar Cayce predicted that the earth would shift on its axis in 1998 but this did not occur because his timing was wrong. Conditions did not change to avert this but it will occur but at another time. The gentleman that made the prediction was a gentleman. It was not in order for it to occur. Time cannot be predicted. Those changes may occur but at a different date. Yet do not feel that they will have to occur.

I do not see the planet Earth being struck by a comet, asteroid or something else from outer space within the next few centuries but it will be divided and it will go on and on. It will be politically divided.

It's a good idea to buy land in South Florida because you will be here. Although it is true that the water will rise, I do not have dates about the water rising. It will not be in your lifetime but it looks like the rising of the water is eminent in Florida. Water from the rising seas will intrude into your community in the next century. (T)

The earth is on an approximate 25,580 year cycle and at the end of each cycle are there great changes regarding the earth and humanity. It has to do with the planet Niburu approaching the earth.

With the earth changes and the vibration and quickening, the people who live beneath the surface at Mount Shasta will still not be able to live on the surface.

The Gulf Stream is gradually losing its ability to bring warm air currents to the British Isles are because of the fresh water polar glaciers melting into the salt water oceans. The salt water helps to bring movement

A huge emission of methane from thawing Arctic permafrost beneath the East Siberian Sea is a possible threat to mankind, not in the near future but it is controlled.

6. Miscellaneous

Information regarding the planet in ages past appeared in Section Q: *The World Before Biblical Times.*

In your study of the earth, various dimensions, spheres etc., the expression "Fluid Earth" is used and it is not water. It is a more hydrogen earth, in your language.

When there is a major disaster such as an earthquake or a tsunami in your world in which many people are killed we are aware of what is to be and we are always there to welcome those who are coming into your world. (B)

The planet Earth is a conscious entity.

Earthquakes can be caused by intelligent entities or sometimes what you might call natural phenomena. The 2014 strong earthquake in Haiti was not caused by intelligent entities. It was natural, not orchestrated.

As some scientists believe, the core of the earth is getting warmer. It is a natural cycle.

Z. DONALD TRUMP AND THE 2016 ELECTIONS

The questions in this section were asked over a period of several years. They were asked by those who attended the meetings. Some questions are very similar to others questions because the same people were not always present at all sessions. Therefore some were not aware of questions which had been previously asked. Since the content of the questions involved contemporary situations or events of the near future, the dates that the questions were asked are included. Some events may have already occurred prior to the publication of this book. Some of the questions were not about the elections or President Trump but the answers to those questions provided information about President Trump.

The questions are presented exactly as they were asked followed by the words of the guide. A few of the questions may have appeared in previous chapters.

I am not aware of any polls that said that Donald Trump would be elected. The only person I know that said that Donald Trump would win was Donald Trump. But right along, the guide said he would win.

I want to assure you that I am not trying to persuade or influence anybody about anything. I am just trying to share with you what has come through from the guide so that you can make up your own mind regarding what you want to believe regarding what has happened, what is happening and what will happen.

Please understand that I am only the messenger. If you do not agree with what is said here, please do not argue with me. Argue with the guide instead.

Around 1990 the guide said that no presidential elections would be important until the 2012 election. It would make no difference who would be elected before that. But since the spirits cannot tell time, perhaps it could also be the 2016 election that he was referring to. On the other hand, perhaps what occurred after the 2012 election was a necessary forerunner to the 2016 election.

FEBRUARY 2015

<u>Are behind the scene powers in American politics so strong and influential that it really doesn't matter whom we elect as our president?</u>

No, because it is already done. But it is someone you do not know [in politics], someone new on the scene.

MARCH 2015

<u>Has the coming presidential election already been determined by the global government?</u>

Indeed it has. The Republicans will take over but the Democrats again will squeeze in. It will be controlled by Republicans.

MAY 2015

<u>Will the next president of our country have an agenda that works for the betterment of mankind?</u>

Indeed. He will be seriously interested in improving your country. At a point, but not completely.

JULY 2015

<u>Is our country run by mostly elected officials or mostly by certain behind the scene powers?</u>

You have many behind the scene powers as you suggested. It really does not matter who is elected president.

MARCH 2016

<u>Do you see any health problems or physical harm coming to Donald Trump because of his anti-establishment position on many political issues?</u>

Indeed, sir. He will be voted and approved and an issue will come from it. Many people would like to dissolve him, especially in Mexico. There will become health problems after a while. I see an assassination attempt on his life. He will run and he will be approved but there is some determination here that is not given. The outcome is decided, definitely.

He will not be in the condition that he is at the present moment. The R party will come into power. The assassination attempt will be made from the government.

AUGUST 2016

Did the Nazis receive technology information from the extraterrestrials through reverse engineering of their crashed UFO's?

Indeed, sir. And so is ISIS. Extraterrestrials are helping ISIS. There are also some who want to defeat ISIS. ISIS will be defeated. It will take some time for ISIS to be defeated. ISIS is gaining weight. ISIS is growing and the dependency [?] is not up to Hillary because she is with ISIS. She has not done anything at this moment to stop ISIS. Have you noticed that, dear sir? And the other man who has a big mouth and is very stupid because he is not knowledgeable. But he will be able to be strong and make a lot of sense and be more encouraging for the future. ISIS will strike again with the magnitude of the Wall Street Towers. They will go back to New York and they are eying at this moment Washington. They are trying to hit the root of your government like they did in Brussels. They are in South Florida now where you are. They are around but they figure that all old people are in Florida. They are going for young people and young children.

NOVEMBER 2016 (2 days before the election)

Will either Hillary Clinton or Donald Trump have any serious medical issues in the near future?

Absolutely, sir. The issue has already started with Hillary Clinton. If you notice, her right eye will tell you that she has Parkinson's. It has not been determined as yet but it will continue. It is not fatal, sir. Donald Trump's health is okay, sir, but not mentally. Mr. Trump is very bright and intelligent and she, Hillary, has trouble remembering. Her memory has not been successful.

Is either one more sincere than the other in their desire to help our country?

Indeed. One has desire to help her pocketbook and the other has desire to help and he is not educated enough as far as he should be.

<u>Will there be something in the recently revealed e-mails of Hillary Clinton that will prove that she intentionally did something illegal?</u>

Is that not so, sir? She will be penalized for that. [Regarding jail], she will not have that direction at this time. But she will be suffering some humiliation, yes.

<u>Does Donald Trump have the desire and the ability to follow through on his promises about making America great again?</u>

Indeed, sir. He does have the ability, much more than the lady. She is evil, sir. Sometime ago I indicated that Donald Trump would be the one to be elected. It still seems that way by a very slim chance. He will be elected by a small number of votes.

<u>Are the Russians trying to interfere with the U.S. elections?</u>

Yes, yes, yes. China is also hacking into the e-mails of various authorities. Russia hacked into Hillary's e-mail.

<u>Will Donald Trump make a good president?</u>

He will make a wonderful president because he will learn to listen and demand attention as he has been doing all his life. He gets his way and he demands attention. As you noticed, he has great control over situations.

DECEMBER 2016

<u>It is said that Nostradamus predicted that Donald Trump would get us into World War Three. What is your reaction?</u>

It was not Donald Trump. It was the lady that would definitely lead us into World War Three. I don't agree with Nostradamus.

<u>Concerning Donald Trump, will he be reelected? Will he finish his term?</u>

Indeed, and he will be re-elected and he will not have any space, or time or energy for himself for another chance. He is going to accomplish everything that he desired to do. Everything he promised to do, he will do. At least he will try. And he will do it with pleasure. He will be successful. You will be proud of him. So will he, as you well know. He will be very proud.

What will be the outcome of Donald Trump being elected president?

You will be happier than ever. He will help all he can. He will try and he will do what he claimed that he wanted to do. You will be lucky and supportive of him and be kind to him. He is a show-off and he has a big mouth, but he is a successful person in business and in other professions that he has chosen. So, take his advice. He is not God but he knows how to get what he wants. [Regarding the alleged groping of the women who accused him], ridiculous, sir. Every pencil has an eraser.

JANUARY 2017

Will the president elect be convicted of any crime?

He will not be convicted of crime but he may not conclude a term. He will be a very wonderful, strong, good human being. He is kind and he is knowledgeable. He will help many that need help. He is for the positive, not the negative. He is very intelligent but an idiot. He will be successful.

You said that the president will do a good job and that he will not finish a term. What will happen to him?

Pressure. He will not die. Pressure will make him disabled. He will try very hard and do very well. At this time I am told that I am not able to discuss at this very moment. Do help him. He is sincere and he is much better than that woman that is up the hill. She was trying to get Iran and she is just negative. She will create a war. It is better she rest.

Will Donald Trump remain in office for four years?

Indeed. You betya. Indeed. In spite of it.

FEBRUARY 2017

Will we have the next world war during Donald Trump's presidency?

I think you need help in not realizing to give him a chance. Don't be misgiving. He is learning. He is sent here, God given. He will keep every promise he made to the best of his ability. He does not like anyone that opposes him because he needs all the help that he can get. He needs it so much. He is desperate. This is his country. He loves his country and he tries to do the best he can. He is not ignorant. He is very simple and kind. He is much kinder than the news broadcasts. And it would not be for me to say that Mr. Trump is not having some issues or forces from Jesus the man. He is kind and forgiving, not knowledgeable, not aware; a simple soul wishing to save his country, mankind.

When you said that Hitler was playing a predestined role and was guided by extraterrestrials, was it the goal of that group of extraterrestrials to take over the world?

No my dear sir. They were following his orders, not their own orders. This is the same group of extraterrestrials that is assisting ISIS today. We must get rid of them. You are on the same path with ISIS as you were with Hitler? They are a fungus. Even though I cannot tell time where I am, I see you getting rid of ISIS within the next ten years, absolutely. There will be less bloodshed. We will end up saluting Donald Trump and be grateful for his thinking on this mismatch. There is a lot of negativity in thinking of Americans about Donald Trump. That will change in history. He will be just like Abraham Lincoln. He will go down in history as a good man. He will not die a good man. People's attitudes won't change now but down the history in retrospect he will be considered different.

MARCH 2017

Is Donald Trump the reincarnation of a powerful past political leader? Is that leader Napoleon?

He has been in power before, in previous lifetimes. He thinks of himself as Mr. Napoleon.

Are many of the current popular music stars, including the popular singer Lady Gaga, instruments of the Illuminati? Is the same true of the media?

Indeed, sir. The same is true of movie and TV stars. The media is very much controlled by the Illuminati. They all get together and make your simple laws. You have something to fear from the Illuminati. You should ignore them or oppose them. Be strong and know what is better for you, each one of you individually. Mr. Trump cares about you and of course he cares about himself. If you try to make him budge he will blame somebody else. He always has someone to blame. He is not controlled by the Illuminati. You cannot control this man. This man is not controllable as this time comes. The fact that he cannot be controlled is a positive thing. No enemy will control him. His mother controlled him. His father could not control him and his children cannot control him. He is what you call uncontrollable. He has a very strong will. Not the brightest but a strong will.

APRIL 2017

<u>As Donald Trump claimed, was the Obama administration involved in tapping his phone lines or of those associated with him?</u>
Indeed, sir. All your phones are tapped. The place in England records every single phone line by satellite. Donald Trump is right in his claim that Obama was directly involved in getting information from tapping his lines. There are no secrets, as you well know. When you tell one person, it is an open book.

<u>Many years from now, when historians look back on Donald Trump's presidency, how will he be treated?</u>
He will be treated as Abraham Lincoln was. He will be treated as a noble, fine man. He has done his best and he has achieved many wellnesses and will be looked upon as Abraham Lincoln is and will be looked upon as a goofball, which he may be. His failures as a president will be considered as the notoriety he has gotten from numerous occasions, mainly the female sex.

JUNE 2017

<u>Is there any truth in the implications that Donald Trump was manipulated or assisted by the Russians during his election?</u>
My dear Mr. Trump has his mouth where his foot belongs and he makes mistakes. But every pencil has an eraser. He is not able to admit he made a mistake by opening his mouth. The Russians weren't even aware of manipulating the elections. The Russians had no involvement with the recent elections. [This seems to contradict a previous statement.]

JULY 2017

<u>What future do you see for president Trump?</u>
I see a light, wonderful future, like Abraham Lincoln, a good soul

that will be regarded later in history as a wonderful, successful person as Abraham Lincoln did when he freed the slaves. He will be regarded as a wonderful president. The knucklehead!

DECEMBER 2017

Who was the most undervalued or unappreciated president of the United States?

Lincoln. Years from now Trump will be considered like Lincoln. Trump is doing what will be valued. He is giving employment. He is getting manufacturing back. He is having success which your newspapers do not appreciate. He is doing much positive. He will not bring your country to war. He is escaping war. There is no question that if the Democrats had won, you would have definitely gone to war. There was outside unseen non-physical influence on Trump winning the election.

FEBRUARY 2018

You said that there would be an assassination attempt on Donald Trump. Has that already occurred or will it occur in the future? Will he be injured in the attempt? Will the attempt be made by the Republicans or the Democrats?

That has already occurred but there will always be assassinations of disliked people. There will be an assassination attempt on him again. I do not see him injured but he is not in good shape health wise like your news broadcasts say.

MARCH 2018

What is the outcome of President Trump's presidency?

Your wonderful president will stay his full time. In fact he is even planning on the next time. He is thinking ahead of you and he will do well. I realize that he is disliked as much as the dear person Abraham Lincoln was disliked. You are going to have him again. But he is doing good and he is not recognized for the good he is doing. Newspapers do not give you proper information. He will go down in history as Abraham Lincoln.

MAY 2018

<u>Will Donald Trump complete his second term as president?</u>
Indeed, sir, and he will do a good job.

OCTOBER 2018

<u>Will Donald trump be the first president to let us know that UFO's have made contact with us?</u>
Indeed. He will be able to tell you but he will not be accepted. His word is usually down and laughed upon and made fun of but he will go down in history to be the first honest president.

<u>A Chinese scientist claims Donald Trump is the reincarnation of Cyrus The Great in the Bible. Is that true?</u>
In a way, yes. Mr. Trump is a very intelligent man. Sometimes Mr. Trump is too intelligent for the people who are against him. He means well. He has done well. He has done miracles. I say to you that for the heart of the Jewish people he has done things to assist you and protect you and make you grow.

<u>David Ecke has been speaking about how there is a select group in Bohemian Grove that selects the presidents as puppets and that there is really no two party system. Is he credible? Is this true?</u>
Yes. They did not decide to select Donald Trump to be president. He was selected by the people that voted for him. He was wanted by the people.

NOVEMBER 2018

<u>Many people try to label Donald Trump as evil and that he is like Hitler. Does he have a pure heart with the direction of this country?</u>
Donald Trump is misunderstood because of his personality. He has a very low personality but he has succeeded and done whatever he promised to do. His personality is his ruination.

DECEMBER 2018

<u>Was Donald Trump chosen to be president by protective spirits because his abrasive personality would dissuade people from worshipping him?</u>
Yes. Not only abrasive but confusing.

JANUARY 2019

<u>Will President Trump remain in office for the remainder of his term?</u>
He will definitely remain and he will do much help and good. He will go down as a famous president.

FEBRUARY 2019

<u>Is Donald Trump working to the benefit of the goals of Cabal or the benefit of the goals of the Alliance?</u>
Donald Trump is working to help and he cares very much about people. Donald Trump will be going down in history as Abraham Lincoln did in his time. He will be recognized and uplifted sincerely. He will be recognized as a great president after he has gone to the spirit world. He will be recognized so by some in his lifetime. He is a wonderful man when you need an enemy.

Chapter 11

CONCEPTS TO PONDER

I, Charles Zecher, refer to the following passages as "inspired writings". I do not know if this information was channeled to me from an outside source or if it was the product of my overactive imagination. As these passages came to my mind, I could feel man abundance of energy that I could not explain. My thinking was certainly supercharged. I do not know if there was some form of telepathic communication from spirits or angels. I can neither identify the source nor can I vouch for the validity of what I say here. Nevertheless, the various concepts appear interesting and perhaps something worthy of consideration. I tried not to judge whether the concepts were appropriate, even those which seemed to run contrary to what I thought I knew. Sometimes the exact wording of statements would automatically appear in my mind. On the majority of occasions, the overall concept would come to mind. On those occasions I would write what came to mind and the writing would come very easily. Then as I would read what I had written, refinements would come to mind. Sometimes the thoughts came so fast that I missed them and was unable to write them down.

THE BANQUET OF LIFE

It has been said that life is a sumptuous banquet that takes place in the most lavish of banquet halls. The dining room is impressively large and magnificently decorated, ornately appointed with plush carpeting, rich draperies, priceless works of art, and furnishings of great splendor. Throughout the hall are numerous elegantly carved dining tables surrounded by perfectly matched chairs., Each table is exquisitely set with delicate china trimmed in gold, drinking glasses of perfect crystal, beautifully crafted silverware and a variety of accouterments of such beauty that even the imagination of the beholder cannot exceed.

As we peer into the banquet hall, we easily note that the arrangement of tables has been designed with specific order. At the far end of the hall, to the left, there are numerous tables around which are seated only people young of age. It is easy to note that these youth are filled with the lively anticipation of what is about to occur. They are so filled with the vibrancy of life and the excitement of the dining experience upon which they are about to embark. The conversation is animated and loud. They can be seen sitting on the edges of their chairs, hardly able to restrain their impetuousness, just waiting for the food to be served. For them, the wait seems endless; they are so anxious to begin.

The entire mid section of the banquet hall is filled with tables as far as one's vision can allow. Around these tables are seated many adults of their middle years of life. The meal has already been placed on the table. The numerous serving dishes are heaped with all kinds of delicious foods and there is an abundance of beverages of all varieties. The repast has begun and these guests are at various stages of the partaking of their meal. A full range of gustatorial sensations can be observed. They are filled, to varying degrees, with the pleasure of such heavenly enjoyment and it appears that nearly everyone wants the banquet to continue forever like this.

At the other end of the banquet hall, there are also many tables. Around these tables are seated only individuals who are beyond the years of the prime of life. They have finished their meal and look so satisfied and contented. Many are sitting back on their chairs with their arms crossed upon their chests. Although they no longer have the passion of the hunger they once had, they do have vivid memories of the experience and the feelings of enjoyment of partaking of the banquet. As they delve back in their memories, many can even recall the time of the excitement of waiting for the food to be served when they were so hungry. As we look around at these tables, we can hear so many people saying as they lean back on their chairs, "My but that was a wonderful meal!" After such a fine meal, some need to rest a bit. So they go to the door behind all the tables and go upstairs to rest a while.

IT'S NOT WHERE YOU END UP IN LIFE THAT COUNTS

In the latter years of life, some people live in the lap of luxury; enjoying life to the fullest extent, travelling wherever they want, doing whatever they want, having plenty of money to buy whatever their hearts desire. In spite of outward appearance, some may be content while others may be miserable. Some may be in good health and others in poor health. Some may have many friends, others with no friends.

There are other people who spend their life's final years living in poverty. Some are practically penniless, unable to procure even the necessities of life. They may even be in poor health and all alone with no one to share their lives with or even care for them. Their possessions are scant and insufficient for making life enjoyable. Just as with those loving with all the trappings of life, some may be content while others may be miserable.

It seems that the majority of people spend the final years of their lives somewhere between those who live in luxury and those who live without the finer things of life.

Whether your latter years are spent in luxury, poverty or somewhere between are of no importance to the real you, the you at the soul level. The important thing is what you did in life prior to your latter years. As we look at those around us in the latter years of life, we cannot observe their lifestyle to measure how successful they really are.

There are people who live in the lap of luxury in their latter years who are truly good souls whom we may admire. They have spent their lives being kind to others, helping whenever they could. In the process of living they gave little thought to their own welfare, but instead placed their focus on those who were in need. They lived by the golden rule.

Other people living in the lap of luxury in their final years are not to be admired. They have spent their lives selfishly, giving little thought to the hurt or harm they brought to others along the way of life's journey. All they cared about was themselves. Their mistreatment or lack of consideration of other people was their means of attaining what they desired and received.

Just as with those living luxuriously at life's end, so it is with those living at the opposite end of the scale. Some should be admired for their actions as they journeyed through life. Others should be pitied. The golden rule meant nothing to them.

Our lifestyles or our possessions are no part of our true selves. It is only what we are at the soul level that is of importance. No one can take lifestyles or possessions with them when they make their transition into the spirit world. They take only their actions with them, including what they have thought about, said to, or done to others. It is with their actions that they must live in the afterlife. It is the consequences of their actions that become the karma of their future lifetimes.

When all is said and done we cannot look at the lifestyles of older people and make any kind of judgment as to whether they are what we might call "good" people or what we might call "bad" people. It is not for us to determine if they are rich or poor in spirit.

SOMETIMES THE ANSWER IS NO

Why doesn't God answer our prayers? We often have wants or needs that we pray and pray and pray for but God just doesn't listen to us. Sometimes our prayers are answered. On other occasions it seems that God just isn't listening? Why doesn't God always help us? Are there times that God is asleep? There are scriptures in the Bible that say "Ask and it shall be given." But we ask and it is not given. Have we proved that the Bible is wrong and is just not telling us the truth?

We often confuse our needs with our wants. We say, "I really need a larger screen television than the one I have." when we really mean, "I really want a larger screen television than the one I have." It is often difficult to distinguish our wants from our needs. We do not know the difference between the two.

Our desires come from our mind. Could it be that God just doesn't give us what we want because the mind of man is not the mind of God? God is both universal and personal; internal and external. That is, God rules the universe and has dominion over all that is, and yet God is within us. Our soul is our true self, our higher self where God dwells. The spirit guide has said that we pray to ourselves. We pray to our personal god, the god that is within us, the god that is part of us. It is our soul that knows what is best for us. If our wants or what we think are our needs run contrary to what is best for us, then we are protected when our prayers are not answered. We are saved from what could be disastrous for us. We must remember that sometimes unpleasantness or even tragedy in our lives is just what we need to point us in the direction that we should go.

We incarnate into the physical life to learn specific lessons so that we may advance in the evolution of our soul. If our wants prevent us from learning the lessons we need to learn, the God in our soul will protect us by not granting our wishes. Sometimes our life's lessons are of karmic origin. If, for example, we have shown extreme haughtiness toward others in previous lives, then it could be that humility is one of our lessons to learn in this lifetime. If we want something that will bring us the opposite of humility and cause to be haughty, then our wishes will not be granted. Our prayers will not be answered.

We must have faith in ourselves; that is, in the god that dwells in our soul. We must have faith and understand that we are provided with opportunities to advance in our spirituality when our prayers are not answered.

WE ARE NOT ALONE

Although it may appear that when we are alone with no one else in our presence, we may think we are alone but in reality we are far from being alone. There is much more than just the physical world that we perceive through our senses. The non-physical world is very real and teeming with life, even more so that the physical world in which we live.

Every place in the universe is abundant with life, not physical life such as we humans but conscious entities that are invisible to us. This includes spirits, angels, animal spirits, elementals and many varieties of entities with which we are unfamiliar. Even our thoughts and the thoughts of others are a form of energy in the world that we cannot perceive through our five senses. Our thoughts populate the world around us. The thoughts of those in our presence are invisibly around us with a life of their own

Our thoughts attract invisible entities around us. Good thoughts beckon beneficent beings. Negative thoughts attract negative beings. Our thoughts can attract assistance and guidance. Although we can do so, it is not necessary to pray for what we want. Just think it.

We must never underestimate the power of our thoughts. Loving thoughts bring loving invisible beings. Hateful thoughts will bring negative beings who may even try to harm us. We must be careful regarding the focus of our thoughts because the kinds of thoughts we have attract the type of entity that reflects the type of thoughts.

We can call upon spirits and we can call for angels for assistance. We must be careful about our thoughts because the kinds of thoughts we have attract the kinds of entities that surround us. Think positive and you will get positive results. When you fear that the results will be negative, you will get negative results. Fear and doubt are your enemies.

Even when we see people around us, they are often not what they appear to be. Amongst us are extraterrestrials who have assumed human form. Our neighbor may not be of origin on this planet. They often have abilities to monitor and access us that far exceed our power. Those from other star systems have abilities that are beyond that which we can even imagine. They can change their form and appearance at will. We refer to them as shape shifters. This is for real.

UNDERSTANDING GOD

There are no words in our language or in any other language that can even begin to explain what God is. In order to have a minimal understanding of God, we have brought the concept of God down to our level of thinking. Since humans are physical beings, we have likened God unto a physical being like ourselves in order to understand God. Even when compared to spirit beings and angels, the abilities of physical humans are severely restricted. Thus, we put unlimited limitations of what God is when we define God as a product of our thinking. In all aspects God is limitless. Our human minds cannot even comprehend the concept of "limitless". Whether it is space, time, or abilities, we cannot conceive "limitless as having no beginning or no end.

Civilizations throughout history have tried to grasp an understanding of God. To do this, it has been necessary to define God in the only terms we know, human terms.

The Bible says that God created man in God's image. The Bible also says, although somewhat indirectly, that man created God in man's image. There are dozens of passages that mention the hand of God. For example, one verse says, "But to which of the angels said 'Sit on my right hand, until I make thine enemies my footstool." Apparently if God has a right side God must also have a left side. If God uses a footstool God must have feet. Moses saw the backside of God. The heart of God and the Godhead are also mentioned. God has a throne that God sits on, so God must have another body part. To the best of my knowledge, nothing is mentioned about God having fingers, toes or hair or even a long white beard. We know that God is male rather than female because the Bible refers to God as He. God also procreates because he has sons and daughters. The minds of humans are so limited that they cannot even begin to conceive the concept of God.

Even the use of pronouns (He, His, Him) to refer to God is human thinking. Instead of "He" or "Him" we might better say "God". Instead of "His", we might better say "God's".

LEARNING TO GET TO WHERE YOU WANT TO BE IN LIFE

All of us, except perhaps a very small percentage who are among the more enlightened souls, have very immutable preconceived notions about ourselves. Sometimes others view specific aspects of our personality in accord with our own views. More often than not, however, those who know us well see us quite differently from the way we perceive ourselves. Considering that there are numerous aspects of our personality, the closer our views of specific aspects of our personalities are to the views of others, the more real understanding we actually have of ourselves. It is quite likely that if you ask others if they understand themselves, most in all sincerity will respond, "Yes, very well." In most instances, this answer couldn't be further from the truth.

The closer our views of the various aspects of our personality are to the views of those who know us well, the greater the potential we will have for a truly successful, happy and fruitful life. The comparison must be made by those who know us well, certainly not by strangers we meet or even by those we do not actually know very well. A person may view himself as being a very interesting conversationalist, for example, because of the amusing anecdotes or stories he relates. Others who are not well acquainted him may find him very entertaining. On the other hand, those who know him well may find him very boring because he keeps repeating the same stories over and over again. There are always exceptions; it could be that a few of those who know him well enjoy hearing the same stories repeatedly.

If you learn to see yourself as most others see you and then make changes to be in accord with how they see you, it is more likely that they will have a better opinion of you and will treat you in a more positive manner. If you feel that you are a very cheerful person, try to discover if others feel the same about you. You might discover that most others see you as a very grumpy, complaining person. That could be a learning point; a point where you could make changes to improve your relations with others.

Think about the following statements you could say about yourself and then seek to see if others would agree with you:

I have a wonderful sense of humor.
I am reliable and you can always depend on me.
People don't like me because I am short and fat.
I am sincere and honest.
I am really sexy and good looking.
I treat others very politely and with respect.
People don't like me because I am ugly.
I pay careful attention to time and always arrive on time.
I am not a controlling person.
I am not hot tempered or argumentative.
My way is the best way.
I have good common sense.
I shouldn't smile because my teeth look bad.
I treat everyone equally.
I do not have an attitude of superiority.
I am a very humble person.
Everybody loves me.
I am an easy going person and easy to get along with.
I am always open to new ideas.
I am not stubborn or closed minded.
I am a good listener.
I speak well and with clarity.
I am not a boring person.
I always treat others politely and with respect.
Etc. etc.

If anyone says something about you that runs contrary to the way you feel about yourself ("You're such a snob."), don't just brush it off. Consider the possibility that there might be some truth in it. The above mentioned are but a few of the many possibilities of how we might consider ourselves and adjust our thinking and behavioral patterns accordingly.

THE BIRTH OF THE SOUL AND ITS ENDLESS EVOLUTION

In the beginning there was just a swirling charge of energy. The energy intensified and swirled to the point where it could no longer contain itself and so it exploded leaving its entire being into a myriad of images of itself. Some call this "The Great Bang". Its entire self was now fragmented. Each fragment or element was a burst of energy, an expression of itself. The fragments were of different intensities and varying vibtrational levels. Little by little the elements combined to manifest as what we might call different forms, some physical or what you could say of lower vibrational level and some not or what you could say of a higher vibrational level. The elementary physical manifestations became the mineral kingdom. As more elements or fragments combined, the vegetable kingdom came into being. Consciousness was imbued into minerals and vegetables.

The fragments further coalesced during the transition from the vegetable kingdom into the animal kingdom when all the aspects came together. The soul gives birth to itself at the transition from the vegetable kingdom. Before the vegetable kingdom, there are just soul fragments. Awareness begins in the mineral kingdom and continues to evolve until all the soul fragments coalesce into the birth of the soul. The soul is continuously in the process of giving birth to itself. We are all both the whole and the fragments of the whole. The evolution of the soul is the amassing of more and more soul fragments. It is infinite in its evolution.

Humans evolve through seven levels, sometimes referred to as seven heavens, the seventh being the highest of all. When we reach the seventh heaven, we are at the God level. At that level we become God. We become the god of a whole new universe. As a god, we then also evolve through seven levels, much higher than the previous seven levels through which we evolved. When we arrive at the seventh heaven, we are at a new god level. We become god again, much more evolved than the previous god level. We are the god of a new universe, much higher than the previous universe for which we were the god. This process repeats itself over and over. Higher-level gods are repeatedly being created. Just as time and space are endless, without beginning or end, so it is with the evolution of all of creation. There is no limit on the level of evolution of all that is.

JESUS

While on Earth, Jesus was a highly evolved soul and thus he was able to perform miracles and healing. He possessed other advanced insights that very few humans have. His level of vibration was such that the Christ Spirit (i.e. what some might refer to as the Holy Spirit or the God Force) was able to enter his body and share his body with him. At the point of entry of the Christ Spirit, Jesus became Jesus the Christ. Thus, Jesus was the Holy Spirit and, since the Holy Spirit was God in spirit form manifested in man, Jesus was man, the Holy Spirit and God. Jesus and God were then one. This is the basis for what Biblical scholars have termed "the trinity".

The Christ spirit is the manifestation of God in form that could cohabit a human body along with the original soul that inhabited that body thus producing what could be called a split soul.

Jesus the man now resides in the spirit world. The Christ Spirit has withdrawn and Jesus is no longer Jesus the Christ. Because of his high level of evolution, (what some may call holiness) Jesus possesses a great amount of spirit energy. It is his high degree of energy that enables him to answer our prayers from the world of spirits. The religion of the person seeking help from Jesus does not matter. Although Jesus was a Jew and Christianity evolved from the life and teachings of Jesus, he will come to the aid of anyone who calls upon him.

THE LOOP OF INFINITY

Time is the loop of infinity, with neither beginning nor end. It just goes on and on. The future is the past. The past is the future. Time continually renews itself. The loop of infinity never ends, always renewing and repeating itself. Repetition is renewal, the loop of eternity. Just like time, space is also infinite. It loops around and repeats itself; no beginning, no end. Time and space blend with energy. Energy exists on the framework of time and space. Energy renews itself continuously. It is endless and vibrant forever. Energy rides on the back of time and space. It is eternal action without beginning or end. Energy is just a single action. A single action is all actions. All actions are a single action, just as time is a single point and space is a single point. Space can be in fragments and time can be fragmented. Yet they cannot be separated from the whole. Time space and energy are regurgitated. Nothing exists except for the loop of infinity of time, space and energy. Time, space and energy flow in all directions. They are all one. All that exists is one.

GOD

In the beginning, God was an endless, timeless sea of consciousness. In the beginning, with this consciousness, God became aware of God. In the beginning, with this awareness, came the creation of Energy and Love.

In the beginning, as always, the three aspects of God were, are, and will always be Consciousness, Energy and Love. It is these three aspects of our creator that some have given the names of God the father, the Son and the Holy Ghost; the Trinity. Although there are misinterpretations, the core of the concept is solid.

The role of Jesus in his Biblical incarnation and in other incarnations as well as the role of other individuals throughout history was, is, and always will be to promote the Love aspect of God. Jesus the man is not God but Jesus the Christ represents the fullness of God regarding the high level of Consciousness, Energy and Love. Jesus the man is a high-energy entity in the spirit world that is able to assist us with our requests. Just ask. Your religion does not matter.

God is Consciousness. God is Energy. God is Love. The more Love you have, the more God you have. The more you have God, the more you are God. The same can be said of Energy.

The more Energy and Love you have, the more Consciousness you have. The more Consciousness you have. The more you have God. The more you have God, the more you are God.

The Energy aspect of God, often called the Holy Spirit, manifests itself as all of creation. Everything that exists emanates from Energy. It makes no difference if we see Creation as physical, thought, emotional or anything we can imagine, it is nonetheless Creation. All of Creation is God. God is God's creation.

Love is not an emotion. It is a force. It is the force which gives us the realization that that we are one with all that is. It is the force, the mortar, which unites all of Creation with Consciousness.

God is the ultimate supreme mind.

Chapter 12

SONDRA REFLECTS

CREATING OUR FUTURE

When we think about our future, we often wonder just where our life's journey will take us. Let us never think of ourselves as the pawns of our destiny. Instead of wondering where our life's journey will take us, let us focus on where we will take our life's journey. May we ever be aware that it is we alone who are the planners of our life's journey. We map our future with each and every action we make. We map our future with each and every word we say. We map our future with each and every thought we have. From this day forth, let each of us strive to plan a happy, pleasant journey for ourselves.

A GREATER MEANING

Search for greater meaning in our lives. Seek increased awareness of the potential that lies within. Seek to nurture the spark of the divine that lies at the very core of our being. Achieve greater awareness of our true self. Think of ourselves as more than just our physical bodies and that which is perceived by our senses. Think of ourselves as more than just our feelings, our desires and our emotions. Think of ourselves as more than just our intellect, our reasoning and our thoughts. Know ourselves for that which we truly are: the creation of God, formed in the image of God with the seed of all of the attributes of our creator.

OUR FREE WILL

Our creator has given a free will to each soul that has been created. As we exercise this free will, we carve out our own unique path to our spiritual destiny. With our every thought, our every word, and our every deed- the spiritual path that we must follow is created and laid out before us. Each soul enters this physical life equipped with a unique set of tools, specially selected to help us proceed down the spiritual path that we ourselves have created. As we look at the people around us, we can see a great variety of individual differences. It is those differences that are the tools we possess to help us make progress on our spiritual journeys. They can be our race, our color, our health, our talents our intelligence level, our physical appearance, our weaknesses, and a host of other kinds of differences, including whether we enter physical life as a man or as a woman.

SPIRITUAL ADULTHOOD

Grow little closer toward spiritual adulthood. Understand that spiritual adulthood means having a full awareness of ourselves. Awareness of both the human aspects and of the spark of the divine within us that leads us to oneness with our creator. Seek to learn more about our attitudes and our emotions so that we might grow in spirit. As we seek greater understanding of ourselves, we cease being slaves to our emotions. Learn to become the masters of our feelings and attitudes. Know that through prayer, the direct communication link to our creator, we can bring great change into our lives. When we find ourselves in the midst of unpleasant personal situations; when we find that things in our lives are not as we want them to be; when we desperately want things affecting our lives to change--then may know that there is something better to do than praying for conditions affecting us to change. Instead of praying for our life's problems to go away, first learn to pray for a change in our emotions and attitudes toward those problems.

THE EARTHLY KINGDOMS

Seek to enrich our awareness of the relationship between our creator, ourselves, and the planet on which we live. As our consciousness expands, we come to more fully understand that all of creation is in unity. All that exists in our dimension has been created for the benefit and for the development of the souls of mankind. As we grow in spirituality, the mysteries of the interrelationships between each element of God's creation can be understood more clearly. The wondrous relationship between the earthly kingdoms of the mineral, the vegetable, and the animal all uniting and working in unison. All placed in our presence to be used for our holy benefit. Each kingdom has been designed and created to work in harmony with the human race. Pause to reflect that everything in our universe has been divinely created in perfect harmony, to be used by each one of us for the development of our eternal souls.

CONTRIBUTE POSITIVE

Recognize the positive and dwell upon it. For as we think positive, then do we contribute positive. If each one of us would contribute our portion of positive to our own small world around us, then the whole world will become more positive; more and more positive each day. Work for the spread of good. God is good. Let God be experienced throughout the world.

A GREATER AWARENESS

Be ever mindful that we are the creation of the divinity and have that spark of the divine within us. We are destined to learn and to grow, destined to fulfill the purpose for which we were created. Seek greater awareness of ourselves and the role that we are to play.

CHANELERS

Let us become channels of kindness by showing kindness to those around us.et us channel forgiveness by forgiving those whom we feel have offended us. Let us channel patience to all by being patient with all in all that we do. Let us channel God's love by thinking with love, speaking with love, and acting with love as we live from minute to minute, day to day, year to year and lifetime to lifetime.

CHILDREN OF GOD

We truly are children of God, formed in the image of God, created to be like God, destined to be one with God. That is a destiny we cannot avoid. We must arrive there. We can make it easy for ourselves or we can make it difficult. The choice is there. But that is our destiny. God has so ordained.

SPIRITUAL PATHS

There are many spiritual paths, each taking the traveler in the direction he should go; each leading to the same end; each seeking greater closeness to our Creator

THE HUMAN BODY

The human body is truly the magnificent, divine expression that has been given to us by our creator for our stay here on this earth. The human body enables each soul to express itself in this dimension as we fulfill our role in the divine plan for which we have been created.

TIME

The time that we call "<u>now</u>" is the present. But it is really the past. Everything that we are experiencing at this time, whether it brings us pain or joy, Is the result of our past thoughts and actions. We are living our past. The time that we call "<u>now</u>" is the present. But it is really the future. Every thought we have right now, And every action we take, determine our future. We are living our future. We can't change the present. It was determined in the past. We can change our future. It is being determined right now. The future is beginning right now.

OUR ADVERSARIES

Each individual in our circles of acquaintances has been created for the purpose of playing a role in the divine plan that our creator has given to us. Let us open our eyes to look around ourselves and take pleasure in appreciating the miracle of all that is wonderful and good in our lives.

Let us also experience the miracle of learning to be thankful for all that which does not seem so good and wonderful in our lives. Our adversaries, our enemies; our problems, our heartaches; our trials and tribulations are all here for good reason. They are all necessary to us. It is they who are our teachers. It is they who provide us with opportunities to master the lessons needed to help us grow in spirit. As we learn from our teachers we grow in spirit and play the divine role for which we have been created.

HEALING

Healing of the body. Healing of the mind. Healing of the spirit. Let us be healed so that we may heal others. Let us heal others so that we may heal ourselves. For as we heal others, we heal ourselves. Healing is a kind thought. Healing is a kind word. Healing is a kind deed. Let us live, eat and breathe thoughts, words and deeds of kindness from this day forth. All that we do with only thoughts of ourselves is selfish and unkind. All that we do with kindness and thoughts of others creates healing. We have been created to be healers. Let us do that for which we were created. Let us heal. Let us begin this very moment.

OUR NEEDS

What if we tried to become like the man who said, "I am indeed the richest man on earth because I live my life so that my needs are few."? What if we looked within and could see all our greed? What if we saw that our wants become our needs, and the more we get, the more we want, the more we need? We have created a life of unending needs. So we never achieve our original goal. We never experience true inner satisfaction. As we withhold satisfaction from ourselves. We make it so that we can never experience the peace that comes from satisfying our needs. What if we were to realize that external needs are really very few in number? What if we concentrated on our inner needs, the needs of the spirit? As we satisfy our inner needs, we achieve inner peace. True riches are those that lie within us.

ONE- LINERS

The more you give, more you get.

You help yourself by helping others.

It's not how far you progress. It's how much you progress.

You don't need religion. You just need the golden rule.

You must earn love before you can learn to love.

When your memory goes you are forced to live in the now.

Losing your memory of past events gives you the freedom from being tied down to them.

Stupidity is not a virtue; neither is ignorance.

I honor myself when I am of assistance to others.

I assist others when I show respect for them.

Being right is not enough. Being polite adds to right.

Before attaining social, emotional, intellectual and spiritual maturity we must go through the process of growing up.

It is not that you are directed by your destiny. It is that your destiny is directed by you.

ABOUT THE AUTHORS

Sondra Perlin-Zecher has been active in the metaphysical field for more than fifty years. She is a clairvoyant, clairaudient medium whose life's work has been devoted to helping others through psychic readings and counseling. She is probably best known as the psychic who solved the Son of Sam mass murder case. She works with law enforcement in solving crimes. As a medical intuitive, she often works with medical doctors in diagnosing problems. Her educational background includes graduate degrees in art, social work and psychology. Her formal training, combined with her psychic sensitivity, has enabled her to provide help to numbers of individuals, medical doctors, and law enforcement officials including the FBI.

Charles E. Zecher has been a student of metaphysics and the paranormal for more than fifty years. His professional career spanned nearly forty years as an educator and school administrator at the secondary school level and universities in New Jersey and Pennsylvania. He is certified as an advanced clinical hypnotherapist. For nearly thirty years, he has worked with his wife in offering programs of interest in their homes in Bridgewater, New Jersey and in Coral Springs, Florida.

Charles and Sondra are former directors of the Central Jersey area Mutual Interest Group of the Association for Research and Enlightenment. They currently sponsor the Coral Springs Metaphysical Group. They have two adult sons and reside in Coral Springs, Florida. They can be contacted at zecher@myacc.net or czecher93@gmail.com.

Printed in the United States
By Bookmasters